PORTFOLIO

ONE GREAT INSIGHT IS WORTH
A THOUSAND GOOD IDEAS

Phil Dusenberry joined BBDO as a copywriter in 1962 and
rose through the ranks to become chairman and chief creative
officer of BBDO North America, transforming it into the
leading creative shop on Madison Avenue and the flagship of
the Omnicom empire. He was inducted into the Advertising
Hall of Fame in 2002. He lives with his wife, Susan, in New
York City and Sag Harbor, New York.

D1282641

One Great Insight Is Worth a Thousand Good Ideas

AN ADVERTISING HALL-OF-FAMER

REVEALS THE MOST POWERFUL

SECRET IN BUSINESS

PHIL DUSENBERRY

PORTFOLIO

PREVIOUSLY PUBLISHED AS
THEN WE SET HIS HAIR ON FIRE

PORTFOLIO
Published by the Penguin Group
Penguin Group (USA) Inc., 375 Hudson Street, New York, New York 10014, U.S.A.
Penguin Group (Canada), 90 Eglinton Avenue East, Suite 700, Toronto,
Ontario, Canada M4P 2Y3 (a division of Pearson Penguin Canada Inc.)
Penguin Books Ltd, 80 Strand, London WC2R 0RL, England
Penguin Ireland, 25 St Stephen's Green, Dublin 2, Ireland (a division of Penguin Books Ltd)
Penguin Group (Australia), 250 Camberwell Road, Camberwell,
Victoria 3124, Australia (a division of Pearson Australia Group Pty Ltd)
Penguin Books India Pvt Ltd, 11 Community Centre, Panchsheel Park,
New Delhi – 110 017, India
Penguin Group (NZ), cnr Airborne and Rosedale Roads, Albany,
Auckland 1310, New Zealand (a division of Pearson New Zealand Ltd)
Penguin Books (South Africa) (Pty) Ltd, 24 Sturdee Avenue, Rosebank,
Johannesburg 2196, South Africa

Penguin Books Ltd, Registered Offices:
80 Strand, London WC2R 0RL, England

First published in the United States of America as *Then We Set His Hair on Fire* by Portfolio,
a member of Penguin Group Inc. 2005
Published in Penguin Books 2006

10   9   8   7   6   5   4   3   2   1

Grateful acknowledgment is made for permission to reprint an excerpt from "Right Field" by
Willy Welch. Used by permission of Playing Right Music.

PUBLISHER'S NOTE
This publication is designed to provide accurate and authoritative information in regard to the
subject matter covered. It is sold with the understanding that the publisher is not engaged in
rendering legal, accounting, or other professional services. If you require legal advice or other
expert assistance, you should seek the services of a competent professional.

ISBN 1-59184-082-1 (hc.)
ISBN 1-59184-142-9 (pbk.)
CIP data available

Printed in the United States of America
Set in Sabon
Designed by Joe Rutt

For Susan, who's written the best chapters of my life

ACKNOWLEDGMENTS

Writing a book, as in writing advertising, is a collaborative effort. No great ad campaign was ever created in solitude. Nor was this book. Thus, I wish to thank the many who contributed to the pages that follow.

First, my enduring gratitude to the folks who make all advertising possible—the ones who spend the bucks: my clients.

Leading the list: Pepsi's Alan Pottasch, my oldest client, not in years but in longevity. Alan and I have worked together for over thirty-five years, slugging our way through hand-to-hand combat in the "cola wars."

For their guidance, confidence, and counsel, a special thanks to Steve Reinemund, Craig Weatherup, Dawn Hudson, Antonio Lucio, Jack Welch, Rudy Giuliani, John Sculley, Lee Iacocca, Mike Glenn, Richard Costello, and the late President Ronald Reagan.

My immense gratitude to all those who gave so generously of their time, tales, and insights—and enriched this book with their unique vision: Roger Enrico, Fred Smith, Peter Souter, George Bryant, Martyn Straw, Bill Katz, Charlie Miesmer, David Novak, Ellen Sills-Levy, and Mike Deaver.

For getting the ball rolling on this project in its infancy, a special nod to Larry Freundlich.

This book—and I—would be nowhere without the fabulous talents of all the BBDOers who worked with me over the years: Ted Sann, Charlie Miesmer, Al Merrin, Don Schneider, Michael Patti, Steve Hayden, Jimmy Siegel, Rick Hanson, Janet Lyons, Allen Rosenshine, Andrew Robertson, Jeff Mordos, John "Ozzy" Osborn, Chris Havard, Andy Knipe, Regina Ebel, Tom Clark, Dick Johnson, Eric Harkna, David Frankel, Gene Lofaro, David Lubars, Len McCarron, Ed Maslow, Phil Gant, David Johnson, Brett Shevack, Bruce Meyers, Al Martin, David Blackley, Marcello Serpa, and Peter Clemenger.

And especially Joe Pytka, whose brilliant film directing always moved the needle on our efforts much further than we imagined. And of course Peter Cofield, whose music always gave our work a fresh and unexpected dimension.

Thanks also to BBDO's June Baloutine and Roy Elvove for their invaluable assistance in this book—and to Karen Lynch, my executive assistant of twenty-two years, for always being there for me.

Most importantly, my unending gratitude to my agent, partner, and friend, Mark Reiter, for shepherding this project through from beginning to end. His wisdom, guidance, and unbounded creativity were a pleasure to behold.

CONTENTS

ONE GREAT INSIGHT IS WORTH A THOUSAND GOOD IDEAS

THE INSIGHT MOMENT

The words weren't working. In 12 hours I was scheduled to stand up in front of Jack Welch and explain to him why General Electric should entrust its entire advertising budget to the nurturing hands of my agency, BBDO, and our cunning theme line, "We make the things that make life good."

Not exactly the "phrase that pays"—and I knew it.

The year was 1979. Jack Welch wasn't JACK WELCH yet, legendary CEO, Wall Street darling, coiner of management mantras like "No. 1 or No. 2 or out." Back then he was a newly minted thirty-nine-year-old vice chairman of GE, one of three men vying mightily for CEO Reginald Jones's job. A new ad campaign that would consolidate all of GE's disparate businesses under a single all-embracing thematic umbrella was one of Welch's ways of setting himself apart from his rivals. The man who could create a new public face for the company could be the man to lead the entire company.

GE had always believed in advertising as an essential tool in its marketing thrust. As far back as the 1950s, GE had sponsored *The GE Theater* with Ronald Reagan as its host. In the 1960s GE was the sole sponsor of the *GE College Bowl,* which linked the company with higher education and leading edge technology. But in the 1970s, the era of conglomeration, as GE grew into dozens of individual business units, each with its own advertising strategy, it was hard to picture the company as having an integrated identity. Whatever hold GE had on the public imagination was the equivalent of a utility: safe, boring, unimaginative. (In fact, GE was such an integral part of the average home—just like a utility—that some people mistakenly used to send their electric bills and payments to GE.) Given its history, the company understood the benefits of advertising to establish an image. But it had lost its way temporarily. So, now GE wanted a new persona.

That's why six weeks earlier Welch had asked for presentations from the two agencies that split GE's advertising work: my agency, BBDO, and our arch-rival Young & Rubicam. It would be a winner-take-all creative shootout. At stake: $60 million.

I was the BBDO executive in charge of the agency pitch. There was a lot riding on this, and not just because $60 million then is today's $450 million. Everyone was geared up for battle. GE was in our sights. If we had eggs, we were putting them all in the GE basket.

But as I stared at the tin-eared theme line "We make the things that make life good," knowing the words weren't working, I wasn't panicked. I wasn't worried. The theme line was the cherry on top of the sundae as far as I was concerned. The reason for my uncharacteristic calm was simple: we were armed with an insight about GE that was irrefutable, irresistible, and (I was sure) unthought of by our rivals at Y&R.

When big companies put their advertising into review, they create a level playing field for all the competitors. They pay them for their efforts (albeit modestly). They arm them with all the market data and consumer research available. They put their top people at the agencies' disposal for questions. That's what GE did too. They didn't see this shoot-out as a pop quiz to establish whether BBDO was better than Y&R. GE was in it for a very good reason: they wanted the best campaign. And like a smart boss, they put all their resources at our disposal.

Three separate creative teams from BBDO fanned out with the same material—and not surprisingly, came back with three different approaches.

The first focused on GE as a consumer appliance company. Even though the consumer sector accounted for only 25 percent of GE's profits, that's how most people perceived GE: it made toasters and irons and ovens. The campaign centered around a line from The Lovin' Spoonful song "Do You Believe in Magic?" and endowed consumer appliances with all manner of life-altering attributes.

The second team's approach was bolder. The idea was "You ain't seen nothing yet," and it promised consumers that the best of GE's technology was yet to come. Clever, I thought, but positioned a little too far into the future. It suggested a capability that GE did not yet have. An alluring promise, but undeliverable.

The third approach materialized when one of our top creatives, Ted Sann, and I looked at reality. As we sat around and tried to think of what people do in their everyday lives and relate it back to GE, it dawned on us that GE is pervasive. To the untrained eye it appeared to be an amorphous giant that manufactured everything from small appliances to lightbulbs, refrigerators, railroad engines, power turbines, space-age plastics, and nuclear reactors. It had a huge equipment leasing operation. It owned iron ore mines in the Rockies. But as we analyzed this smorgasbord of operating divisions, we began to see this pervasiveness as a plus. No matter what you do in your life, GE is part of it. So, we needed to demonstrate to people that GE is a *positive* part of their lives.

A problem well stated is a problem half solved because it forces you to stretch for an insight rather than a quick-fix idea. In this case, the insight was asking, "What does GE do to make life better?" Once we posed the right question, the answers came flooding in from everyone on the creative team. GE makes clock radios . . . which wake you up. GE makes ovens . . . which bake the bread you eat. GE makes the light-bulbs . . . that let you read to your children. GE makes the audio equipment . . . that sends your daughters dancing. It makes the engines . . . that bring you home.

We were on such a roll that our senior creative directors Charlie Miesmer and Dennis Berger, both amateur guitar-pickers, set the answers to song: "We wake you to the sun, We make your daughters dance, We bake your bread, We light your way . . ." The only thing missing was a closing theme line. As I say, "We make the things that make life good" wouldn't cut it.

That's what was running through my mind as I left the office at 9 P.M., hailed a cab on Madison Avenue, and desultorily gave the cabbie my address. As we honked, bounced, and stalled our way through traffic, a beautiful thing happened. Maybe it was the last pothole, but the theme line, full-blown, popped into my head. "GE . . . We bring good things to life."

It wasn't Shakespeare or Yeats, but I knew in my heart that it would ring like poetry to the folks from GE.

By the luck of the draw, the next morning BBDO was chosen to present first. Given the chance to pitch first, I'll take it. Not only is the audience fresh and attentive, but if your presentation is on the mark, you become a tough act to follow. Everyone's work has to stand up to yours.

We were so confident of our theme line—and the strategy behind it—that we decided to lead off with it and let it spearhead our entire pitch. We would sink or swim with this one insight: GE is a valuable part of everything in your life. At the conclusion, as the conference room lights slowly went up, we splashed the "We bring good things to life" slogan across all the screens. I kept my eyes pinned on Welch, hoping to spot a thumbs-up or -down in his facial expression. I didn't know him well at the time—none of us did; he was the new kid on the block and a wild card at that—but I thought I saw stars dancing in his eyes. When he came up to shake my hand, he was fairly cool. "That was pretty good," he said. "How long would it take you to get these commercials on the air?"

"Six weeks," I said.

"Can you do it in five?" he asked.

That's when I was sure we had won the business, even though Y&R had yet to present. Two days later Jack called to confirm what we already guessed. All of GE's advertising was now ours, and we had five weeks to get something on the air.

I could wax eloquent about our resourcefulness in getting an integrated slate of commercials and print ads into the marketplace in less than forty days. I could slyly mention that winning and keeping the GE account helped my career immensely, securing for me a promotion and an exponential increase in compensation. I could note that the GE win set BBDO on an unprecedented new-business winning streak, including marquee accounts such as FedEx, Frito-Lay, Visa, Mars, HBO, Pizza Hut, Polaroid, and Apple Computers, that left our competitors shaking their heads with envy.

But this is not a book about my career, or BBDO, or for that matter, advertising. You won't learn how to write persuasive copy here. Or compose a 60-second short story for Michael J. Fox and a can of Diet Pepsi. Or convince Michael Jackson to donate his biggest hit for your client's commercial. Or stuff three midgets into a tiger costume for a long-forgotten FedEx spot. You won't get pious lectures about the decline in advertising creativity and the constant vigilance required to maintain standards. Nor will you get sentimental yawnings about advertising's good old days, before slashed fees and advertising consultants and TiVO machines that skip commercials. You also won't get any blue-sky musings about the brave new world of interactive advertising, broadband marketing, and so on—any of which may be outmoded between the writing of these words and your reading of them. As I say, this is not a book about advertising.

This is a book about insights in business—how we get them, how we recognize them, how we keep them coming.

Insights as opposed to ideas. There's a difference. Ideas, valuable though they may be, are a dime-a-dozen in business. That's certainly the case at ad agencies where ideas (not all of them good, mind you) are the currency of the realm and even the mailroom people spit out ideas as if they were candy from a PEZ dispenser.

Insight is much rarer—and therefore more precious.

In the advertising business, a good idea can inspire a great commercial. But a good insight can fuel a thousand ideas, a thousand commercials. Our GE theme line, "We bring good things to life," endured for twenty-four years, from 1979 to 2003, during which BBDO created thousands of commercials and print ads for GE. It endured even as Jack Welch, through more than 1,700 acquisitions, dramatically steered the company away from its core manufacturing base into new core areas, such as the financial marketplace (GE Capital) and broadcasting (NBC). The theme line endured even as Jack sold off the venerable low-margin small appliances business of irons and toasters that had become the "face" of General Electric. It endured because its basic underlying truth did not change over the years. At the risk of overstating the value of "We bring good things to life," I would argue that it was more than *just* an effective advertising slogan. It also expressed the fundamental rationale for Welch's company: every business GE goes into must provide a benefit to some consumer constituency, must make people's lives better. That's the muscle that grows from a powerful insight.

More than anything else, an insight states a truth that alters how you see the world. In the 1980s, a Nebraska minister named Robert Fulghum delivered a sermon, "All I Really Need to Know I Learned in Kindergarten," listing nineteen nuggets of advice that every schoolchild hears, such as: Share everything. Play fair. Don't hit people. Don't take things that aren't yours. Warm cookies and milk are good for you. Take a nap every afternoon. When you go out into the world, watch out for traffic, hold hands, and stick together.

Fulghum summed up by saying, "Take one of these items and extrapolate it into sophisticated adult terms and apply it to your family life or your work or your government or your world and it holds true and clear and firm. Think what a better world it would be if we all—the whole world—had cookies and milk at three o'clock every afternoon and then lay down with our blankets for a nap. Or if all governments had a basic policy to always put things back where they found them and to clean up their own mess." Fulghum's insight—that we acquire all the wisdom we need early in life, not later—was so compelling that his parishioners faxed copies of the sermon to friends (this was in 1985, before the Internet), the *Reader's Digest* reprinted it, and eventually it became the lead title of a slim volume of other Fulghum sermons that sold more than 11 million copies. It was quite a phenomenon at the time, transforming Fulghum into a mini-industry as author and lecturer. The essay inspired hundreds of parodies, even plays and musicals, two of which made it to Broadway. Google Fulghum's title on the Web and you'll find 183,000 listings, the vast majority of them Web sites of psychiatrists, educators, child psychologists, marriage counselors, and family therapists who reprint Fulghum's 374-word essay in its entirety as if it were *their* philosophy. But that's the allure of a powerful insight: the moment you hear it, you can't see the world in any other way.

Insights come in all shapes and sizes.

Management guru Peter Drucker is hailed and admired as "the man who invented business" largely because of seven decades' worth of essays on management in more than thirty-five books. But if you pore through Drucker's books hoping to find a treasure trove of specific ideas and practical advice on how to run a business, you will be sorely disappointed. That's because Drucker doesn't traffic in ideas. Insights are his currency, and his books reveal him to be a man who is a virtual insight machine. Drucker won't tell you how to make a cold call, but he will get you thinking about the implications of cold calls and whether your business is too dependent on them and what that says about how you treat your old customers. Drucker won't tell you how to fire an unruly employee, but he will get you thinking about the criteria for employees to keep and employees to jettison. His insights usually take the form of Socratic questions that make you look at the world through sharper lenses. When Drucker famously advised a CEO of a big multinational company to ask himself, "If you didn't own this business now and had a chance to buy it, would you?" he was doing something far more valuable than listing reasons to keep or fold a division. He was teaching the CEO how to think, much like the ancient saying, "Give a man a fish, and he'll eat for a day. Teach a man to fish, and he'll eat for a lifetime." Drucker was helping the CEO see the world from a new perspective—with a rigor and logic that is impossible to refute. The best insights do that.

Insights can arrive in the form of sound bites.

Warren Buffett, the most admired and imitated investor of modern times, is famous for his secretive ways. He never gives away investing ideas, mostly because investors watch his every move. Any Buffett pronouncement has the potential to move markets—and erase a little bit of his edge. If you study his much-quoted letters to Berkshire Hathaway shareholders, which he has been writing since 1971, you will be amazed at the paucity of investing *ideas* they contain. Buffett reveals nothing about how, when, or why he buys a given stock. But even though he's chary with ideas, Buffett, like Drucker, is an insight machine. His insights often take the form of pithy one-liners. I remember a few years ago when the long-term value of Gillette stock (a BBDO client since 1929) was being questioned in investing circles. As Gillette's largest shareholder for many years, Buffett was asked why he was holding onto the stock. He said, "I go to bed feeling very comfortable just thinking about two and a half billion males with hair growing while I sleep." As an investment idea, it's useless; Buffett reveals nothing about his take on Gillette's management or the stock's relative value. But as an insight about Gillette's fundamental business—razors and shaving cream—it was both eloquent and mind-altering. It reminded me that Gillette not only had a great enduring brand, but it made a product that customers needed and used *every day*. Buffett's insight was obvious—Gillette was in a great business—and the way he phrased it confirmed it.

Insights sometimes reveal themselves through jewel-like analogies.

Buffett is a master of this, too. Back in the late 1970s, he led a public discussion of the relative values of CBS and Capital Cities. CBS at the time was the most glamorous of the three major networks, the shining brainchild of the broadcasting legend William Paley, home of Walter Cronkite and *60 Minutes* and *M*A*S*H* and the NFL. Everybody watched CBS; it was the Tiffany network. Capital Cities was this runty amalgam of local TV and radio stations and newspapers that had been quietly built up in Albany, New York, by the unknown duo of Tom Murphy and Dan Burke. Buffett was taking the then-contrarian view that Paley's reputation was oversold; Murphy and Burke were by far the better managers. He had numbers to back his position—Cap Cities stock had grown tenfold during the most recent ten-year period while CBS had actually gone down. The audience wasn't swallowing the argument until Buffett said, "Imagine that CBS and Capital Cities are two cargo ships—CBS loaded with cargo, Cap Cities a little bare—leaving port on the same day. Ten years later they return. The CBS ship and its cargo are unchanged. The Cap Cities ship, on the other hand, has miraculously grown into a bigger vessel and it is bursting with valuable cargo. Now, who's the better captain?" Buffett's insight: let's focus on results, not image or reputation. But an insight isn't worth a damn if you can't express it in a way that people *get it*.

Insights sometimes come from the most unlikely places. Baseball manager Casey Stengel provided me with one of the more useful management insights for a boss in the ego-riddled world of advertising. On any team he managed, Stengel accepted that one third of his players liked him, one third hated him, and one third were undecided. "The secret of managing," he said, "is to keep the guys who hate you away from the guys who are undecided." As a quotable line, it is mildly amusing. As a piece of wisdom, it hovers between eye-opening brilliance and head-slapping obviousness. But what kicks it into the higher sphere of true insight is the fact that it inspires ideas you can act on. A manager who accepts Stengel's premise will be alert to the cliques and cabals that form in a ball club over a long season and take steps to keep the undecideds away from the players who hate him—on the field, on the road, in the clubhouse. A manager who doesn't accept it will soon be an ex-manager. That's the true value of an insight. It initiates a chain of events that impels you to do something no one else is doing.

An insight also has the capacity to take something that you know in your head and make you feel it in your gut. For example, I play more golf than is healthy for my back, my brain, my self-esteem, and my marriage. I've read dozens of books on the subject. I've taken lessons from some of the best pros in the business. I've taken to heart every piece of unsolicited advice my playing partners have offered, and have been irresponsibly slow to discard these suggestions. I've even taken three days of private instruction in Charlottesville, Virginia, with sports psychologist Bob Rotella to edit and cleanse all my accumulated golf knowledge.

But the most insightful statement I've ever heard about the game came from a pro who was helping me search for my ball in thick rough among a grove of trees off the fairway (of course) at Blind Brook Country Club in Purchase, New York.

Like most golfers, I love to pull out my driver on the tee and hit the ball as far as possible. Like most golfers, sadly, I am not consistently straight with my driver. It is, after all, the hardest club to hit well. I'm much more consistent with a 3 wood—shorter yes, but straighter. I know this about the club and myself. I also know that the value of hitting a ball a long way off the tee is vastly overrated in golf—because 70 percent of all golf shots take place within 100 yards of the pin. Meaning: work on your short game; that's where shots are saved or lost.

Yet all that knowledge falls away when I'm standing on the tee looking at a wide tempting greensward and a pin 410 yards away. Common sense and the laws of golfing probability would suggest that I pull out the 3 wood, knock it straight down the fairway 220 yards, and then deal with the 190-yard second shot in my usual fashion. But no, I don't do that. Against my will and better judgment, I pull out the driver, which in its most ideal mode produces a shot that is 15 to 20 yards longer than my 3 wood. Of course, five out of ten times, I do not achieve an ideal result with my driver, producing instead an unsightly rip that launches the ball in a screaming arc to the left, where it plops far off the fairway, often obstructed by trees or drowned by water, and farther from the pin than if I had kicked the ball off the tee.

Such was the case when I finally found my ball under six inches of thick grass at Blind Brook. That's when the pro said, "Phil, let me ask you something. What if I told you you could pick up your ball and place it in the middle of the fairway over there, except that it would be twenty-five yards farther away from the pin than we are here? And you could do that right now without losing a stroke? Would you do it?"

"Of course," I said. "Who wouldn't?"

"Well," he said, "that's the situation you'd be in if you had hit anything but your driver."

Suddenly the clouds parted. The sun was shining. The veil of darkness that had fogged my judgment vanished. The golfing gods had kissed my brow with wisdom and everything was revealed. I suddenly was blessed with an insight: short but straight *is* better than long and off the mark. In truth, the pro wasn't telling me anything I didn't know or hadn't read in different form in dozens of books. But I had never been able to internalize this wisdom, at least not deeply enough so that I could resist going to my driver when I should be employing a safer club. The pro's insight was not his little tip to hit a safer club. His insight was to couch the advice in the form of a compelling either/or choice—you could be here *in trouble* or you could be there *safe and pretty*; it's totally up to you—so that it was the first time I was made to feel in my bones what I knew in my head. Golf is a game dominated by the spectre of second chances—that's why we award ourselves mulligans and do-overs and relive each round shot by shot. The pro's insight was to show me that I could give myself a second chance, before I needed it.

If I seem a little obsessed with the notion of insights, as opposed to ideas, it's because insights are the brick and mortar of the ad industry—and also its Holy Grails. We live and die on insights. We seek them like hungry bears after honey. And when we come across them, we treat them with reverence and awe. There's a scene in the movie *What Women Want* (one of the rare films that accurately capture life at an ad agency) where Mel Gibson, who has been magically blessed with the ability to hear women's thoughts, makes a suggestion about a Nike campaign to his new boss, Helen Hunt (hired away from, of all places, BBDO). Hunt is shocked and impressed, telling Gibson, "That's insightful." The scene exists—and sticks in my mind—because *insightful* may be one of the highest compliments you can hand out in the ad business, sometimes even better than hearing "That's a great ad!"

I've always found some irony in advertising's playful, carefree image, that the industry somehow functions in a creative playground at the expense of professionalism and disciplined thinking. In this fantasy, agency account executives are forever entertaining clients, either by pounding down martinis at

"21" or bonding at the Harvard Club. The creatives are slightly more dissolute and unruly, perpetually goofing off in the office, tossing Nerf balls at tiny hoops by day and draining coffee cups by night, as they dream up evermore-phantasmagorical scripts and scenarios for the clients' ads.

In many ways, nothing can be further from the truth. The best ad agencies are remarkably disciplined machines, usually governed by clear operating philosophies and codes of thinking—and, unlike at the vast majority of American companies, these codes are written down! As far back as the early 1960s, my agency, BBDO, wrote out its creative philosophy in what it called The Four-Point Process—and the agency's leaders made sure every employee and every client understood the thinking behind it. The specifics of BBDO's four points are not relevant here (not yet at least), but the fact that they were codified in writing (and long before mission statements became a corporate fad) surely distinguishes the typical ad agency from most businesses. I'd wager that of America's 7.2 million commercial enterprises, big or small, at least 7.1 million of them do not have any corporate philosophy or operating instructions written down for their employees. They've never given a moment of thought to how they sell or brand themselves or present their product to the public or differentiate themselves from the competition. Nothing's in writing, and very little is actually in their minds. They don't have time or money to conduct research about their product or service or customers or competitors. In turn, they have no information to react to. Which explains why they're just winging it from day to day.

I'm not extolling ad agencies as the perfect model for running a business. But there is something that the best agencies do that *does* have value for anyone in business. The best ad agencies are great at coming up with insights that can reshape or save a company. The best agencies are great at tackling the thorniest business problems—and solving them. And they do this over and over again—it's the business they're in—in large part because they have a system for identifying problems and coming up with insightful solutions that cure the disease, not merely relieve the pain.

The system is not complex or elaborate. If you had to draw a schematic of what agencies do for clients, it would be a simple linear matrix of research, analysis, insight, strategy, and execution. I'd sum it up with the clumsy acronym RAISE—except it doesn't mean anything and it suggests that there are hard and fast rules for creating ads. There aren't. However, at its finest moments the matrix moves from one component to the next in balanced, fluid harmony.

It begins with a problem. A client—let's say it's a beer company—wants to increase sales (a familiar problem; who doesn't want to increase sales?).

The first thing you do in dealing with any business problem is *research*. You collect data so you can understand the problem, or at least approach it more knowingly. Before you can deliver a message to customers that incites them to buy more beer, you have to understand something about the customers and their relationship to the product. You ask, Who buys our beer? How often? What do they like about it? Why do they choose us instead of another beer? And so on, assembling data about the customer, the product, the competition, and the market.

Once assembled, the data demands *analysis*. As you pore over the numbers and opinions, an interesting tidbit sticks out. Let's say it's the fact that 80 percent of the beer is bought by 20 percent of the beer-drinking public. It's the old 80/20 rule in action. Whenever it comes into play, you cannot ignore it.

Smart analysis will bring this salient fact to the fore, and it should lead to an *insight* about the brand: our beer drinkers are extremely loyal to the brand. So, if we want to increase sales, we should tap into that loyalty. We need to persuade our existing customers to remain loyal to us. That's a valuable insight because it (a) focuses you *toward* a very specific market and (b) has the concomitant benefit of steering you *away* from the always costly tactic of stealing customers from your competition. Avoiding a bad decision is often more valuable than making a good decision. (As someone said, the best trades in baseball are the ones you don't make.) When you can accomplish both with one insight, it's a home run.

Once the insight materializes, you develop a *strategy* for the brand that, in a perfect world, can be summed up in a sentence or two—as if it were the brand's "mission statement." In this case (since I'm recalling a real-life episode in the marketing history of Schaefer beer), the insight and strategy led to the slogan "Schaefer . . . the one beer to have when you're having more than one," which endured for nearly two decades.

From here, it's a simple matter of *execution,* of creating great ads without veering off strategy. I'm being only half-ironic when I say that execution is an afterthought. In my experience, if you have a great insight and strategy, great ads practically write themselves. My colleague Charlie Miesmer reminded me that the first TV commercial he ever wrote was for Schaefer beer. By then Schaefer's "one beer to have . . ." slogan had been firmly established in the marketplace for ten years. The phrase was a classic, a fixture in the beer marketer's lexicon, to the point where people had been hearing it for so long that it had almost lost its meaning. But the insight behind it—that Schaefer beer drinkers are loyal, multiple imbibers—was still true. If loyalty was the chief virtue underlying Schaefer beer, he could tug at that emotional heartstring—and use the slogan to move things along.

Recalling a poignant scene from Stanley Kubrick's *Paths of Glory*, in which a young French girl sings a song in a tavern that brings tears to the eyes of hardened soldiers, Charlie set up a scene, reminiscent of an NFL locker-room hazing, among Schaefer truck drivers where new drivers have to sing the Schaefer theme song. Everybody's laughing because none of the young drivers can sing. Then a fresh-faced rookie (played by Larry Kert, the original Tony in *West Side Story*) stands up on a table. His sweet tenor voice is so clear and moving as he sings "the one beer to have when you're having more than one" that the hall falls into silence and tears well up in the drivers' eyes. It was Charlie's first TV assignment, it won a Clio, and it was nothing more than a commercial showcasing the beer's slogan (in effect, a celebration of a theme line, an ad about advertising). But that's what happens when you are armed with a strong insight and stick to your strategy. The ads often do write themselves.

This is how it always works in the advertising business: good *research* demands brilliant *analysis* which inspires blazing *insights* that lead to groundbreaking *strategies* and award-winning *executions*.

Except when it doesn't, which is a disconcertingly large part of the time.

It doesn't work because you can't predict when you'll capture lightning in a bottle, and even if you do, you can't guarantee that the client will be smart enough to recognize the lightning when he sees it. Or brave enough to play with lightning when he *does* recognize it. Insights do not adhere to a strict metronomic beat that begins with research and ends with execution. Insights materialize at any point along the matrix. Sometimes they are the product of elegant research and analysis. But just as often they appear because of a casual remark by the client about what he or she *really* wants, or in response to a clumsy execution of an ad that is so *lacking* in insight that it inspires you to fill in the blank. Or sometimes it's little more than trusting your gut, relying on instinct, feeling moved by a notion and assuming that the rest of the world will be equally moved.

I say this because, as much as I take pride in our insight-delivery "system," I'd be exaggerating if I claimed that our clients hire ad agencies, and particularly BBDO where I worked, for our research and analysis skills. We're not McKinsey & Co. with dozens of Harvard MBAs crunching numbers 24/7 so that we can write mammoth reports that justify enormous fees. We create campaigns that our clients absolutely love. Campaigns that drive sales, change the image, shift attitudes, sometimes alter the entire revenue landscape of a corporation. Anything less and the work doesn't get on the air and into print . . . and the client loses hundreds of millions of dollars . . . and we lose a client.

But if we're not pocket McKinseys, we're also not fools. We know the value of research and analysis. We poll consumers and conduct focus groups. We sift through the data that our clients provide and that we generate ourselves. More than anything else, we listen to the client's take on the data, and we listen to anyone in-house who's taken the time to *think* about the research.

If you look closely, you'll see that almost every successful area of endeavor follows this RAISE matrix to achieve its ends. Some endeavors don't know they're doing it. Some, like us wild and crazy guys in advertising, do it in loosey-goosey fashion, generating insight by blurring the line between instinct and analysis, head and gut.

The most fanatical loyalists to the RAISE process are people in politics, who are so slavishly devoted to polling data that they would not countenance any insight or strategy that isn't supported by the data. This isn't necessarily a bad thing. When you're selling a candidate in an election campaign, the voters have only one opportunity to buy—on election day. It's the year's biggest "one-day-only sale." So you poll and crunch numbers until you think you know everything on the voters' minds. Of course, having all the information at hand does not guarantee that you will use it wisely. Gleaning the perfect insight from perfect data is never a sure thing. Even Bill Clinton's most perfervid detractors in the Republican party will admit to his political skill and discipline. He never made a big political decision without first polling to see how it would play with voters. His real genius, though, was extracting insights from the data. That, I believe, is why he was so devoted to polling—he knew he could interpret the data more shrewdly than his competitors. In the 1992 presidential election, when all the data screamed out that voters cared only about pocketbook issues, which was where the incumbent George Bush was weakest, it was Clinton's team that had the insight to focus on the economy—and never waver from that message, even in the primaries when Clinton was being assailed for his personal indiscretions, his draft dodging, his dim-witted brother, his "Slick Willie" persona, you name it. "It's the economy, stupid" became the Clinton rallying cry, reminding the candidate to never go "off message" no matter what people said about him. A simple insight, obvious in hindsight, but so powerful it helped a man become President of the United States.

I got a strong taste of insight in the political arena eight years earlier with another president, Ronald Reagan. In 1984 Michael Deaver, Reagan's deputy chief of staff, at the suggestion of an old friend, Jim Lake, called to invite me to lunch at the White House. I was so nervous all I could think to say on the phone was "Great. What are we having?"

Deaver, it turned out, wanted BBDO to handle the advertising for President Reagan's reelection campaign. As I picked through a tuna and tomato salad in the Executive Dining Room, I explained that (a) we couldn't handle the assignment at BBDO, which had a long-standing policy against taking sides in politics, and (b) it was too big for me to handle alone. But I promised to do the next best thing: find someone who could. I called Jerry Della Femina about helping out. Jerry proposed that we assemble an ad hoc agency of the best people we could find, which was rather insightful in itself. It took some of the political stigma out of the assignment. We weren't choosing sides, or declaring our political affiliation, or trashing the Democrats. We were merely saying yes, at specially reduced rates, to a White House request—and getting to flex our creative muscles in the biggest game of all, a presidential election. This was greater than selling pickles or cereal or shoe polish. We called our all-star squad The Tuesday Team (named for election day) and gathered at the White House for our first meeting with the President.

Right from the start Dick Wirthlin, the President's chief pollster, had given us all the White House's research and polling data. The numbers told a simple story that wasn't hard to interpret. People liked the President. They were happy with the job he was doing. The economy was back on track after the "malaise" years of the Carter administration. Unemployment was down. A tax cut had worked. The stock market was surging. The nation was at peace. America's standing in the world was high again, after the humiliation of the Iran hostage crisis. You didn't have to be a political pro to read these numbers with a big smile on your face.

As advertising professionals we knew the proper campaign for a candidate with these positives was to take the high road. The research backed us up, consistently telling us that Americans felt uncomfortable when their president hit below the belt. With so much good news to emphasize, we aimed to win by a landslide, not a mudslide. At the same time, we could see that Walter Mondale, the Democratic nominee, was running a negative campaign. And positive beats negative every time in the ad effectiveness book.

But we were still lacking that singular insight that would set this analysis into motion—and give us the Big Idea for our first two assignments: (1) a kick-off ad campaign inaugurated by Hal Riney's memorable "Morning in America" spots; and (2) a 20-minute film to be shown at the Republican convention that summer in Dallas, an assignment I took on myself.

All that changed at that first White House meeting when Ronald Reagan suddenly entered the room where we were nervously waiting. Before we had a chance to swallow hard, he said, "I understand you guys are selling soap and I thought you'd like to see the bar."

Ronald Reagan never entered a room without spinning off a one-liner; it always broke the tension. In this case it provided our insight moment.

We were so focused on all the good things happening in our country, we had forgotten that people would associate the good news with Ronald Reagan. More important, we had forgotten that, no matter how you felt about his policies, the President had an extremely winning personality. While we were struggling to get a handle on how to package the positives, the President's quip woke us up. Our "product" wasn't America at peace or in prosperity. Our product was Ronald Reagan, and he was a helluva lot more than a bar of soap. Here was someone we could wrap in red, white, and blue. Here was someone beautifully playing the role of the nation's grandfather. Here was someone standing in sharp contrast to his predecessor. With this "product" front and center in any advertising, we could celebrate America and the Reagan administration's first four years. We could rightfully ask, "Why would we ever want to go back?"—and not be afraid of the answer.

It was a copywriter's dream, neatly fitting the marketing requirements they teach you at Harvard Business School. We had a solid product benefit: "Leadership that's working." "Leadership" has always been a firm platform to stand on. "Working" was our proof of claim.

And so I dreamt—in a hurry. In film terms, 18 minutes is a lot of time to fill, and I needed a concept big enough to carry it. As I closed my eyes and tried to will the right images and the right sounds to the front of my mind, I kept hearing the President's voice behind images of all the events that had taken place during his first term in office. We could use footage of the most momentous occasions of his presidency: Normandy Beach, where he led the commemoration of D-day; the historic Korean and Japanese trips where he cultivated our Asian allies; the Economic Summit in England, and the visit to Ireland, his ancestral home. And all of this would be narrated by Ronald Reagan himself. If we did it right, there wouldn't be a dry eye in Dallas by film's end.

Now, you have to remember this was 1984. Commercially polished advertising that centered on a near-shameless appeal to the voters' most noble instincts and emotions—rather than their wallets, their fears, their prejudices—was not the norm in presidential advertising. (And four short years later, in Bush *vs.* Dukakis, it would revert to vitriolic form again with the infamous "Willie Horton" ad and the Democratic nominee in a goofy tank commander's helmet.) But I have always believed that when a creative mind is given freedom to roam at will, the place where it characteristically spends its time is the human heart. So, I was very comfortable tugging at the voters' heartstrings. And armed with the insight that Reagan was our product, I was extremely confident that our pitch would play to the masses.

Within days, I started writing the script as our editors Bob DeRise and Tommy Maniacci started assembling film. All of us on The Tuesday Team knew that Ronald Reagan had a special ability to inspire a sense of confidence and security. We conveyed this in clips of the President visiting our troops in Korea; eliciting smiles and cheers as he mingled with our fighting men and women; capturing private moments with Mikhail Gorbachev; festive shots with Russian children during his historic nuclear control mission to Moscow.

We shot miles of original footage. Less than two weeks after the President popped his head into our meeting, I found myself standing on a beach in Normandy with a cheering throng of thousands. We had just flown in from Ireland where we had filmed the President visiting his ancestral home in Ballyporeen, Ireland. It was a moving occasion, but nothing compared to the main event, the focus of the President's trip: the fortieth anniversary of the D-day landing where he delivered one of his finest speeches. That trip and the accumulated imagery let us capture his optimism *and* the measured gravity with which he played his role in history (and taught this son of a Brooklyn cabdriver that motorcades and military helicopters are the only way to travel).

Working nights and weekends with our editors, our producer, Arnie Blum, and our account supervisor, Sig Rogich, we watched the film begin to take shape. We paced our cuts to the reassuring rhythms of the President's speech patterns, making the film a natural outgrowth of his real character. We sought to balance the public qualities of Reagan's leadership and his personal qualities of warmth, humor, and compassion. We included testimonies from Margaret Thatcher, backdrops like the Statue of Liberty, and the incomparable sound of Ray Charles singing "America the Beautiful."

When we screened it for the President at his ranch in Santa Barbara, even in rough cut form, there was no doubt it was a moving piece. During the Omaha Beach segment one of the Secret Service men turned away to wipe a tear as the President himself dabbed his eyes and said, "I didn't think I was supposed to cry at these things."

When the film aired in front of 12,000 rabid Republicans at the Dallas Convention Center and to 40 million Americans watching on television, it delivered the desired effect. And much more. The unapologetic emotional tone and sunny imagery of the film became the signature for the rest of the campaign's advertising and established a consistent uplifting message for the more than sixty ads that our Tuesday Team produced up until November. It also unnerved the Mondale-Ferraro ticket so completely that they never found an effective message to counter us.

But it all began with the Reagan-inspired insight that *the President is the product.*

We bring good things to life.

The one beer to have when you're having more than one.

It's the economy, stupid.

The President is the product.

If in citing these examples I make it sound as if every insight can be reduced to a cheery advertising sound bite, well . . . it's not too far from the truth. The problems an advertising agency tackles are big problems—and they are familiar to anyone in business. And if you can't express the problem's solution in a pithy phrase—so that you can repeat it relentlessly until it sticks to the roof of your mind—you haven't solved the problem.

Everybody in business knows the troubles I've seen, because they've seen them too.

- There's the problem of *parity*. In a world where eight beers cannot all be the driest, where eleven golf balls cannot each travel the farthest, where five automobiles cannot all deliver the smoothest ride, and worse, even if they do, the distinction isn't important enough to make a difference in the consumer's life, how do I differentiate myself from the crowd?

- There's the problem of *moving the needle*. In a world of mass markets and economies of scale, how do I sell more stuff so that it has a measurable impact on my business?

- There's the problem of *launching*. How do I tell the world I've arrived? That I'm here?

- There's the problem of *competition*. How do I fight off or attack my competition?

- There's the problem of *mission*. How do I express what I stand for?

- There's the problem of *image*. How do I establish an image, how do I change it, how do I improve it? How do I go from worst to first?

These are universal business problems, as serious to the budding entrepreneur with two Laundromats in Kansas City as they are to a master marketer like Nike's Phil Knight. They both want to stay in business, build market share, open new income streams, cement relationships with old customers, and attract new ones. What's important to note here (and serves as my sly way of establishing an adman's bona fides) is that when smartest-guy-in-the-room types like Jack Welch and Roger Enrico and Bill Gates and Fred Smith and Steve Jobs and Andy Grove need to deal with these universal issues, they invariably turn to advertising agencies for answers—and they spend hundreds of millions of dollars to support our conclusions.

What they're paying for, more than anything else, is our insight. All we need is one.

This book explores and explains how insights are born. Yes, I'll write it in part from my perch as an adman. After all, I've helped sell everything from pizzas to razors to automobiles to soft drinks. I know how to sift through the morass of confusing information and come up with the "phrase that pays," the nugget that breaks through the clutter and reaches consumers in their hearts, their guts, and their wallets. And I've seen how other successful professionals have done it too. Every man and woman who's ever had to sell something can relate to this, and vice versa. In the course of these endeavors, I've dealt with presidents and supermodels and pop idols. (We're not only the guys who set Michael Jackson's hair on fire for Pepsi, we followed that up with a commercial featuring Madonna that created such an uproar that it only ran once.) That experience ought to count for something.

But I am also writing from the vantage point of a manager. As the chairman and chief creative officer of BBDO's North American operations, overseeing 3,500 talented "knowledge workers" in a pressure-cooker milieu, I've learned that you can't legislate insight. You can't make your people be creative on cue all the time. But you *can* orchestrate insight. You *can* create a favorable environment for it. You *can* steer people toward it and demand it—and you *can* reject it when it doesn't meet your standards. That, too, ought to count for something.

What I want to show is simply this: when you're in search of an idea, big or small, there is a singular moment when insight rears its lovely head. The moment may pass in an instant (like Ronald Reagan entering a room and exiting) or it may sail over you unnoticed or it may smack you in your frontal lobe. I don't have guaranteed rules to help you recognize these moments—although I have some suggestions (such as, if it sounds like Mark Twain could have said it, keep it)— but I can aim to help you create and re-create the conditions where insight moments occur with milk-of-magnesia regularity.

Let me illustrate the difference between an insight and an idea—where they come from and what they are.

One reason why people treat insights and ideas as the same thing is that they often come serendipitously—out of small private moments or casual remarks or, perhaps, simply when we're standing on our front lawn getting angry.

This is what happened to Michael Deaver in his first year as Ronald Reagan's White House communications director in 1981. First thing every morning at his suburban Washington, D.C., home, Deaver would go out to his front lawn to pick up *The Washington Post, The New York Times,* and *The Wall Street Journal.* He'd scan the headlines. There he would read about a downturn in the unemployment rate or trouble in Eastern Europe or Congress threatening to hold up legislation. As he read, he had the depressing thought, "This is my day. I'm going to spend all morning dealing with these headlines, explaining the Reagan administration's position on each. My whole day is dictated by the need to *react* to these."

That's when it hit him. What if he could gain control of the news cycle rather than let it control him? That question was his big insight, and it gave him an idea.

Deaver's job was communicating the Reagan message, and he had learned a lot from the 1980 presidential race. He learned that you win only with a disciplined message and that you can't say anything just once. You have to pick a theme, stick to it, and hammer it home repeatedly. (This is something that all of us in advertising should know.)

As he thought about it, he realized that the President's schedule was both fixed and flexible. It was fixed in the sense that there were inviolate dates six to nine months out on the President's calendar where he had to be at an economic summit in Europe or make a state visit to Japan or receive a foreign leader at the White House. There were also fixed domestic events such as speeches at business and political conferences, which were locked in a year in advance. Not everybody built their calendar, but the leader of the free world had to. That, Deaver thought, could be an advantage. If we know where we have to be, we have a head start on everyone else.

He rushed to the White House and walked into Chief of Staff James Baker's office to announce that he was forming a group that would meet at Blair House, the vice president's home, at week's end. Its job would be to map out Ronald Reagan's schedule six months out. They would meet each Friday to update the schedule as they lost a week. He called it the Blair House Group. Its job was to think in long sweeping news arcs—to see the narrative arc of a message and figure out ways to deliver it over several months, to stick to it, and to make sure the media got it. This is how the White House could gain control of the news rather than being controlled by it.

His thinking was simple but counterintuitive. You don't win if you're constantly moving forward into the future; you're only playing catch-up. You win by working backwards, by mapping out your schedule six months ahead to see where you *want to be* and then figuring out what you have to do and say to get there. Thus, the White House message arc was invented.

A quarter century later, when everyone—not just politicians but CEOs and advocacy groups—is sophisticated about staying "on message," spinning the news, and staying three steps ahead of the media, this may seem obvious. But it was new back in 1981. No matter what you think of Ronald Reagan and his policies, there were many reasons he was known as the Great Communicator. Deaver's "control your message" insight was one of them.

Now, here's an *idea* born of serendipity that happened to us at BBDO in 1981, perhaps the same moment that Deaver was standing on his front lawn.

We were struggling to come up with a new corporate image commercial for General Electric. We already had the GE "We bring good things to life" slogan working, but we needed to show a GE product or service powerful enough to speak for the whole corporation.

The meeting was going nowhere. Every road had turned into a dead end and we decided to call it a day and resume the next morning. Bart Snider, then GE's advertising manager, muttered something about GE inventing the lights for night baseball games many years before. I perk up when the subject is baseball, and a light suddenly illuminated the dark outfield of my imagination.

I raced back to my office and called Ted Sann, our GE creative director. We locked the door and wrote the spot in less than two hours. We re-created that summer night in Lynn, Massachusetts, in 1924 when a group of GE engineers joyously arrived at the local ball field, still dressed in business suits and ties, to play what we called one of the most historic baseball games ever. We decided that the eagerness with which they played would be matched by a Keystone Kops ineptitude. (They're GE engineers, after all, not Ty Cobb.) A well-dressed young man with pomaded hair studied a thick paper portfolio, issuing instructions. Something momentous was in the air. Suddenly, banks of klieg lights came on from platforms built by GE engineers, allowing the game to continue into the darkness. Thus, in our telling, was night baseball born. The exuberance with which the lights were greeted made viewers feel that they had gone back in time to witness an exquisite moment in American history. The spot did its job, creating massive goodwill for GE. It ran as part of GE's corporate campaign for thirteen years.

But it wasn't an insight. It was just an idea that was well executed.

That's the difference between Deaver's brainwave and our "Night Baseball" commercial. Deaver's notion was an insight that changed how an administration operates. It told people in the White House that they could wrest control of the news cycle back from an aggressive media empowered by the investigative triumphs of Watergate. And like all big insights, it inspired a tidal wave of ideas that brought the insight to life—from constructing the President's schedule six months out and working backwards to creating vivid visual tableaus as backdrops to the President's speeches to reinforce the arc's message.

On the other hand, our "Night Baseball" idea was just that—a notion overheard as a meeting winds down. It didn't inspire a raft of other ideas. It stood alone, illustrating a human side of GE's engineering excellence as a happy symbol of the entire corporate enterprise. It supported the insight that GE brings good things to life.

When you think about it, insight is a precious gift—and not just in the workplace. It's the reason in times of moral crisis that we turn to ministers and rabbis and priests; in times of personal pain that we turn to psychologists and therapists; in times of emotional confusion that we turn to a wise friend. The best counselors have the tools and experience to assess our situation and see it from a different perspective. If we used their insights properly, our marriages would be more stable, our children would be easier to raise, our friendships would be more durable, our careers would proceed seamlessly from one success to the next. That is the ideal state, the perfect world, I'm trying to capture in this book.

I originally thought I'd structure this book to the stately cadences of my RAISE matrix. I'd write about insights through the prism of research and analysis and strategy and execution. But then I realized that I'm not particularly proficient in the mechanics of research and analysis. I don't crunch numbers. I don't conduct polls. They are merely means to an end (important means, to be sure, and I will give them their due). But I'm much more fascinated by business problems and their eventual solution.

As a veteran of serious marketing wars who's sat in countless conference rooms hearing out clients' woes, I've had to deal with all the challenges that businesspeople face. We'll toss them up like a baseball here and take a healthy swing at hitting them out of the park.

Shall we begin?

CHAPTER 1

ALL THINGS
BEING EQUAL

America is a big nation, so big in fact that it is not just one enormous economic market. It is a collection of many different economies. In order to visualize and understand these various economies, we often resort to "branding" them, giving them names that collect all the chaotic forces fighting for recognition into one intelligible grab bag.

When America began its drift away from making things to serving people, someone described the new scene as the *service economy*. From there it was a short leap to the *leisure economy* and the *knowledge economy*. In the 1970s, when we realized how perilously dependent we were on dwindling energy resources, we saw the world through the prism of the *oil economy*, and then the *scarcity economy*, which led naturally to the *environmental economy*. When we started borrowing more than we saved, we created the *debtor economy* and then suffered through the *inflation economy*. We've enjoyed the *convenience economy* and evolved with the *spiritual economy*. One company has become so dominant and life-altering that pundits have named the *Wal-Mart economy* after it (although I like to think Wal-Mart has succeeded by exploiting the *value economy*). Obviously, we remain in the *digital economy* and we have no idea how big the *Internet economy* will become. A book in 1997 claimed that the *entertainment economy* was the mega-media force that would shape our lives. As I write this I'm looking at a cover of *Business Week* devoted to the *innovation economy* while an American president is touting the wonders of the *ownership economy*—which perhaps will be the cure for the *outsourcing economy*. Andrew Robertson, BBDO's worldwide CEO, branded the swelling torrent of media and the scarcity of time to consume it as the *attention economy*.

I'm not mocking these attempts to brand our business environments. These are all legitimate descriptions, although they are profoundly colored by how we earn a living and what really matters to us. I guess if you loved running a pizzeria, your world would be governed by dough, cheese, tomato sauce, and pepperoni. You'd be living in a *pizza economy*.

As for me, an advertising professional, I have my own economy to worry about. Let's call it the *parity economy*—a world where all products and services are perceived as equal, with differences so miniscule that they do not dent the average consumer's consciousness. I have spent every hour of my waking life thinking about the parity economy and what I can do to help my clients escape its pernicious clutches. It even infects my dreams. I worry about parity not only when I'm awake but in my sleep.

The dream is always the same. Actually, it's a nightmare. In it there is a tightly coordinated marching band, consisting of beautifully synchronized trumpeters and trombonists and drummers. There are also high-stepping baton twirlers in my dream. And strutting majorettes and jumping cheerleaders. It is a glorious festive affair, and the number of participants exceeds 20,000.

The only thing unusual about these energetic participants is their uniform. They aren't dressed in the traditional garb of a marching band. Rather, they're dressed in the costumes of America's best-known brand-name products. They're a marching brand, not a band. One hundred eight brands of cigarettes lead the pack, followed by 800 brands of fragrances and 230 brands of cereals. And this is where the nightmarish part begins. The cereals, like the fragrances and cigarettes, are remarkably similar. Froot Loops is strutting next to Loop de Loops, Honey Nut is paired with Nut'n Honey, Cracklin' Bran with Oat Bran, Bran Flakes with Raisin Bran with 40% Bran, Bran Flakes with Corn Flakes, and on and on.

It's a marching band of marching brands.

Now it's passing the VIP reviewing stand which is jammed with the creative directors of all the leading ad agencies. Somewhere I'm among them. I know it's paranoid to think that all the brands turn to stare at me as they pass. But in my nightmare, they do.

The band abruptly comes to a halt, members in the rear comically slamming into the ranks in front of them. Suddenly a discordant mélange of 20,000 instruments is playing different tunes in different keys at the same time. The noise is grating, and as it grows in volume, the decibel level becomes painful—like millions of fingernails scraping across a chalkboard.

This is the moment when I wake, a bit shaken but grateful that it was only a dream.

But was it?

If nightmares are our fears projected on the screen of our

sleeping minds, the vapid sameness of the 20,000-piece brand-name band is totally appropriate for someone like me. This parity among brands is indeed a nightmare sufficiently chilling to disturb the peace and induce night sweats.

I have devoted my career to solving a simple marketing riddle: How do you separate your client's brand from everyone else's? How do you distinguish it from the pack? How do you provide that brand with a character that leverages it a full notch above the competition in the public's mind?

And so the dream makes perfect sense. In the clear, cold light of wakefulness, when I am alert and rational, I know that consumers must deal with this marching band every day. They are assaulted by the painful similarity among brands of perfumes and soaps and beers and cars. They are drummed senseless by the mind-numbing spectacle. They are the citizens of the parity economy. As am I. That's why the age of parity is my nightmare.

Today's marketplace is cluttered with products that are no better and no worse than their competitors. Even with advances in technology that materialize each week, the outstanding product benefit you invent today will almost certainly be copied by everyone else tomorrow.

It wasn't always like this. When an automobile company would introduce a new model with standout design or driving features, that automaker was guaranteed at least a five-year window of unchallenged freedom to exploit that advantage. That's how long it took auto companies to copy and catch up to a competitor: five years. That changed in the 1970s with the emergence of Japanese automakers, who could copy any American innovation and bring it to market within three years. By the 1980s, with the Japanese copying not only Americans but Europeans as well, the auto industry became a mishmash of parity—with everyone copying each other in ever-shrinking time frames. Three years after Chrysler came out with the groundbreaking and enormously successful minivan, not only were the Japanese copying it, but so were the Americans.

The salt in the wound is that all too often your new product benefit, which you have spent years perfecting, is not valued very highly by the consumer. We have found time and again that when our clients' research and development departments have told us, "Here is our latest miracle," the consumer has yawned. "No big deal. My shirts are white enough. My floors are clean enough. This is not important enough to make a difference in my life."

The truly disconcerting aspect of parity among products and services is how it metastasizes into parity in advertising—advertising that looks and sounds and feels like everyone else's advertising. This is hard to fathom, even perverse, when you consider that advertising's only purpose is to differentiate brands in the consumer's mind and to minimize whatever brand parity exists.

But it happens all the time. The reflexive churning of clichés, the autonomic allegiance to the tried and true, the zombie-like adherence to the "rules" are also part of the nightmare in which the marching band struts its banal stuff.

Eventually, even the band members drop of exhaustion. The mindless tune they've been tooting up and down the avenue finally fails to attract anyone's attention. After all, consumers inevitably spot the copycats. They get wise to the word weasels and their claims rationalizing some flimsy point of difference that barely scrapes by the lawyers. They know when they are being conned. They learn that each of eleven brands of golf balls cannot possibly travel the farthest; that eight beers cannot all be the driest; that five automobiles cannot all deliver the smoothest ride. The consumer, having been exposed to an avalanche of similar products, touted to similar claims and tunes, correctly surmises that all of them cannot be unique.

When everyone is the best, no one is the best.

This is how superlatives—the most valuable words in any communicator's rhetorical arsenal—gradually yield their authority and power. Suddenly being the "strongest" or "fastest-acting" or "longest-lasting" or "most reliable" or "friendliest" no longer packs a wallop, because these words have been attached to so many similar products in so many similar messages that the consumer can no longer correctly associate the superlatives with the product. Think about it: When was the last time you saw or heard the word "best" employed in a convincing or memorable advertisement? The word has been so overused and abused, it has been drained of all its resident meaning. For advertising purposes, "best" is practically obsolete (one exception: Gillette's "The Best a Man Can Get" is still working in its second decade).

This is how language becomes impoverished. This is how messages become muddled. This is how imitation becomes the lingua franca of marketing. This is how my chosen field, the advertising industry, joins the parity economy.

I shudder to admit that all this imitation, while being the sincerest form of flattery, is neither unwilling nor accidental. It's genuine, spawned by real advertisers unabashedly telling their agencies, "Do me one of those Apple spots" or "Give us something along the lines of the Nike campaign." The other guy talks calories in his ads, so you talk calories in yours. The other guy talks horsepower, so you talk horsepower. The other guy adds a miracle ingredient, so you add one too. All the faces in the marching band blend into one. All the tunes echo melodies you've heard elsewhere. And then it's no surprise that sales suffer—that you move the needle in the wrong direction—because the public gets confused. And pretty soon boredom sets in. And then you're dead.

What's truly insidious here is that when a genuinely unique client comes along, offering a product or service that has never been seen before, your mind is so geared to detecting parity and fighting it that you might not notice that parity, for once, is not part of the client's equation. Parity is absent. That's what happened to us at BBDO in 1984 when we were invited to pitch the HBO account.

HBO wasn't HBO back then, the home of *The Sopranos* and *Sex and the City* and *Curb Your Enthusiasm* and a $100-million miniseries produced by Steven Spielberg and Tom Hanks. For one thing, it was known as Home Box Office. The bulk of its programming back then was showing major (and not-so-major) movies a few months after their theatrical release, much of it family-friendly viewing, some of it edgier or as HBO liked to say, "uncut and uncensored." It broadcast live performances by big-time as well as undiscovered comedians, complete with racy subjects and salty language. It put on championship boxing matches, with cameras and microphones in each corner between rounds giving viewers images and sounds they had never witnessed before. And it repeated these programs endlessly throughout the month.

And that was the problem. Home Box Office was a radical concept at the time—a paid subscription TV service. So, when subscribers felt they had seen all the new programming that season, they'd become disenchanted, call their cable company, and say, "Disconnect me from HBO." Just like that. HBO's challenge was first to keep their existing subscribers from walking out the back door and, second, to bring in new subscribers through the front door at a faster clip than they were leaving. It was the classic bathtub riddle you faced in grade school. If you're losing x amount of water down the drain, how fast does the spigot have to run to keep the bathtub full? Our job was to create advertising that did both jobs at once—clog the drain and speed up the spigot. It had to bring in new customers by introducing them to HBO and it had to keep good subscribers in the fold by reminding them why they subscribed in the first place.

As we listened to the HBO executives explain their business goals, my mind was racing, turning over every word they said, hoping to find some supercharged phrase that would help me identify the one product benefit, large or small, that would break through the parity barrier. And then it hit me. Parity? Parity with what? With regular television? With movies in theaters? With other basic cable channels? With magazines, books, records, concerts, amusement parks, and other myriad forms of entertainment? What was HBO comparable to?

That's when I realized that the insight had already walked through the door, that *there was nothing out there like HBO.* All my training and experience fighting parity was pointless in this case—because parity wasn't in the mix. HBO was presenting a set of circumstances and features unlike anything we had seen before.

The economics of HBO were certainly unique. You had to pay to get it. This was unprecedented to American television consumers, who were so accustomed to free TV that they thought it was written into the Bill of Rights. Complicating that, HBO was a premium pay channel. You had to hook up to basic cable first and *then* you paid extra to get HBO. In effect, consumers were being asked to (a) work a little harder than usual and (b) go into their pockets twice simply to watch television. I was also intrigued by the idea that any advertising we created for HBO would be running on television channels such as ABC, NBC, and CBS that HBO was competing with. It was like using a Coke bottle to advertise Pepsi. Or *USA Today* taking out an ad in *The New York Times* saying, "Hey, read us, not the paper you're reading." This suggested to me that we couldn't say anything too negative about the networks—we couldn't slam them as a retrograde inferior product. The closest we could come would be saying something on the order of "We're not the channel you're watching right now. We're something else." But even that notion emphasized HBO's uniqueness.

More important, HBO's programming mix of movies, live comedy, the occasional sports special, and (oh yes) no commercials was 180 degrees different from anything on traditional TV. The only thing HBO and network TV had in common was the device people used to watch the channels, that is, the television itself. Everything else was night and day.

I calmly turned off my brain, looked up at the ceiling to whisper "Thank you, Lord," and sat back to relax at the realization that I was facing one of those rare occasions when parity is not an issue. The insight is much more apparent, much closer to the surface. But still you have to see it, seize it, and know how to run with it.

We almost didn't. As we prepared our presentation that summer for what would be the biggest account review of the year, we lapsed into old habits, still thinking in terms of parity. We took a few wrong paths in preparing our pitch. One of our false starts was to establish HBO as "the entertainment center"—because we saw it as a pure entertainment channel. No news, no local sports. Just entertainment. We took a Billy Joel song, "The Entertainer," and dreamed up some fun words to go with the tune. But then we saw that we were falling into the same old parity rut, trying to identify a little morsel of distinctiveness and exploit it. Entertainment wasn't an insight. A lot of stuff on free TV qualified as "entertainment." In the end, all we were saying was, "Hey, we're like the other guys, but we're a little better."

That's when we came back to our senses and committed ourselves to the insight that walked through the door: there's nothing out there like HBO. In fact, that more or less became the theme line of our pitch: "There's no place like HBO."

None of the five other agencies competing for the business took that position. None of them exploited HBO's uniqueness. They all presented parity-inspired concepts attempting to give HBO a small edge over the competition, when in fact HBO was the only game in town. We won the account.

Twenty years later BBDO still has the business, although it's evolved slightly to deal with the 500-plus channels that constantly threaten to lure eyeballs away from HBO. Even with over 30 million subscribers, HBO still has the same bathtub drain challenge of adding new customers at a faster rate than it loses customers. But the new theme line, "It's not TV, it's HBO," still hinges on the same insight—that HBO has eclipsed parity, that it's unique, that there's still nothing else like it.

That notion gave rise to one of my favorite commercials produced during my years at BBDO. It's called "Chimps" and it is the first commercial to ever win an Emmy Award. It begins in the Grebe Preserve in Africa with vignettes of friendly chimps in the jungle. An older chimpanzee scratches his chin and moves his lips, only the voice is that of Marlon Brando's Don Corleone from *The Godfather* saying, "Tataglia's a pimp. He never could have outfought Santino." Next is a young chimpanzee, swinging on a branch, in the voice of Tom Hanks from *Forrest Gump*: "Momma says, 'Stupid is as stupid does.'" An enraged chimp quotes Peter Finch's Howard Beal from *Network,* "I'm mad as hell and I'm not going to take it anymore." An older chimp employs James Earl Jones's voice to tell a younger chimp that "The Force is with you, young Skywalker." A wild group of chimpanzees, banging sticks, chant, "Toga, toga, toga . . ." from *Animal House.* What's going on here? Why are chimpanzees quoting memorable lines from great movies? Quick cut to a woman writing in her journal: "Their inexplicable behavior continues. Ought to go now. *Braveheart* is on." She's identified as world-famous animal researcher Jane Goodall, "HBO viewer since 1978." As she settles down to watch *Braveheart,* we see chimpanzees outside her window watching too. Then the graphic: "It's not TV. It's HBO."

I cite HBO here as the exception that proves the rule—the rare marquee brand that transcends parity. I have a hard time coming up with other marquee names that do the same. Perhaps the Disney theme parks; there's nothing else like them either. But in every other arena parity defines the struggle between big-name brands. It's certainly the guiding issue in

Wal-Mart *vs*. Target, or Pepsi *vs*. Coke, or Toyota *vs*. Honda, or Mercedes *vs*. BMW, or *Time vs. Newsweek,* or Budweiser *vs*. Miller, or Crest *vs*. Colgate. These are not mere commodities. These are mega-brands with billions of dollars of advertising, image-making, and brand equity supporting them. And yet, despite the multibillion-dollar investment in each, these brands still have to prove every day of the week that they are *not* the same as every other store, soft drink, car, newsmagazine, beer, and toothpaste.

Ironically, even ad agencies, whose job is to clear a path through the fog of sameness for their clients, suffer from parity issues. All ad agencies are not alike (of course!) but that doesn't mean they are not perceived that way, or that whatever differences they have should be significant to clients. Before we can execute strategies that depose the tyranny of sameness for our clients' products and services, we have to solve that problem in our own world as well.

Every agency attacks the issue in its own way. But it's safe to say that no agency prospers and grows unless it has a guiding philosophy to deal with parity. At BBDO, I like to think we have had a recognizable—though not predictable—signature for the kinds of advertising we created. We fight the war on parity not with logic alone. Yes, we can construct a rational sales argument as well as the next guy, but our primary objective has always been to create a dramatic showcase that appeals to the consumer emotionally and, more important, entices the consumer to enter the picture.

We want the consumer to know that we are talking to him or her directly as an individual, not as a demographic, and that we understand the kind of life he or she leads and why our brand would mesh perfectly with that life.

We see it as a marriage of *logical persuasion* with *emotional drama*. Not everyone does it this way. But we like to think of it as our creative signature, our strategy. We expect two things from it: We want consumers to tell themselves in the most rational way, "I get what you're saying. I understand what your brand offers me." And then we want each consumer to feel emotionally, "In my gut, I like what you're saying. That's me you're talking to. That's my life."

If we can accomplish these two not-so-simple objectives—if we can get the consumer to *accept* our logic and then to *feel* it emotionally (by crying, laughing, or whatever)—then we have created an unassailable combination. It's a one–two punch. The logic is the haymaker to parity's head. The emotion is the roundhouse right to the gut that puts parity down for the count.[1]

For example, the logic of the "Chimps" commercial is that it reminds people of the simple fact that HBO has perennially been the place where consumers can see great movies, and see them so often that they can remember the best lines. The emotional part—in this case, a sophisticated appeal to the funny bone—is using chimpanzees instead of human beings to express this point.

What's missing here, of course, is the commercial itself, its execution. You don't see how carefully the chimpanzees were cast and photographed, or how diligently their facial expressions and lip movements were synchronized with the soundtrack (they actually looked like they were talking), or how

---

[1] If you're a baseball fan, think of it in terms of a great fielding shortstop who can hit .315 *and* knock in 50 home runs a year. Lots of shortstops have hit .315, but only Alex Rodriguez (when he played shortstop as a Texas Ranger) did that *and* hit 50 home runs. That's how he broke parity and became the highest paid player in baseball history.

much effort it took to clear the rights to the films and to sign up Jane Goodall, not to mention filming in the African jungle. I promised in the Introduction that this would not be a book about advertising, so you're going to have to take my word for it that the execution of our insight was as good as it gets, or at least up to our highest standards.

That's the unspoken subtheme in this book, and I will deal with it here for the first and only time. At every step of the process, from research to execution, you need creative people. Their decision on whom to cast, the lighting, the music, the photography, the style and size of the print must always serve the ethos of breaking parity. Production details are not extraneous to the message. In the end, they become the message.

To debase these details, or to minimize them, is to leave the job half done. It is a sin. And sins such as copycats, fake slices of life, freaky soundtracks, neurotic quick-cuts, random editing, and most virulently, clichéd words and pictures are daggers pointed at the heart of strong insightful work.

Getting to the point where our execution matches the visions in our heads isn't the product of a one-trick pony or one-man show. Everybody helps—from the media buyers who showcase our ads in the best possible environment, to the research people who don't just count heads but get inside them, to the account management people whose intellect and intuition keep us glued to the right course and aimed in the same direction as the client. And then there are all the people who execute the work, bring it to life, and maintain the competitive edge. That kind of achievement doesn't come from a computer, or a chart, or a committee in a crowded room. Most likely it is going to come from one creative person's crowded mind—from a person who has nightmares as well as dreams.

Deciding to be a "creative" agency—that is, we're gonna do things our way and they're gonna be different—was the only way we believed we could survive in the parity economy. And thrive.

I used to think that I was the only person who had to worry about parity. After all, the chairman of FedEx doesn't dream of marching bands populated by same-seeming services and products the way I do. He's got other reasons to lose sleep— such as his 113,000 employees, his fleet of 700 jets, and rising jet fuel prices. He hires guys like us to solve his parity problem—to create a message that differentiates FedEx from UPS and DHL.

I used to think that way. Then I walked into my favorite wineshop in Sag Harbor, Long Island, where my wife and I have a weekend home. The proprietor was reading a book titled *Bang*. It caught my eye because it was written by a friend, Linda Kaplan Thaler, who runs her own ad agency. Although Linda has had many successes, she's probably most famous for coming up with the remarkable AFLAC duck commercials to sell supplemental employee insurance. Her book was about "getting your message heard in a noisy world" (I guess she was dealing with the *clutter economy*). It's a lively recap of all the problems she's solved for clients who need to get noticed—by coining phrases like "Kodak moment" and easy to remember jingles like "I don't want to grow up" for Toys 'Я' Us. I figured Linda's book would appeal to marketing directors at big companies and other businesspeople with big ideas and big budgets. I didn't think it would appeal to a small wineshop owner.

"Why are you reading that?" I asked.

"I thought I could learn something. Every business can use a bang now and then," he said.

As I thought about him later that day, it dawned on me that maybe he had parity nightmares too. When you think about it, a liquor store is close to a pure parity play. It's a door, a counter, some shelves to hold the bottles of booze, some racks to hold the wine bottles. The vast majority of the product line can be found in any other liquor store, whether it's an $8 bottle of chardonnay or a slightly more upmarket bottle of Glenlivet single malt Scotch. So what differentiates one store from another?

That's what the store owner was pondering when he picked up a marketing book about getting your message heard.

A book like *Bang*—or this one for that matter—wasn't going to give that store owner ideas about how to run a wineshop. But it *would* show him how others have tried to stand out from the crowd. And once people see how others have set themselves apart, they see the sneaky deleterious effect of parity. They get *ideas;* they swell with the ambition to be a little different too. It might be good for business.

I don't spend much time thinking about how to run a wineshop, but once the question enters the frontal lobe, some quick off-the-rack solutions come to mind. I would offer *free delivery,* which in a world where "time is money" provides a service that saves people time without costing them money. I would set up *wine tastings,* which lures people into my shop with the promise of educating them about a tricky subject. I'd improve my *selection,* maybe even to the point of specializing in one type of wine so that I could legitimately brag that I had the best selection of, say, Oregon pinot noir in the world. (Nothing fights parity better than being the "best in the world" at something, anything.) I'd set up an *Internet site.* I'd offer *daily sales*—for example, 15 percent off every Italian wine on Mondays, 15 percent off every American red wine on Tuesdays, and so on through the week. Anything to distinguish myself.

But even then, I know that in the parity economy, whatever bit of differentiation I can establish and use to my advantage is fleeting. There's always someone else either chipping away at my edge, or establishing their own uniqueness, or quite often, simply copying me.

For example, a few blocks from my home in Manhattan is another wineshop called Best Cellars, which was designed to be like no other wine store in the world. The concept is simple: it sells only one hundred wines (thus flouting the merits of offering a lot of choice) all priced at under $20, arranged not by region or grape but by color-coded flavors, set in stylish type fonts, such as "juicy," "smooth," and "big" for red wines, "fizzy," "fresh," and "soft" for whites. The insight behind this daring approach is a good one. To most people, buying wine is like taking an essay test, where one has to describe one's taste preferences, price range, attitude toward different regions, maybe even one's lifelong drinking experience. You're not buying a bottle of wine; you're channeling a life's worth of alcohol consumption. Best Cellars turns the essay test into multiple choice: all you have to do is get yourself to the right flavor and category and choose one of the five or six wines available. Instead of retail shelves, the store displays the wines via a prize-winning design of back-lit cubbyholes in vertical rows of nine. The store has even taken price out of the equation because no bottle exceeds $20. Maybe best of all, it creates a staff of experts (how tough can it be to master one hundred wines?), which gives the store a valuable claim to superb in-store service. The concept worked well enough that Best Cellars soon expanded to Seattle and Boston.

But then the parity economy exerted its gravitational pull on Best Cellars. A wine merchant in Washington, D.C., had the brilliant insight to hire one of Best Cellars cofounders and copy virtually every retailing element that Best Cellars had developed. He situated his store on fashionable Dupont Circle and called it Grape Finds. I know about this because the controversy ended up in the U.S. Court of Appeals, with Best Cellars suing Grape Finds for copying its proprietary ideas (a legal concept called "trade dress"). In the end Best Cellars acquired Grape Finds. But that's part of the parity economy too; if it's too costly to differentiate yourself *again* from all the me-too copycats, don't try to beat them at *your* game. Buy them.

I don't want to get bogged down in the intricacies of wine retailing—the subject here is not the "wine economy"—but get used to my wineshop owner from Sag Harbor. From time to time he's going to be making cameo appearances because he's emblematic of the challenges that any businessperson faces. He could be anybody—a one-store proprietor or the CEO of a giant consumer goods company. He deals with customers every day. He sells a parity product. He has competition, seen and unseen, everywhere. At any given point in time, he deals with the universal problems of selling more stuff, letting people know how to find him, creating an image for himself, understanding what his customers really want, trusting his gut, reinventing himself, and keeping the insights coming so he grows.

The American marketplace is dominated by two giant warring impulses. First, the *democratizing* urge that seeks to prove that "all men are created equal," that you're no better than I am and I'm no better than you. It's a bedrock American principle—determining how we choose our leaders (one person, one vote) and how we lead our lives (equal rights, equal opportunity). It's also a paradox: it elevates us as a society while diminishing us slightly as individuals. Then, the *competitive* urge that simultaneously seeks to refute this. We all want to establish ourselves as being a little better than the next guy. Whether it's something as trivial as the car we drive or as crucial as the level of professional service we provide, we want to prove that we are not like everybody else, that we're slightly unique, and therefore slightly more worthy of other people's honor, trust, tribute, and loyalty. This is how great organizations, great brands establish themselves.

In the remaining pages, I'll point out all the forces that are working overtime to bring you, your business, your product or service, your image, your message, and your future down into the great equalized maw of sameness where you are indeed everyone's equal. And then I'll show you how to think your way out of this trap.

CHAPTER 2

PUTTING YOUR FAITH IN RESEARCH

Insights do not appear in a vacuum. They appear when you start assimilating information. This is true in business and in life. If you're a parent of a teenager who's troubled about something, you can't assume that, as a parent, you have some innate gift that sees with 20/20 clarity into the core of the teenage brain and soul. You have to assume that you're clueless because that forces you to gather information. You call up the child's teachers, coaches, and friends to ask, "What's going on?" You may even ask your child some innocent questions about his or her day. Then you start sorting out the evidence until an insight about what's *really* on the teenager's mind emerges. In other words, you conduct research. That's the primary source of information. And information is where insights begin.

Research, of course, comes in many forms. And they're all legitimate *if* they produce valid insights. Everyone works differently at the game of research.

Some people are obsessively diligent about it. They leave no stone unturned in their search for meaningful information. They need to know everything about a problem so they can conduct intense analysis of the data. They do not feel secure if the data are incomplete. They think they're missing something, that their analysis will come up short.

Others trust their intuition. They can isolate one morsel of information from a messy pile of research and know that *this morsel is the one that matters*. Their gut tells them to ignore all other inputs.

Roger Enrico got his big career break early on at PepsiCo by spotting a gold needle in the haystack of marketing data that no one else was seeing.

The year was 1973. Enrico was working at Frito-Lay in Dallas as the young brand manager of Doritos. The brand came in three flavors then: the original Toasted Corn, Taco Flavored, and the newly introduced Nacho Cheese Flavor. Nacho Cheese, being the newest, intrigued Enrico because it was already selling well. What he wanted to know was how many consumers actually tried the new product versus the other two mainstays: Toasted Corn and Taco. He couldn't tell from the existing data because the numbers were all rolled into the total Doritos brand. So he asked his ad agency at the time, Tracey-Locke, to provide him with data on the trial rate of the three individual flavors. "Trial rate" is marketing speak for the percentage of people who are trying your product for the first time. In reality, it's a painstaking research process that takes at least two months to complete. But in the end, it gets the job done and gives you accurate data.

What the research told Enrico was that the main flavor, Toasted Corn Doritos, had a 40-percent trial rate (meaning four out of ten consumers tried the product for the first time), Taco Flavored was also near 40 percent, and Nacho Cheese was lagging at 10 percent (meaning only one out of ten people actually tried it). The Nacho Cheese trial rate should have depressed Enrico. But as he compared it to overall sales, an interesting contradiction emerged. Nacho Cheese had the same level of sales as the other two more established flavors. Enrico thought, "I didn't pass calculus, but my arithmetic isn't that bad. If sales are the same with 10 percent trial against 40 percent, then people must be buying Nacho Cheese Doritos a lot more often or in larger amounts. So let's not concern ourselves with the repeat rate. Let's focus on that first-time consumption rate. People are buying Nacho Cheese four to one. The upside here could be 400 percent. We've got a monster hit on our hands and don't know it. We've got to relaunch Nacho Cheese Doritos!"

That was Enrico's initial reaction. But as with many of us, when the research comes back with an obvious truth, our first impulse is to mistrust it. Enrico thought, "It can't be this easy. The world is not so generous to young Italian marketing guys. You can't just step into a new job, ask one question, and get a new killer brand handed to you on a silver platter."

So Enrico did what any fresh-faced executive who didn't have a track record yet to trust his gut would do. He called up his ad agency and told them to repeat the process. "It can't be this good," he said. "Consumers must be confused. They probably don't know one flavor from another. You've got to do the research again so we can see if the results hold up the second time around." And then he called a meeting—a four-day brand planning conference at The Wigwam in Phoenix, Arizona, where the first presentation centered on the latest research results on Doritos. The results were exactly the same as the earlier survey: Nacho Cheese outsells the others four to one.

This was the moment when Enrico's soft and fuzzy hunch

turned into a solid-gold insight. "The conclusion is obvious," he told his team. "We should take all our advertising and commit it totally to this new flavor. We should get behind this product and relaunch the hell out of it because we have been given gold from heaven."

Thirty minutes into the planning conference, he adjourned the meeting for three days of sunshine, golf, dinner, and hanging out. "What else is there to talk about?" he thought. "If we talk anymore, we'll ruin it."

When Roger's team returned to Dallas, he ordered them to put all their energy into relaunching Nacho Cheese. Then he went to his boss, Jim Groebe, and presented both the research and his plan. Groebe agreed that it made sense. Next he went to Groebe's boss, the head of all sales and marketing at Frito-Lay, for approval. The sales and marketing chief didn't like the idea because he feared that concentrating on one brand would shortchange the other two. So he told Roger to continue marketing and advertising *all three* flavors.

When you have a big insight—even if it's only about Nacho Cheese Doritos—you have to protect it at all costs, even to the point of insubordination. Roger decided to go to the wall for what he believed. He went back to his team and told them to keep going: focus on the one flavor, focus on Nacho Cheese. They directed their ad agency to create commercials that didn't even show the other two flavors. When Roger showed the spots that he planned to air to Groebe, he was told, "You're on your own here, Roger. It's the right thing to do, but you're out on this limb by yourself." Then Enrico went to Groebe's boss and showed him the spots. With each commercial that ignored the other two brands, he could see the sales and marketing head becoming more steamed. As the presentation ended, the man leapt to his feet and reminded Roger in the harshest terms that since the spots did not reflect the direction he was given, they cannot go on the air.

Enrico shot back that they'd bought a "roadblock" on all three networks for Sunday (a roadblock is a media buy that airs a commercial at the same time on multiple channels so that viewers can't miss it). "These commercials are going on the air," he said. "If you stop the buy, then next Monday morning you won't have a marketing team. We're out of here." Enrico conveniently neglected to mention that he had never checked this threat with his team.

The marketing chief looked at Enrico in disbelief and said, "You're serious, aren't you?"

"Dead serious," Roger said.

"Well, I think you're wrong about this, but I have to admit, I like your determination. Go ahead and run them. And you'd better be right."

The commercials ran on Sunday night and sales immediately took off; in fact, they doubled within a year.

I tell this story at some length because it demonstrates the awesome power of research properly assessed and courageously applied. This "trial rate" episode was the defining moment in Enrico's fledgling career. Some years later, he became PepsiCo's chairman and CEO. The Doritos episode also became a legendary story that seeped into the PepsiCo culture, an example of how the company wanted its executives to act: that it's okay to stick your neck out, that you're courageous enough about a conviction to quit over it. Today, Frito-Lay is a money-machine that dominates the salty snacks category. Pound for pound it is one of the most profitable enterprises on Earth, up there with Intel and Microsoft. And its single most profitable product thirty years later remains . . . Nacho Cheese Doritos.

The kind of research Enrico relied on was disciplined, quasi-scientific (in the sense that it was repeatable), and fairly sophisticated. That's fitting because marketers, by definition, rely more heavily on research of consumer habits than any other industry.

It's equally true in the advertising business, which has a long complicated history of research.

We've all heard the cliché about advertising: "Only half your advertising budget works. The problem is you don't know which half." Well, the history of research in the advertising industry is basically the history of advertising people striving overtime to prove which half of the ad budget is working.

It started as far back as the 1920s with a researcher named Daniel Starch who argued that the only advertising that worked was advertising consumers noticed and remembered. He famously wrote in an article in 1923 that "An advertisement, to be successful (a) must be seen, (b) must be read, (c) must be believed, (d) must be remembered, and (e) must be acted upon."[1] Starch set up a service to tell advertisers how many people could recognize their ad in magazines they read. In doing so Starch launched what was, at the time, the most labor-intensive activity in the history of social science research. Hundreds of researchers were sent out into the streets, loaded down with packets of magazines, with the sole purpose of finding out how well consumers could recall a

---

[1] For the moment, let's ignore the inherent fallacy in Starch's argument. It implies that each individual opportunity to notice and recall an ad exists independently of other exposures to that ad. It doesn't account for the accumulated returns of repeat exposures to an ad, which is at the heart of creating awareness and building a brand.

client's ads. This was the birth of research devoted to the *audience*. And it cannot be overstated how influential Starch scores became in the minds of anyone who created ads or paid for them. This influence eventually extended beyond the world of magazines and into television where the Chicago-based Nielsen firm told advertisers how many people were watching their commercials, who they were, and where they were watching them. A New York outfit named Arbitron conducted similar research about the radio audience.

There was also an intense period in the 1950s and 1960s when research was devoted to *products*. Advertising agencies like BBDO established test kitchens and research "laboratories" as sophisticated as anything the client had back at headquarters. Mostly, agencies tested to find unique characteristics in the product that could be highlighted in advertising. Over time this sort of research had the ironic consequence of turning insight on its head. Instead of waiting for the client to create a product with attributes that could then be advertised, some clever agencies searched for characteristics that were *missing* from the product—so they could then help the client create a product that could honestly claim the attribute in advertising. One example: the invention of Chunky Soup, a product of BBDO's test kitchen, which allowed Campbell's to advertise big chunks of meat and vegetables. Thus: "Chunky—the Soup That Eats Like a Meal." This "reverse engineering" approach produced comical consequences, none more so than the agency for Viceroy cigarettes, which came up with a technical demonstration that proved cigarette smoke in the mouth killed bacteria (assuming that this was a desirable attribute). Mercifully, the bosses at British-American Tobacco agreed that this would be stretching credulity with the Federal Trade Commission. They opted not to market Viceroy for its bacteria-killing properties.

Product-based research at ad agencies, noble as it was in helping clients improve their products, eventually went the way of the dinosaurs. Agencies couldn't afford to compete with their clients' burgeoning research labs, and soon clients stopped looking to their agencies for new product ideas.

The next phase in the history of research focused on *brands*. What were people's attitudes toward a brand? What did it mean to them? How did they feel about it? It was research aimed at establishing more highly evolved conclusions than whether a product was "better" or "worse." It was designed to get under a consumer's skin, and to probe how advertising altered people's attitudes, positively or negatively, about a brand. It's still going on, but to a much lesser degree at advertising agencies (which with their reduced fees can ill afford to maintain deep research departments). For the most part, brand research has now been outsourced to specialist firms. In fact, research has become a burgeoning business unto itself, with companies like Gallup, MRI, and Interbrand dedicated solely to the research process. If clients want sophisticated brand research, they can just go out and buy it.

There was also a phase from the 1960s to late 1980s when research fell under the sway of social psychologists. This was *social and psychological* research, which focused more on the end-user of the products than the product itself—on people rather than brands. The goal here was to learn more about the people who used the products—their demographic and psychographic characteristics—so advertisers could tailor their media messages to connect with people who had these characteristics. Politicians still rely heavily on this approach. They identify their electoral base and then customize their message to appeal to that base. Personally, I value this kind of research. I like any information that tells me what consumers are thinking, what moves them, what makes them choke up or laugh or swell with pride. If it makes you *feel* something, I can use that information, and turn it into a powerful brand appeal.

Not everyone thinks this way. Today, we are surely in the era of research that relies on *technology*. It is the era of the Universal Product Code and the infrared scanner. And in that sense we have come full circle with research. A wise man once pointed out that there were two critical events in the history of market research. The first a hundred years ago when we discovered that we could ask consumers questions. The second, more recently, when scanner data taught us that we didn't have to ask questions. Armed with scanner data, credit card receipts, ZIP Codes, and a powerful computer, a marketer can pretty much identify the name, address, income level, and social status of everyone who buys his product. That doesn't mean, of course, that all this information is being put to use. My hunch is that the vast majority of corporate data has been shoved into company vaults for decades—untapped, unexplored, unanalyzed, unproductive of insight. Sort of like the scandalous discovery during the 2004 presidential race when 100,000 hours of terrorist surveillance tapes were found languishing untranslated and unanalyzed on FBI shelves because there weren't enough Arabic translators to get to them. Mind you, this is data involving national security, America's highest priority. It's no better at any company. Even giant marketers haven't scratched the surface of all the useful research they possess—because they can't. They don't have the time or resources.

As an ad guy who relies more on wits than data, I take some cold comfort in that fact. There's still hope for those of us who favor instinct for our insights.

I feel sheepish devoting this many words to research. People who've worked with me would say that Dusenberry and research are two words that should be separated by miles and miles of dead space. They would scoff at the notion that I am a research maven or a data-busting connoisseur, poring over trial rates and re-use numbers all day long. That's not what I did at our agency, nor was I known for it. But in reflection, I realize that I was always conducting research in my own way. When I was eavesdropping, or buying the client's products in a store (even though I could receive them for free), or driving the client's cars, or testing the competition's offerings, or going back into the archives to look at old campaigns, or having lunch with the former CEO or brand manager (smart people who either retired or left the client's employ), or talking about all of it with friends over dinner. All that was research. In my own way.

In truth, I do all that because the only research that matters to me (and to most creative people) is the research that inspires ideas and leads to insights. And the research that consistently delivers insights is the research that lets consumers air out their problems.

I learned this in my first days at BBDO. The agency had an elegant proprietary research technique called PDS, or Problem Detection Study. It was BBDO's belief that *consumers are most honest and accurate about their feelings when they are complaining*. When consumers describe a product or service, they tend to be guarded or less than candid. Rather than react to the product or service itself, they play back to you what they've learned about the product through advertising. Which tells you absolutely nothing new. Therefore, if you want the truth from consumers, get them to register their *complaints* about the product.

Consumers love to complain—and they're at their most candid when they do.

The technique grew organically out of what was then the agency's well-known "four-point process" for developing effective advertising: (1) know your prime prospect; (2) know your prime prospect's problem; (3) know your product; and (4) break the boredom barrier. Pretty basic stuff. PDS attacked point number two, and it worked like this: Ask the average consumer what he wants in a bank and he's likely to say something innocuous, such as "friendly service." But ask for his greatest complaint about a bank and you'll hear something entirely different: "The lines are too long." Or, "When I ask for a loan, they make me feel like a beggar." Or, "The application process is endless."

Ask a consumer what she wants in a credit card, and she'll say, "I want to buy anything I like with it," a typical playback from previous advertising. But if you ask that same consumer what's wrong with her credit card, she's more apt to say, "Not enough places take it."

That was our research philosophy back then: Don't tell us what you like. Tell us what's wrong, what you dislike. That's an emotional response. And we can work with that. It lets us create emotionally charged advertising (thus achieving point number four: break the boredom barrier). More important, it allows us to preempt the customer's affection, and solve that customer's biggest problem; all the goodwill customers feel about the category accrues to our brand, not our rival's, because we are addressing what really matters to the consumer.

Maybe it was because I made my bones at BBDO, where problem detection was part of the agency DNA, but problems are how I define my research.

Out of problems come insights. Take the Chunky Soup case. If you asked consumers what they liked about soup, they would serve up the usual pat answers: soup is hearty, soup is nourishing, soup warms you up. The answers we've all heard since soup advertising began. But when we asked consumers to complain about soup, the answers were entirely different: the pieces of meat are too small, the vegetables are skimpy, it doesn't fill me up. The insight here practically jumped onto our plate. From there it was a hop, skip, and a jump to the birth of Chunky, and the perfect answer to what mattered most to the soup customer.

The biggest fallacy about research is that *you need to spend a lot of money to get it.* You have to hire research professionals and their squadron of field workers who scour the supermarket aisles, conduct phone surveys, and pay people to show up at focus groups. Not necessarily so. You can glean valid research simply by listening to people on the street. If your gut tells you that what you're hearing is *true,* or if you keep hearing the same thing over and over again, you are already conducting legitimate research.

Peter Souter, our talented creative director at AMV/BBDO in London, tells the story about how the most simple research yielded a winning insight. The client was Britain's National Health board, which wanted to mount a massive anti-smoking campaign, targeting young people, especially teenaged girls. The logic in the U.K., as in the U.S., was that if you can stop kids from smoking early in life, they won't pick up the habit as adults—and billions of pounds in national health costs will be saved each year.

Tobacco is one of the most heavily researched categories in the marketer's playbook. It's a product that, like soda and beer, is purchased in multiple units every day by the same consumers. People don't buy a pack of cigarettes on a whim one day and then wait to buy another pack two months later. They buy the product daily, with the metronomic consistency of people buying a newspaper or showing up at the corner deli for their morning coffee. They also buy the product in bulk quantities—cartons, boxes of cartons. With all this purchasing going on, data accumulates, patterns emerge, and a ton of knowledge about the tobacco consumer becomes manifest. There's not much about their product and their public that cigarette manufacturers do not know.

Cigarettes are also one of the most brand-reliant categories. Smokers have a strong commitment to their brand of cigarette, not just for reasons of taste (which, as a former three-pack-a-day smoker of Marlboros, I can attest to) but also because of the imagery and positive emotions they associate with their favorite brand. When I lit up a cigarette I felt like the rugged Marlboro man; it was the fuel of my ambition as a young advertising man. Every line of cigarettes has some branding agenda going on behind it. Some obviously are more successful than others (think Marlboro *vs*. Winston in the U.S., one a dominant brand, the other the *former* leader). The branding investment in cigarettes would be chilling if it weren't so breathtakingly efficient. The cigarette manufacturer's branding is awe-striking, involving billion-dollar budgets and years of painstaking, relentless, down-to-the-smallest-detail branding tactics as insidious as Merit cigarettes sponsoring women's bowling leagues because their research showed that housewives who liked to smoke also liked to bowl. (I'm glad I wasn't around when the marketing people came up with that insight.) There's even some branding going on with people who buy generic cigarettes (they don't care about taste or brand imagery; they care about price—and that can be turned into a branding attribute too).

Don't get me started on cigarettes. The bottom line is that there is an enormous amount of brand equity in cigarettes and, in turn, an equally enormous amount of consumer loyalty and emotional attachment to cigarettes. Smoking, after all, is a habit—a habit so powerful and pleasurable that people continue to do it even when they know it can kill them. Smokers absolutely love their cigarettes.

This is what the anti-smoking campaign in the U.K. was up against: an installed branding base, heavily funded for decades, for many lines of cigarettes; powerful consumer loyalty; and an addictive feature (nicotine) lodged within the product that kept consumers using the product even when it was not in their best long-term health interests. Those are powerful obstacles unmatched by any other product on Earth; neither alcohol, gambling, nor sex has the controlling sway over us that tobacco does. The only thing harder than getting people to start smoking or getting smokers of one brand to switch to another is to get smokers to quit. The average smoker tries to quit nine times; not even dieting has a failure rate that high.

How do you fight this when you're dreaming up an anti-smoking campaign? You can't focus on the health hazards, obvious as they may be. Young people think they're invincible. They have no concept of mortality. You can't scare them "straight" with the threat of lung cancer.

You also can't dissuade them from smoking by claiming that it's "uncool." Decades of advertising, not to mention shrewd and relentless product placement in movies since the 1930s, have done too good a job establishing smoking as "cool."

Nor can you make an issue of the cost of cigarettes, or that they make you unkissable to a nonsmoker, or that smoking is largely banned in indoor public venues nowadays. None of these issues are compelling to a smoker; they are mere hurdles to the fulfillment of the smoking habit, not reasons to quit. A more vivid insight, a stronger truth was required.

Virtually nothing in the extensive research data on smoking and smokers revealed a vivid insight that could make a jot of difference. A stronger—and newer—truth was required. To get that, Souter concluded, he needed more data, more information, particularly about his target audience: the young women of England. With all the conventional data proving fruitless, Souter was left to rely on unconventional research.

A young female assistant took it from there. She left the agency's office on Marylebone Street, found a café in the shopping district, and parked herself at a centrally located table so she could eavesdrop on the conversations of the young women at neighboring tables. It didn't matter whether they smoked or not. She wanted to know what was on their minds. She sat there for five days, writing down impressions and every stray bit of conversation that landed on her ears. She heard the girls talk about school and work and parents and boyfriends and favorite clubs and singers and CDs and movies. But as the days mounted up, one dominant theme emerged: the girls were obsessed with their appearance. The assistant's notebook was filled with dialogue about shopping for clothes (especially jeans, underwear, and shoes), about haircuts, about shampoos and skin creams and makeup and eyeliners and nail polishes and fake nails and lipsticks and diet supplements and cosmetic surgery and . . . well, you get the picture. Nothing commands center stage in the idle young female mind more powerfully than *how she looks*.

As soon as the assistant returned with her notebook, Souter knew that the big insight accompanied her. Coupling this new research with the client's existing information about smoking's deleterious effects on our appearance, Souter and his team put all their money on the simple insight that *smoking ruins your looks*. It not only stains a woman's teeth and rots her breath, but it reduces the luster of her complexion, adds wrinkles around her eyes, and crinkles the skin around her mouth. The end result was a fabulous series of prize-winning ads that hit the young women of England where it really hurt: their vanity. Forget that cigarettes may shorten your lifespan. Ignore how they make you a social pariah in some circles. Focus on how they make you physically less attractive. That's enough to make a young woman stop smoking.

In hindsight, making the connection between smoking and a woman's fading looks may seem obvious. But until that young assistant returned from the café with her notes, no one had ever made the connection before. That's the beauty of good research. It reveals a useful insight in a matter of seconds. Without research, you could be wandering in the wilderness, blind and insight-deprived, forever.

What's most arresting in this example, though, is the simplicity of the research. It cost nothing. It required no expertise other than the patience to sit in a café for five days. It demanded none of the painstaking analysis that so much number-crunching research requires. The data were overwhelming; the insight was hitting you over the head. It is the sort of research that anyone—whether in a giant company or a sole proprietorship—can do. All you need is the gumption to push away from your desk, walk outside into the street, and start absorbing the world.[2]

There must be something about research in cafés and pubs that brings out the best in the creative folks at AMV/BBDO—because that's where they found the insight that led to one of the greatest TV commercials in U.K. history. The client was Guinness, maker of the popular stout beer, which had a long tradition of advertising since 1929 when it debuted with the slogan "Guinness is good for you." That claim eventually ran afoul of regulators who regarded it as overreaching. And in the ensuing years, Guinness had fallen upon fallow times in their advertising. They were looking for AMV/BBDO to tighten up their message. A new and memorable image was needed.

To begin their research into the product, the creative team of Tom Carty and Walter Campbell retreated to a local pub where they could watch their client's product in its most ba-

---

[2] The ads reminded me of the "Keep America Beautiful" campaign from the 1960s, spearheaded by President Lyndon Johnson's wife, Lady Bird Johnson. There, too, the ads preached cessation of an inappropriate activity—in this case, littering. In the same way that it might be hard for any American born after 1980 to imagine a time when people were permitted to smoke anywhere—in movie theaters, on airplanes, in hospitals and doctors' waiting rooms!—it might also be hard to imagine a time when littering *wasn't* a crime, when Americans would literally heave bags of trash out of their car window as they drove along the highway. The "Keep America Beautiful" campaign changed an entire nation's behavior. What the anti-smoking and anti-littering insights have in common is the compelling link between ceasing an activity and maintaining beauty. The link is obvious only in hindsight.

sic form of consumption. As they observed the patrons ordering Guinness and the barkeeps fulfilling demand, they figured out that it took a full 120 seconds to (a) pour a pint of Guinness properly so as to achieve the perfect equilibrium between thick brown stout and white frothy top and then (b) wait for it to settle. They believed that the waiting part was an unexploited Guinness virtue. That people would be willing to delay gratification until the beer rested perfectly in the glass said something wonderful about Guinness. The waiting, thought Carty and Campbell, might be worth celebrating. That was their insight, which they expressed in a theme line that repeated a hoary cliché: "Good things come to those who wait." But the commercial they created to illustrate the virtue of patience was anything but a cliché.

Carty and Campbell wanted to make a surfing commercial, drawing the parallel with the wait for a pint of Guinness to settle and a surfer's wait for the perfect wave. The commercial begins with a close-up of a Polynesian surfer. The commentary is adapted from *Moby-Dick*, alluding to Captain Ahab's relentless search: "He waits that what he does. And I'll tell you what. Tick follows tock follows tick follows tock." (In a 60-second spot, where every tenth of a second in the final cut is fought over, it's a leisurely 10-second beginning, disorienting the viewer but also pulling him or her in.) Then cut away to shots of surfers out in the ocean on their boards, waiting . . . waiting . . . waiting. Cue the sound of percussion instruments. A big wave is approaching. Suddenly, quick suggestive images of white horses appear. The horses (inspired by paintings by Eugene Delacroix and Walter Crane showing white horses mingling with waves) appear to be riding the waves. The waves, horses, and music build to a crescendo. The surfers celebrate in silence on the beach, falling over each other in the sand. Something wonderful and heroic has happened: the perfect wave came in, the surfers were there to catch it, and we witnessed the whole thing. Cut away to a product shot of a pint of Guinness draught, complete with white foamy top, and the theme line "Good things come to those who . . ." You know the rest.

The "Surfer" commercial, which aired in 1999, did wonders to rehabilitate Guinness's image. No longer was Guinness associated with men in pubs who drank themselves into a hooligan stupor. Suddenly Guinness was chic, a badge product that said Guinness drinkers appreciate quality. The commercial, virtually unknown to Americans, became the equivalent of the famous Macintosh "1984" commercial; Brits voted it the greatest TV ad of all time! (You can see it online at the agency's Web site at www.amvbbdo.co.uk.)

And it all started with two men conducting a little client research in a pub. No cost. No elaborate methodology. No meetings to get budget approval. Just a few orders of Guinness and the occasional glance at your wristwatch.[3]

---

[3] The ad itself is beautifully executed and, although no one's quoting budget numbers, is believed to be the most expensive commercial ever shot in Britain—well over $2 million. But that's the power of a clear unequivocal insight (regardless of the fact that it came out of a pub crawl): the client will stake you a large sum to express it. I could take mind-altering drugs for ten years and not come up with an execution like this. But I admire the way it breaks the rules. It doesn't show the product until the 55th second of the 60-second spot. That means it's trusting the viewer to hang in there through 94 percent of the commercial to find out who's the seller and what he's selling (in a spot that preaches patience, that argues "good things come to those who wait," I guess that's appropriate). It's also shot in black and white (the costliest commercial of all time and it doesn't offer the viewer the sensuous beauty of color!). Most of all, I love how it gives the viewer credit for having a brain. A spot that alludes to Herman Melville and Eugene Delacroix in order to sell beer is not talking down to the consumer; it's talking up.

A second big rule about research is that you have to trust what it's trying to tell you. No matter how raw it rubs you or how it upsets your hard-won biases, if you trust the people who conducted the research, you have to accept their conclusions—and work with the information. There's no point in ordering up the research if you're going to dismiss it when it upsets your expectations. However, beware: research is a guide, not a god. Those who worship at the altar of research and follow it blindly—without shrewd analysis—often find themselves heading the wrong way down a one-way street.

I learned this the hard way with the Pepsi Challenge back in the late 1970s and early 1980s. If there's one account I feel more attachment to than any other, it's Pepsi-Cola. The account has resided at BBDO for more than forty-five years (which in this age of change is saying something), and I've worked on it for nearly thirty-five years. It is one of advertising's glamorous marquee clients—with big budgets and lots of freedom to make eye-popping commercials. It's also one of the most influential accounts, a true trailblazer, the first to focus on the consumer who uses the product (the Pepsi Generation) rather than the product itself (more about this later).

That's a mouthful of superlatives for a brand that—let's face it—is practically a synonym for the underdog, the perennial number two. But that had always been Pepsi's position in the soft drink universe. A runner-up to mighty Coca-Cola. So much so that when people found themselves in a No. 1 *vs.* No. 2 scenario, they always described it as a "Coke *vs.* Pepsi situation." When your brand enters everyday language for its "two-ness," you know where you stand. You're reminded of it every day.

By 1977 I had been living with this "condition" for all of my creative life with Pepsi. I hated being number two. But then something strange started happening in the Pepsi hinterlands beyond Madison Avenue. Specifically in Dallas, where the local Pepsi bottler was taking it in the chops from Coke, getting mercilessly outsold, 8 to 1. He needed some marketing drama to stem the tide. He needed something stark and stunning and revolutionary. He needed a tourniquet to stop the bleeding.

Surprisingly, the answer came straight from his own backyard: a series of blind taste tests scrambled together by a Dallas ad guy named Bob Stanford. This is the moment, however crudely, that the Pepsi Challenge was born. It was crudely patched together, but it was disarmingly honest in its revelation. It showed that consumers, even lifelong Coke drinkers, preferred the taste of Pepsi. As a local commercial, it was research brought to life on film. And an insight we stumbled into.

It was also a "Wow!" heard from Dallas to Detroit and throughout the entire soft drink universe.

Pepsi volume, Pepsi share, Pepsi leadership scores all soared in the Dallas area and throughout Texas, and then the results started migrating to other low-volume markets where the Pepsi Challenge ran. If you were getting slain by Coke, the message said to local Pepsi bottlers, try marketing the Pepsi Challenge.

As promising as the results were, it took everyone at headquarters a while to accept, much less embrace, the entire Challenge phenomenon, to trust the research and follow what it was telling us. Some of it, of course, was institutional inertia. Pepsi had been number two for so long, we couldn't believe that maybe for the first time in eighty years Pepsi ac-

tually had a strategic advantage over Coke that we could exploit. As BBDO picked up where Bob Stanford left off, we
also faced a creative conundrum: What kind of ads are we going to produce? Are we going to scrap years of breakthrough
award-winning commercials to show taste tests in shopping
malls? Could we afford to abandon two decades of precious
brand-image equity for a 180-degree turn in our advertising
approach? Could we afford *not* to?

There were a lot of issues to consider before we could trust
the research on a national basis. Making taste tests the
centerpiece of Pepsi's advertising was a declaration of war
against Coke. This would not be treated as another backyard
skirmish. This was a frontal assault on the market leader. If
we did it, we had to go all the way. And we had to be prepared for Coke to retaliate with heavy muscle. The implications if we erred were considerable: a huge black eye for the
Pepsi brand. Meaning: a hit in market share, which depresses
profits, which brings down the stock. A lot was riding on our
insight. Even with the results slapping us on the forehead, it
was still difficult to trust the research.

In the end, though, we went with the research findings.
Working with Pepsi's director of creative services, Alan
Pottasch, we created a series of "Pepsi Challenge" spots—
deliberately crude taste-test dramatizations—and took them
to Vic Bonomo, then Pepsi's president. I have to admit he
wasn't excited by the idea. He loved the "generation" advertising we had done that had brought Pepsi close to parity with
Coke. But he could add up numbers as well as anyone else. He
was sick of being a runner-up. He was willing to go to war.

The lines in the sand were drawn. The cola wars had be-
gun. Five years of nonstop Pepsi Challenge commercials were

under way. They weren't creative milestones, but, boy, did they move the needle. They put Pepsi at the same table with Coke, literally and figuratively. They made taste an issue. They made loyal Coke drinkers *consider* the heretical notion of trying Pepsi. And they dramatically increased Pepsi's market share in the U.S. from 23 percent of the cola market to 36 percent.

The stunning irony of all this is that the Pepsi Challenge was originally intended only as a *short-term* promotion, a quick hit designed to jump-start Pepsi sales in low-volume markets. But Coke felt so threatened, and took the Challenge so seriously, that they mounted an all-out ad blitz in an effort to blunt the Challenge's thrust. Most of their spots were taste-test spoofs—and downright goofy (two monkeys comparing Pepsi to Coke in a shopping mall). These only brought more attention to our campaign. If Coke had ignored the Pepsi Challenge, it would have gone away. But Coke kept it alive.

More important, the Pepsi Challenge—coupled with our image-building spots—induced Coca-Cola into the biggest marketing blunder in American business history: the introduction of New Coke. "After eighty-seven years," wrote Pepsi-Cola CEO Roger Enrico, "the other guy blinked."

A lot has been written about New Coke, most of it in head-shaking puzzlement. No one knows for sure why Coca-Cola's management made this terrible error. As a keenly interested observer, I have my own theory: *Coke trusted our research.* They saw that a certain type of cola formula (slightly sweeter with a different balance of brown spice notes) was winning blind taste tests. They figured, not illogically, that this was the formula that cola drinkers preferred. So they decided, again not illogically, to give it to them—in the form of New Coke (which everyone agreed tasted a lot like Pepsi). But what was right for us was not necessarily right for the other guy.

It went down something like this: The cola folks in Atlanta created New Coke and then replicated our taste tests. All their tests, however, were done blind. They put the new cola (which was formulated to win taste tests) in an unmarked can and, not surprisingly, people said they preferred the taste. Case closed. Let's go to market. Unfortunately, that blind taste approach canceled out Coke's huge branding edge, the "halo effect" of the Coke logo pasted on a bright red can. And that made all the difference.

They failed—stunningly—to consider the hold that the old Coke had on consumers. When you introduce a new product, you're also taking away from the old one—in which case, it's a good idea to ask your existing customers how they feel about it. In Coke's case, of course, they weren't just removing any old product off the shelves; this was a beloved icon that is surely the most visible branded product in the world. The uproar among millions of loyal Coke drinkers, astonishingly unanticipated by Coke executives, planted the entire company in a self-induced crisis of unprecedented proportions.

After months of scrambling, Coca-Cola management recovered. They phased out New Coke, relaunched the old Coke as Coke Classic, and within five years regained much of the market share they had lost.

But the Pepsi Challenge had done its job. Pepsi was now *more* than a contender. It says so in the research.

My third point about research is that *anyone can do it*.

Before I attacked this chapter on research, I conducted a

little research myself. I visited veteran New York City market researcher Ellen Sills-Levy at her ESL Insights offices at 40th Street and Lexington Avenue. Ellen, with whom I've worked on various projects for thirty years, is the kind of researcher who gives the lie to the notion that research is not a creative act. She has the two qualities any great research professional needs: skepticism and curiosity. Over the years she has done everything from creating standard questionnaires for the man on the street to working undercover as a factory worker in a Mitsubishi auto plant to find out why female workers were suing the company. She has posed as a loan applicant to report on how a bank treats its customers and run hundreds of focus groups. She's observed people in their environments to determine how they use a client's products. She's followed people during a typical day to assess their daily habits and patterns. She even uses techniques that probe a consumer's unconscious, from intense 4-hour sessions revolving around Jungian archetypes (one of which led to the creation of the Traveller's Insurance umbrella logo) to an exotic technique we developed at BBDO called Photosort, which asks people to look at carefully selected photographs and express their emotional responses. It's a great way to visually personify a brand. There's not much in-the-trenches market research that Ellen Sills-Levy hasn't seen or done.

And even she's convinced that everyone in business can and should be doing more research on their own.

Small business owners, she points out, have one huge advantage over giant corporations: regular intimate contact with their customers. That's why big organizations have to spend so much on people like Ellen Sills-Levy to conduct research—because they're so far removed from their customers. They don't see them walk into the store once a week. They don't know them by name. They don't talk to them or ask about their children. But a small business owner can do that. Problem is, so few of them actually exploit this edge.

It's easy to see why. When you're running your own business (and it's no different if you're running your own department within a bigger organization), you've already got enough to do. You've got customers to worry about, assignments to finish, orders to push through, deliveries to check up on, complaints to correct. And those are just the day-to-day micromanageable items. You also have to think a little further out (certainly more than one day ahead) about cash flow and meeting a payroll and paying your basic bills. And those are the items within your control. There are also factors beyond your control, such as unreliable vendors, customers who owe you money, and competitors out to steal your lunch. With all these pressing issues, it's easy to see how anyone can forget to take time, catch a breather, and think about research. It's not at the top of most people's minds.

For example, another wine store, another town. A friend of mine was dining in a restaurant in the suburban village of Bronxville, New York. He ordered a bottle of white wine with dinner. He liked the wine so much that he wrote down the vineyard and vintage. The next day he walked into the village wineshop and asked the proprietor if he carried the wine.

"Never heard of it," said the owner. "But let's see if I can get it for you." The owner looked up the information in *Beverage Digest* and announced that my friend could have a case in a week.

My friend thought it was odd that a wine store owner—someone who theoretically should have an intense self-serving interest in wines—would not be intimately familiar with the wine list at a popular restaurant just a few doors down from his shop.

I thought it was more than odd; it was close to entrepreneurial malpractice.

If I were that owner, I would be in that restaurant once a month quizzing the maitre d' on what wines were selling, what new items he was adding to his wine list, what he was removing. That's precious information. Where else could I find more reliable data about the drinking habits of the local populace? I could use that information to make sure I carried the most popular wines—not so much on the off chance that I'd have them in stock if and when someone asked for them, but rather because these were proven winners—wines that people loved. If I stocked them, it was a safe bet that they wouldn't gather dust on my shelves.

The more I thought about it, I realized that this is the sort of research I could repeat with other restaurants. What would stop me from talking to other popular establishments in the neighborhood, studying their wine lists, learning what bottles were flying out of the cellar, and stocking them in my shop?

Research so simple it's a sin to call it research. It's more like common sense. Yet I wonder how many shopkeepers would do that.

But the daily grind of details isn't the only reason people have a blind spot about research. They also have a knowledge bias: they think they already know their customers well enough. They can see what's going on in the sales figures, in what's selling and what isn't. What more do they need to know? Answer: plenty.

When Tiger Woods, after winning eight major championships in six years, famously fired his golf coach, Butch Harmon, he said he didn't need a coach anymore. He could do it all on his own because he could see what he was doing right or wrong from the flight of the ball. "Ball flight tells you everything you need to know," he explained. That may be true for a pro like Tiger Woods. And maybe not. When your ball flight goes awry, you still may need a fresh eye to tell you how to correct it—even if you're Tiger Woods.

It's the same with research in business. When things go off track, you can't find all the answers solely in the sales figures or in what you've been doing all along. You need to step back and get some fresh feedback from new sources, such as your customers, vendors, competitors, and friends. Quite frankly, you should be listening to anyone who can tell you something you don't already know.

Let me repeat: *you need to learn something you don't already know.*

This should be self-evident. However, so much of what passes for research is little more than people seeking information that confirms their biases, their goals, their inclinations, and their decisions. It has nothing to do with acquiring new information. In a sense this is another form of "satisfaction research"; it only tells you what you're doing right. This is not how great insights materialize. Insights come from owning up to what you're doing wrong and addressing those problems in ways that matter.

When I asked Ellen Sills-Levy if she ever encountered this "blind spot" in her clients, she told me about a bank in Connecticut that was preparing a major push to lure new customers from rival banks. The bank hired her to find out what customers were looking for in a bank. The bank was expecting her to talk to their customers and draw up a list of positive attributes that the bank could then claim in its marketing materials. In the course of her research she uncovered the disturbing news that the bank's existing customers hated the bank's fee policies, its substandard service, its long lines, its staff's inability to answer questions or negotiate directly with them, even its monthly statements that one customer described as "dysfunctional." She came back from her researching foray and told the bank, "Don't bother trying to lure new customers yet. Because if things stay the way they are now, you'll lose all the new customers a few months after they see how you operate." Not exactly the answer the bank bargained for, but the research provided a big insight: You've got so many problems, you're not ready to open your doors to new customers. Fix yourself first, then troll for customers. Not the other way around. It not only saved the bank millions of dollars in wasted marketing costs, it literally saved the bank.

Then there was the drugstore chain that asked her to explain the huge disparity in per-square-foot sales from one store to the next among their branches in upstate New York. She visited the branches, saw that some had perfect displays and product layout, while others were unkempt warehouses with little visual appeal. Same stores, but totally different retail environments. She went back to the client and asked the simple question "Have you ever visited these stores and observed the difference?" They answered no. In her mind, that explained everything. No one in top management had ever bothered to see who was doing things right and who was literally messing up. Her insight: You don't need me yet. You need to get out and see your world. That will tell you everything you need to know.

Then there was the CEO who was so enamored of his personal taste that he believed that if he liked something, the whole world would automatically like it too. Ellen's job was to come up with research data that confirmed the CEO's whims. Research to prove a hunch is certainly valid, but more often than not it's a fallacy: there's no rational reason to believe "if I like it" that "everyone else will like it too."

All of these—people who never leave their desks, people who think their whims are universally followed—are variations on a knowledge bias that hinders research.

Perhaps the biggest obstacle to acquiring solid research, though, is people's mistaken belief that they're not equipped to do it properly. They think research is a complicated technical operation best handled by professionals (like Ellen). That might be true if we're talking about, say, medical research. But marketing research is more art than science. In its best form it's applied common sense.

We see this bias all the time with clients. When we talk to them about research, their first question is about which technique we'll be using—surveys, telemarketing, focus groups, and so on. Actually, technique is our last consideration. First, we have to figure out what we're trying to learn. That will tell us how to extract the information.

Let's return to our wine store in Sag Harbor. If I were that owner looking for an insight that would provide a major spike in business, I don't need a Ph.D. to know that I should be focusing on at least five categories that make a difference.

The first is my product line. Am I offering merchandise that appeals to wine buyers? Just as record stores have walls devoted to the Top 40 CDs and bookstores have best-seller sections (and these top sellers usually represent more than 50 percent of a store's sales), I can research what the top-selling wines[4] are—and make sure I stock them. Better yet, I can create a special section for them and steer customers in their direction.

The second is my pricing. Am I perceived as high priced, bargain priced, or fairly priced? I can determine this by comparing my prices with another store. If I'm charging more than a rival, it's good that I know that before my customers figure it out.

The third is my service. I don't know any serious businesspeople who intentionally offer bad service. They all think their service is good (if not great). Unfortunately, the customers may not share that opinion. If there's a gap between the servers and the served, that's worth researching.

The fourth is my environment. Do people like the way I present my wares? Do they feel comfortable shopping in my retail environment? I can tell this simply by watching customers wander the aisles. Where do they linger? What do they ignore?

The fifth is my competition. What are they doing that I should be doing? I'll never know until I walk through a rival's store to see what he's doing that I'm not. Research doesn't get simpler than that. David Novak, the successful CEO of Yum Brands (Pizza Hut, Taco Bell, KFC) spends as much time in competitive fast-food stores as he does in his own. This way

---

[4] This is easy now. Internet search engines such as Google let you find any piece of information you want. What used to take several frustrating trips to the library in the not-so-distant past now gets solved in one or two mouse clicks. For example, every fact in this chapter was either obtained or checked in less than 30 seconds via Google.

he's seeing firsthand what the competition is up to, sampling their products, checking their stores. Like that famous line in *The Godfather*: "Keep your friends close—and your enemies closer."

This is hardly an exhaustive list, but isolating just one of these five categories and exploring it will make me smarter. It might even provide an insight. But that's really up to me now.

That, more than anything else, is what research provides. It puts you back in the driver's seat. It lets you regain control of your brand, your business, your destiny. The rest is up to you.

CHAPTER 3

MOVING THE NEEDLE

When you boil it all down, the purpose of any business insight is to improve conditions so that your business performs better. In my line of work, the goal has been to create great ads for the client so that sales pick up. I can't express it any simpler than that. Clients advertise with one overriding objective: sell more stuff.

How they get there varies from client to client, campaign to campaign. But the objective never changes: move the sales needle.

Notice that I didn't say "make the needle jump." That's too grand an objective for most clients. It suggests that it's easy to make enormous incremental leaps in business. From my experience, it's not easy. Nor is it necessary. You don't need to reinvent the wheel, or ravage your competition, or leapfrog overnight from seventh in your industry to number one. Those are very expensive goals, with little guarantee that they can be accomplished. Moving the needle is an infinitely more modest, achievable goal, but it's a shrewd one.

I learned this early on the Pepsi account. Coke and Pepsi are two classic parity products in look and taste. The main difference between the two is the brand imagery created by their advertising, which viscerally connects the consumer to one over the other. These are the ties that bind, and there's nothing you can do that can shatter these bonds overnight. No matter how great your advertising, you can't make one brand leapfrog the other with one creative burst. But then again, you don't need to. The global soft drink market generates $75 billion in sales. If we can create an ad campaign that improves Pepsi's global share by 1 point, that increase is worth $750 million. That's what I call moving the needle.

It's no different for any of our clients. If we can help Pizza Hut sell one more pizza a month to each of their 17 million customers . . . well, you do the math. That's 204 million more pizzas sold in a year. Multiply that by the average $9 price of a pizza, and you've increased Pizza Hut revenues by nearly $2 billion. That's moving the needle.

It's the same with one more bucket of Kentucky Fried Chicken each month for each KFC customer, or one more monthly transaction by each Visa cardholder, or one more overnight package sent by each FedEx customer. The numbers add up. And you begin to see that, particularly with clients that have large and loyal customer bases, this "edging up" can make a huge impact. That's moving the needle.

It gives you the confidence to take small steps versus a risky giant leap. You don't have to be like everybody else and swing for the fences (which increases your chances of striking out). You can settle for good solid singles and still make progress. This was the logic underpinning a series of spots the Tracey-Locke agency produced for Frito-Lay in the mid-1980s with the comedian Jay Leno. Their mission? To get each salty snack customer to buy one more bag of Frito-Lay chips each month. So they faced Leno to the camera with an open bag of Doritos in his arm. Between bites of the product,

Leno described how easy it was to eat Doritos. They're small, they're tasty, and each bag contains a lot of them. But don't worry about eating so much that you'll run out. "Munch all you want," said Leno. "We'll make more." He wasn't describing the product's virtues and superiority to the competition. He was urging the consumer to *consume more.* I can't recall too many products, if any, from beer to gasoline to cigarettes to soap, that based their advertising on urging you to buy *more* of the product. It was an unusual approach. A blatant appeal to the consumer to help us move the needle.

When I stop to think about it, it's amazing how much energy I devote to thinking about moving one needle or another.

Consider my mental gyrations on a typical Manhattan workday in advertising when I was running BBDO's New York office. In many ways, it's a "move the needle" festival.

I wake up, shake out the cobwebs, and commit myself to some exercise. A little cardio, where I'm trying to move the needle on my heart rate—get it up to a point where it's challenging me—and burn off some calories. Afterwards, I may step on a scale—definitely want to move the needle there in the right direction.

Shower, shave, eat breakfast, and get off to work. No needles there (phew!).

I leave my apartment, hail a cab, and like most "commuters," even Manhattanites whose commutes are measured in blocks rather than miles, I'm mentally calculating the best route to my office. I may suggest an alternate route to the driver. I may even curse him under my breath for making the wrong choice and getting stuck in traffic. I'm looking at my watch, counting the minutes tick by. In effect, I'm measuring time and trying to figure out how it can be done better—how the needle of my commuting time can move in the right direction.

At my office building I stop at the coffee bar. The line is long and I can't help wondering why the employees drawing simple cups of coffee can't speed things up. Even in a coffee line, I'm projecting how to move the needle on customer waiting time (which is the single most important factor in customer satisfaction).

Finally, I get to my office at 9:30, grateful for sanctuary from what has already been a needle-filled morning. But the office offers little relief. On my desk are sales reports from clients and test scores on spots we're thinking of running. More indicators of which way the needles are moving. I tap the computer to check the company's stock price (a very important needle). I call the doctor to see what the blood test says about my cholesterol (also a very important needle). A few minutes later, I pore over the CFO's reports on budgets, salary recommendations, billings, and expenses. Another case of the needles.

It's noon. I'm so stressed out that I decide to relax with a round of golf at my club. I hop into a cab to pick up my car uptown and then take a relaxing drive north of Manhattan to Westchester County. Golf may be a game, but it comes with a sharp statistical edge. For all but the most nonchalant players (who don't care if they get better), it is an orgy of needles that need moving. Golfers are constantly trying to move the needle on their handicap (the universal measurement of a golfer's ability against par; the lower the handicap, the better your game). But they also think in smaller terms—in the game within the game. A golfer might play a round aiming to move the needle on the number of fairways or greens hit in regulation, or the number of three-putts avoided, or most simply, the number of balls lost. An improvement in any one of these areas will improve his score. At the end of eighteen holes, he will add up the number of strokes and enter his score in the club computer, which lists his last twenty rounds of golf and keeps a running tally of his rising or falling handicap. The computer literally tells him, with incontrovertible bluntness, which way the needle is moving on his game. If I wanted to get away from the moving needle, the golf course was the wrong place.

And so it went for the rest of my day. When I drove back to Manhattan, I was calculating the fastest route home. When I got home I calibrated how much time I'd need to return the two dozen phone calls that had accumulated while I was on the golf course. In that light, my day is a dance between life and myself to the tune of "how can I improve the situation and make a difference?" Once you're aware of it, almost any situation becomes a moving-the-needle scenario.

You may think you're insulated from the challenge of moving the needle, that I'm somehow a little more wiggy about it than the average citizen. You may think that, but you'd be wrong. There's a moving-the-needle scenario wherever performance can be measured and people want to improve. Whether you're a dieter trying to lower your weight, or a mother trying to help your kids score higher in math class, or a heart patient trying to lower your blood pressure, or like me, a golfer trying to lower your handicap, you are trying to move some needle.

It's amazing to me that a lot of people don't see the world this way. But I like to think that they're just not thinking in my terms. The basic dynamic behind moving the needle is (a) identifying the needle and (b) deciding if it's worth moving. We do this all day long without thinking about it. Imagine you're a concerned parent who wants your child to achieve better grades in biology. Without really articulating it to yourself, you go through an intuitive analysis and come up with a solution. You look at the child's report card and see an unacceptable grade in biology. You identify that as a specific area for improvement. Then you decide how much improvement is reasonable. Going from a D to an A in one reporting period, for example, might be unrealistic—that is, trying to move the needle too far too fast. But improving to a B, maybe even B+, makes sense. You discuss the goal with your child and you both agree. Then you analyze what the child has or has not been doing. Is it a case of not paying attention in class, not spending enough time on homework, not getting one-on-one time with the teacher, or not getting enough parental help at night? It could be one or a combination, but the analysis reveals a course of action—say, at least 1 hour a night more homework devoted to biology and 30 minutes every other night with you and the child working together. If the child sticks to the plan, a better grade will follow. The needle will move.

We do this sort of analysis instantly and intuitively with lots of everyday challenges. But we lose some of that clarity of purpose in the workplace. Perhaps we don't feel we "own" a work problem the way we "own" our problems in real life. It's someone else's problem, and so our concentration is slightly diminished. Perhaps we don't feel like we fully control our destiny. If we have an insight, we have to run it by our superiors and get them to approve it. That, too, dims our enthusiasm. Perhaps we're simply not looking for insights that improve business conditions. We're so lost in the details that we can't see anything else.

Whatever the reason, the challenge of moving the needle—of defeating the status quo in a significant way—is the engine that drives all growth in business. Not incidentally, it's also the engine that drives analysis in the workplace. After all, you have to identify the *needle* and decide if it's worth *moving*.

Let's extend this moving-the-needle image a little further with the following exercise.

Imagine that your desk at work is covered by gauges. You see them first thing each morning when you settle in your chair. They're like the gauges on an instrument panel of a small plane, each dial measuring a vital function such as speed, altitude, battery life, RPMs, distance traveled. Only in this case, since the gauges are on your desk, they're measuring your business's vital functions—everything from yesterday's revenues to cash flow to the status of your credit line to travel costs to employee morale, even your company's name recognition and reputation. The list could go on forever. But looking at the dials tells you precisely how your business is doing.

Well, gathering information and conducting smart research is like installing a dozen telltale gauges on your desk. As I said in the previous chapter, a lot of businesses aren't so diligent about this. But let's assume for the moment that they're addressing the problem. What next?

Simple answer: you read the gauges and analyze what

they're telling you. And then you figure out which readings matter, which don't. If you're driving a car and the fuel gauge is near empty, that's a serious problem that needs addressing. If the windshield wiper fluid gauge reads low, that's not quite so serious. You can survive without wiper fluid; you can't move without fuel. One's a needle that needs to be moved; the other can be tabled for later.

It's the same in business. Sometimes you look at a gauge and see a condition that could be improved but isn't urgent. Other times you see a gauge that's screaming out a crisis. A smart manager knows the difference.

That, in essence, is how we have always analyzed the client's marketing data and our own research. We're looking at the information with one singular purpose: Will this yield an insight that moves the needle? And will it move it in a big way?

Case in point: In the mid-1990s the Mars candy bar account came loose. Mars had been at a couple of ad agencies around town, but now a big chunk of their advertising, more than $200 million in billings, was up for review. They invited us to pitch the business. I looked at three years of their commercials, emerging befuddled.

I shared my thoughts with Allen Rosenshine, BBDO's worldwide chairman. "Allen, I don't see why Mars is coming to us. Their work is nothing like the creative we would do for them."

We concluded that an account this large and prestigious couldn't be ignored. We'd be fools to pass it up.

Most companies do not require motivation or insight to go after new business. You see a prospect, give it your best shot, and hope that life is fair. But Mars was a very independent, privately held company (the second-largest private company in America, in fact), controlled by the descendants of the legendary Frank Mars. They were competitive, conservative, and used to doing things their own way. They would be tough customers. More important, if we gave them the kind of work we were known for, would they recognize its value? Would they kill it? Would they be fighting us every step of the way? Or would they be our partners? Was it worth it, even for $200 million (which, by the way, would *really* move the BBDO billings needle)?

This hesitance provided us with an insight for our pitch. We would present to the Mars people our kind of work, not the kind of work we thought they would buy. We decided to give them something we believed was right for Mars *and* in line with our creative philosophy. If they chose us, we'd know that Mars was ready for a big change.

The existing commercials for Snickers, Mars's top brand, struck us as odd. The commercials were dull, predictable, and poorly executed. They didn't have the wit or sheen that you'd expect from a super-brand like Snickers. The commercials showed young firemen and lawyers, out on the job, extolling the nutritional value of Snickers if you happened to be so busy working that you skipped lunch. They were practically selling Snickers as serious health food.

This explained why Snickers sales had flattened out. Snickers had been the number one candy in America for twenty years, well ahead of Reese's Peanut Butter Cups and Kit Kat and Milky Way and Reese's Pieces. But at the time of the account review, the brand had fallen into second place behind Reese's Cups (owned by Mars's arch-rival Hershey).

We looked at the name—Snickers—and agreed that the product should be associated with *fun*. Humor was the way to go. That, in itself, was insightful. Sometimes you get so lost in the marketing data and sales targets that you forget to step back and *see* the product you're trying to sell for what it really is. A candy bar called Snickers should not be treated with solemnity.

The other danger of pitching a new account—perhaps greater than the temptation of giving the client what you think they want rather than what you think they need—is the urge to trash everything they have previously done. You know the drill. It's called the "not invented here" syndrome. If you didn't come up with the idea, it can't be good. But there was something in Mars's strategy that appealed to us. We liked their positioning of Snickers as a viable alternative when you just can't break away for a solid meal. That was smart; it was their execution that fell short.

So BBDO's Charlie Miesmer and his group kept the strategy and came up with scenarios where people were trapped in humorous situations and couldn't get out. Our punch line was "Not going anywhere for a while?" And the scene always ended with someone enjoying a Snickers bar. We positioned the product as heroic rescuer of bored and hungry citizens everywhere.

The beauty of this approach—a tight strategy but played for laughs—was that it freed our imaginations to run wild. (That's a common creative paradox: the narrower your focus and the more precise the positioning, the more room you have to roam.) We had a football coach addressing his team in the locker room before a game. "Okay, listen up," he says.

"We're going to do the team prayer, but we've got to be politically correct about it. Father?" And a priest appears, saying, "Bless you all." "Rabbi?" And a rabbi does his bit. Then a Native American shaman. Then a Muslim cleric, and a Buddhist monk, and so on. Meanwhile we cut to a player who clearly feels trapped, while the voice-over says, "Not going anywhere for a while?" And he starts swallowing down a Snickers bar.

All the spots paid off with: "Hungry? Why wait?"

In another spot we showed an older man working all day on his hands and knees painting an elaborate design in the end zone before a football game. He finishes, proudly examining his handiwork. A player runs over to admire the job with him. "That's great," says the player. "But who are the 'Chefs'?" The man has misspelled Chiefs. Closing shot has him surveying his faulty work, mumbling, "Great googily moogily." Voice-over: "Not going anywhere for a while?"

Then there was a bald man mentally willing hair growth in front of a bathroom mirror. He grunts and strains. Boing! A long single follicle miraculously sprouts on his shiny pate. It worked! He'll keep straining until he has a full head of hair. "Not going anywhere for a while?"

We did the same with a telethon to sell cologne named after the 7'8" Bulgarian basketball player Gheorge Muresan. The telethon host begs viewers to call and buy, while a bored telephone operator chews on a Snickers. Then there was the optometrist with a waiting room filled with sports referees, none of whom can pass the eye test (a play on the average fan's belief that all game officials are blind). A bored nurse bites into her Snickers.

We had fun with the concept. Our only concern was Mars's

willingness to swallow our radically new direction. Fortunately, company management was in transition; a new generation of younger managers was taking over. They laughed at all the right places—and we landed the account.

To the untrained viewer, the "Not going anywhere" campaign was nothing more than a stream of eye-catching scenes that made people smile. But if you drilled a little deeper, you saw a tightly focused concept designed to move the needle. The spots were aimed directly at the product's main consumer: young males. That explains the heavy use of sports themes. Also, the spots aimed, with some subtlety, to expand people's notion of when to reach for a Snickers. Not just when you're hungry. But also when you're bored (which is a lot more common than you think). If we could persuade each young male in America to try Snickers as an antidote to ennui, while at the same time goading loyal Snickers lovers to eat one more bar a week, the needle would start moving again.

In any marketing situation, the client is always facing a "Lady or the Tiger" choice of (a) am I going after new customers or (b) am I trying to get old customers to buy more. Confronted with such a choice, most clients ask us, "Why can't I do both?" These commercials took aim at both old and new. The insight was so solidly on target to young males and so simple that it easily translated into print ads. For example, we ran a full-spread ad in the 1997 *Sports Illustrated* Swimsuit issue (the print equivalent of the Super Bowl and a great place to find young male eyeballs) showing a single picture of the man looking at his faulty handiwork, with the thought coming out of his head, "Great googily moogily."

The campaign ran for five years and did its job well.

Within two years Snickers was back as America's number one selling candy—where it remains today. There's only one job tougher in business than stopping the slide of a number one brand that has lost its momentum; it is getting the brand to make a U-turn and regain the top spot. If you identify the right needle (in this case, the one attached to young male sweet tooths) and know how to make it move (that is, make them laugh and talk their language), the job's a lot easier.

Not every product has the enormous scale advantages of Mars or Pepsi or Pizza Hut or FedEx or Gillette or Frito-Lay, where a tiny tremor across the vast customer base makes the needle jump. And even if it does, selling one more unit per customer per month may not be the way to move the needle.

We faced this issue in the 1980s with Campbell's Soup. Sales of canned soup were flat and the folks at Campbell's, the perennial category leader, were mystified.

Canned soup is the quintessential nonperishable food product. It has a shelf life measured in years, not days. When people stock their larder for winter, they load up on soup. When people head to the hills because the world is coming to an end, the first thing they buy is a truckload of cans of soup. And Campbell's was, by far, the perennial champ in this category. It was hard to figure out where Campbell's had a problem. I don't know many brand managers who would object to consumers buying their product in multiples of six, eight, or ten cans at a time. But that's what Campbell's consumers do.

Campbell's, over the years, had done a superb job convincing consumers of the comforting wonders of soup. And yet here we were faced with the unsettling fact that sales were flat. A little bit of this could be attributed to new competition from in-store brands, from niche brands of "gourmet" and organic soups, and an aggressive push from then upstart Progresso. But still Campbell's controlled more than 70 percent of the canned soup category, a dominant market share that, in theory, should have inoculated them from competitive sniping.

The flat sales mystified Campbell's because there was no on-the-street indication that consumers' preference for the Campbell's brand had declined. But the cans weren't moving off the shelves at a desirable pace. So, first thing, we ordered up some tracking research on how customers were using the product. When we opened up hundreds of kitchen cabinets throughout America we made an interesting discovery: they were loaded with cans of Campbell's soup. This highlighted something we rarely encounter in consumer marketing: customers were buying cans of soup, but not using them up. They would store them away and forget about them. When we presented the data to Campbell's and explained why people weren't coming back to the stores to refill on soup, it was as if the seas of darkness parted. Now both of us could see why people stopped coming to the stores to refill their soup supply.

In terms of analysis, this information didn't leave much room for ambiguity. It revealed a disconnect between the purchase rate and the consumption rate. The insight was clear. We had to get customers to stop thinking of canned soup as the default form of sustenance—something you ate only when there was nothing else in the cupboard. We had to get them to start using the product they bought. We had to get them to open up their cabinets and eat more soup.

The needle we needed to move had less to do with sales and more to do with the use-up rate. We had to stoke consumption rather than buying.

It was an intriguing distinction, which made for an interesting advertising assignment. Most advertising aims to make you go to the store and pluck the client's product off the shelf. But here we needed advertising to get people to reach onto their own shelves and pluck out the product that was already there.

That was our insight moment. In articulating the problem, our creative people came up with a simple theme line that defined the entire campaign: "Reach for the Campbell's. It's right on your shelf."

It was the first campaign we ever worked on that didn't urge the consumer to rush out and buy our product. We simply reminded consumers to use it. Same movement, but different needle.

If you're lucky, the urge to move the needle gets drilled into you very early in your career. That's what happened to me. Like most creatives in advertising, I stumbled into the field with a motley smattering of talents, useless in most professions, but somehow ideal for the ad business.

I grew up in Brooklyn, the oldest son of a cabdriver who took pride in being the slowest driver in New York. I went to Midwood High School, where I excelled at football and baseball and my classmates included Woody Allen and Erich Segal (author of *Love Story*). I got a baseball scholarship to Emory & Henry College in Virginia, but the scholarship money disappeared after one semester, so I had no choice but to come home to Flatbush and figure out what to do. I went straight back to Virginia to work at a radio station, where I did everything from deejay work to writing the copy for our local advertisers to selling time on the station. (Station rates were very attractive, "a dollar a holler" as we put it.) Someone told me that I was good at the copywriting part, which encouraged me to send around samples of my writing to bigger radio stations in the New York area. The station managers all wrote back saying the same thing: "We don't hire copywriters at a radio station. You must go to what is known as an advertising agency." The program director at WNEW went a little further than the others. He took the liberty of critiquing my copy, basically saying it was terrible and I had no future in writing. I was crestfallen for a moment, but it somehow made me redouble my effort to get a radio job up north.

I was twenty-one years old when I finally got hired by radio station WGSM in Huntington, Long Island. To augment my income I moonlighted as the in-store announcer for the now-defunct E. J. Korvette's department store.

"Ladies and gentlemen," I would intone from an upstairs booth overlooking the main sales floor, "for the next fifteen minutes only, in the hosiery bar, three pairs of lovely sheer nylons, only ninety-nine cents. But you must hurry. This is for the next fifteen minutes only."

This was the magical moment when I discovered the awesome power of moving the needle. The instant that I uttered these words over the public address system I could see throngs of women below me drop what they were doing at the makeup counter or the handbag department and scurry like ants to the hosiery bar.

"Amazing," I thought. "I just have to say it, and they jump."

This was the moment when I first saw a direct connection between persuasive language and people actually being persuaded—that if I chose my words carefully, limiting them to hot-button phrases such as "three pairs" and "99 cents" and "15 minutes only," people would respond. Until you see it with your own eyes in real time, you may never truly believe that what you're doing is actually moving the needle.

It wasn't long before every department head was rushing up to my mezzanine perch, begging me, "Do my ad, do my ad."

That's when I knew I had a future in advertising.

Moving the needle means something different to everyone.

On a gross level to any of us involved in sales, it means an uptick in units sold. But even when applied to sales, moving the needle has subtleties. For example, in a very large global business, it's not simply a matter of selling more. You have to sell more so that it has an emphatic and measurable impact on the entire business. A local promotion by a Pepsi bottler, tailored specifically to regional buying habits, may shrink inventory or increase quarterly sales for that one region, but it may not make a dent in global Pepsi sales. The local bottler is thinking he did a great job in his territory, while Pepsi's CEO back at headquarters won't even register the gain until all his local bottlers do the same.

That highlights another subtlety about moving the needle. Sometimes you can get by with a small insight. Other times only a big insight will do. The insight that moves the needle for a local Pepsi bottler—say, linking your autumn Pepsi promotion to the high school football teams in a football-mad county—will not be the insight that moves the needle on global sales, or for that matter even U.S. sales. To accomplish that, you need a big sweeping umbrella insight that covers everyone. It's the difference between running for local sheriff and running for president. A simple pledge to reduce drunk driving might elect a sheriff, but you need a grand vision—or an enormous promise that at least 50 percent of the voters care about—to win the presidency.

Whether we know it or not, we live in a move-the-needle world. Computers make it easy to accept this, because they are maniacal measuring machines. They are omnipresent, always ready to tell us whether we're making statistical progress or falling behind. Even as I type these words, my Microsoft Word program is telling me at the bottom of the screen that this is the 29,585th word in this book. See? With each keystroke, I'm moving the word-count needle.

In such a world, everything can be seen in terms of the simple question: *Does it move the needle?* It forces us to confront whether our decisions are making a large incremental difference or a marginal one.

In that light, your insights do not merely move the sales or revenue needle. They can work their magic in the warm and fuzzy areas too.

For example, if you're on top of your game, you can move the needle in employee morale and self-esteem. You can literally lift your people's pride in the company they work for. That's what Avis did back in the 1960s and 1970s with their legendary "We try harder" campaign. The slogan not only positioned Avis beautifully as the appealing underdog to the category leader, Hertz. It not only made a national virtue out of being number two. But the campaign also did triple duty by inspiring Avis employees. They were proud to be known as the people who try harder. If you could have measured Avis employee morale at the time, the needle would have flown off the meter.

Moving the needle is practically like a religion to me. Once you "accept it in your life," it begins to infiltrate everything you touch or that touches you. As a manager of creative people, I have always urged our people to move the needle on every aspect of a commercial. That's why, even with a fool-proof concept and great writing, I would insist that we sweat the smallest executional details—the edit, the sound mix, the music, the special effects—always in search of that little bit extra, that slight nudge forward on the quality meter. At some point during my tenure as agency creative director, this instinct became institutionalized; people joked that the initials BBDO stood for "Bring it Back, Do it Over."

We even try to move the needle in casting a commercial. That sounds transparently smart—casting can make or break a spot—but the truth is, casting is one of the more hit-or-miss aspects of making commercials. Agencies look at hundreds of actor reels, audition dozens of candidates before casting a commercial. But they rarely treat casting as a way of moving the needle of a commercial's impact. Most of the time, they have a picture of someone in mind when they dream up the spot, and they cast the actors who most closely resemble that mental picture. They don't think of casting as a way to go orbital.

I know. I used to think this way. I didn't have time to audition everyone. I didn't have the budget to hire a big celebrity. I had to get the commercial finished on time.

A lot of that changed in 1987 when one of my colleagues, Michael Patti, wrote a Diet Pepsi commercial called "Apartment 10G." A young man answers a knock on his apartment door. It's a beautiful woman asking, "Can I borrow a Diet Pepsi?" He looks in his refrigerator, sees an empty 2-liter bottle of Diet Pepsi, and asks, "How about something else?" The woman begins to beg off, "Listen, if you can't . . ." at which point he jumps out the window into a rainy night, climbs down the fire escape, dashes between cars in heavy traffic across a street to a Diet Pepsi machine. He returns with a can of Diet Pepsi, hands it to the woman, only to see her equally stunning roommate appear in the doorway, asking for a Diet Pepsi too.

The spot could have worked with any fresh-faced young actor with a gift for physical comedy. There are plenty that fit the bill. But when someone in a creative session suggested Michael J. Fox, we all looked at each other and knew that casting the hot young star of *Family Ties* and the *Back to the Future* film series was taking a good idea and improving it by at least 20 percent. A simple casting decision would move the needle for Diet Pepsi, both in the spot's impact and in sales.

This was hardly the first time a movie star made a commercial. Celebrity endorsements have been with us since P. T. Barnum in the 1880s. But using Michael J. Fox was the first time a celebrity had appeared in a commercial with a story line, a 60-second mini-film. Using Fox was optional. But in hindsight, not using him seems unimaginable. That's the pay-off from pushing, pushing to move your own quality needle.[1]

This experience taught us that a celebrity used with light-ness and wit is a great way to move the needle. But only if it's appropriate—meaning, take the celebrity out and the spot would be significantly diminished. We saw this when we used the late Ray Charles in a string of Diet Pepsi spots, singing "You got the right one baby, uh huh." Our first spot and my favorite has Ray playing the piano, singing the praises of Diet Pepsi. (Hey, if you have Ray Charles, you're a fool *not* to put him to work at the piano.) He turns to the camera, announc-ing "Nothing tastes as good as a Diet Pepsi." An off-camera assistant hands him a can of Diet Coke. He sips, then says, "Okay, who's the wise guy?" A memorable blind taste test (and Diet Pepsi wins!).

---

[1] In hiring Michael J. Fox and paying him whatever he wanted, we were getting good value. Using him not only gave us a skilled actor who could complete a scene more quickly and better than we imagined, but we also got all of the positive emotions that people attached to him. In effect, we were getting the afterglow from his popu-lar TV and film characters for free. But you have to be careful associating your prod-uct with a celebrity. You can get burned if the celebrity embroils your client in his or her controversies—as we learned when we made another Diet Pepsi commercial with Madonna and her song "Like a Prayer." But if you're clever and have your reasons, you can even move the needle by casting someone with negative associations. One of the earliest examples of the daring celebrity endorsement, notes the advertising scholar James B. Twitchell in his book *Twenty Ads That Shook the World,* was the famed English beauty and actress who made Pears soap a phenomenon in Britain at the end of the nineteenth century. Lillie Langtry, writes Twitchell, "declared, 'I have much pleasure in stating that I have used your soap for some time and prefer it to any other.' [Pears soap] saw to it that everyone in the civilized world heard what she had to say. [They] did not have to mention what really activated Ms. Langtry's words: she was best known as King Edward VII's mistress. In a sense, she was dirty. But in a contrary sense she was not as good as royalty, she was better. She was what royalty *wanted*."

Perhaps the spot would be cute with any blind person. But with Ray Charles—whose blindness did not require explication—it lifted off into the stratosphere. That's moving the needle.

The best thing about moving the needle is that, over time, if you keep your eye on it, you begin to see things that everyone else is missing.

When Roger Enrico became CEO of Frito-Lay, after years of running Pepsi-Cola and waging war with Coca-Cola, he finally inherited a company that was the undisputed state-of-the-art leader in its category. Frito-Lay controlled 40 percent of the entire salty snack market. It had the best product line, the best branding, the best distribution, the best sales force, the best advertising . . . everything was the best. It was one of those quietly admired companies—off the radar, not the object of cultish adoration like Intel, Microsoft, and GE were for their innovation and management.

Yet despite this dominance, Enrico had also taken over a company that in less than a decade had lost a fifth of its market share. It was a gradual erosion, which is often hard to see, and it came at the hands of small local competitors nipping at Frito-Lay on their home turf, using price and volume to steal market share.

Like any newly installed CEO, Enrico knew his job was to stop the bleeding and regain market share—a classic move-the-needle mandate. But as he looked at Frito-Lay and acknowledged that it was the best of the best, he wondered why he felt confident that he could do better. The company was already great. Was it possible that it had maxed out at 40 percent market share? Was its best days behind it? Was there no way to move the needle up?

As he considered this, Enrico wondered if you could put a number to Frito-Lay's market share in less obvious categories, such as research and development and selling capability. He concluded that, as the dominant brand driving the category, Frito-Lay controlled a 90 percent share of the entire industry's R&D, and an 80 percent share of the selling capability. That's how deep Frito-Lay's resources were. When he compared those figures with the 40 percent market share, it didn't add up. The spread between the company's capabilities and what it was delivering was too big.

That's when the insight hit him. "People," he told his senior management, "we are under-leveraging this company."

The company had been so intent on accomplishing the tough task of moving the needle one-tenth of a margin point here, another tenth there—what Enrico called "optimizing," getting the most out of your existing business—that it had lost sight of the bigger picture. As one veteran told Enrico, "I get it. We've been working on the wrong side of the decimal point."

Enrico thought that was an insightful way of putting it. If you're working on the right side of the decimal point, you're moving the needle in fractions, in tenths and hundredths. If you're working on the left side of the decimal point, you're moving the needle in whole numbers, whether it's one, two, or ten percentage points. According to Enrico, the right side of the decimal point is managing. The left side of the decimal point is leadership. The right side is about today and yesterday; the left side is about the future. The right side is about continuous improvement. The left side is a major reach forward.

A good business does both. It optimizes what it already has through adept management. But at the same time, it looks for new growth platforms—new products, new territories, new market shares to cultivate. These require bold leadership.

This insight gave Enrico a new way of looking at market share—and guided him to make daring initiatives with salty snack products way beyond the friendly confines of the U.S. market in Japan and India and Eastern Europe. These were, as he calls them, "new growth platforms." You may know them as game-changers.

That, more than anything else, may be the real payoff from getting into a move-the-needle mindset. It forces you to come up with a big insight, because sometimes a little one won't do.

CHAPTER 4

THE INSIGHT RESUMÉ

YOUR INSIGHT RESUMÉ

Pepsi and Apple CEO John Sculley liked to say, "Having a point of view is worth fifty IQ points." He said that to encourage frankness and honest debate among his people. If that's true, then having a useful insight must be worth one hundred IQ points—because an insight brings meetings to a close, finishes off fractious debates, and gets people to stop *talking* and start *doing*.

Everyone's capable of having insights. You probably had your first insight as a young child when you realized that you could pit your mother and father against each other to get what you wanted. If one parent denied a request, you asked the other (the insight was "divide and conquer"). Eventually you learned how well this tactic worked—or didn't. And you adapted. As you got older you had other insights about "managing" your parents. You knew never to ask your father for the keys to the car when he was stressed out or angry; you approached him when he was in a good mood. And so on. When you're a child so much of your mental energy is devoted to solving problems on the home front that you practically become an insight machine.

But we somehow lose that ability as we get older and enter the workforce. The problems we face at work aren't so immediate or well defined as, say, getting a bike or stretching our curfew to 1 A.M. (When you're a kid those things *really* matter.) And so we lose that crucial need to keep coming up with insights. Maybe it's because no one is articulating the problem for us or challenging us to solve it. Maybe we're too far down the ladder to feel that our insights matter. We're not invested in the problem, so we don't feel connected to the solution. Maybe we're too timid to float our ideas in public. Whatever the reason, we are suffering from diminished insight capacity. We are giving up one hundred IQ points.

This is never a good thing in business or in life. It puts us at a perpetual disadvantage with our more insightful peers.

Before you can appreciate how insightful you can be *now,* it helps to understand how insightful you have been in the past. Here are twenty-four quick questions to help you compose your own insight resumé:

1. What is the first insight you remember?

2. What is your best insight?

3. What made it great?

4. What was the problem it solved?

5. Can you connect the dots that led to this insight?

6. What is your second-best insight?

7. Again, why? What did it solve? How did it come to you?

8. What is your dumbest insight?

9. How would you characterize your ideas?

10. What's your creative signature?

11. Who are insightful people you admire?

12. Who are your creative mentors or role models?

13. What do you have in common with these role models?

14. When all else fails, to whom or what do you turn for inspiration?

15. What criteria do you employ to judge the merits of an insight or idea?

16. Who are your heroes?

17. Have they ever turned up in one of your concepts? If so, how, when, and why?

18. What is your ideal creative activity?

19. What is your greatest fear?

20. Describe your ideal client.

21. What's your favorite year?

22. A year to forget?

23. How do you stay in creative shape?

24. Define luck.

MY INSIGHT RESUMÉ

Your insight resumé aims, like any resumé, to let you put your best forward. It is the curriculum vitae of your creative life. Here is mine.

1. WHAT IS THE FIRST INSIGHT YOU REMEMBER?

At the age of fourteen, I looked at the facts and decided I was too young to die. As a high school freshman at Brooklyn Tech, I rubbed a nasty Flatbush gang member the wrong way (actually, I did more than rub; I coldcocked him in a cafeteria brawl). Seeking revenge, he and his buddies threatened to have me "clipped" one day after school. "Clipped" meant killed, and I didn't think they were kidding. My insight was, "If you can't beat 'em, leave 'em." So I pleaded with my parents for a quick transfer—which I got—to safer Midwood High School in another part of Brooklyn. And that, to quote Robert Frost, has made all the difference. I still find it interesting that my first memorable insight was inspired by fear and was all about self-preservation. Perfect preparation for the advertising business.

2. WHAT IS YOUR BEST INSIGHT?

Realizing that even though my heart wanted me to become a major league baseball player, my size and talent were conclusive evidence that I couldn't make the grade. A deficiency in something you love is hard for many people to accept. My insight was really about accepting the truth.

3. WHAT MADE IT GREAT?

This insight saved me a lifetime of frustration. It made me realize early on that there were limits in life, and helped me accept the notion that no matter how much you want some-thing, you cannot do it on hearts and wishes alone. You need some tools to make it happen. This doesn't mean you shouldn't shoot for the stars; you just need to know what it takes to get there and whether you have enough of "it."

4. WHAT WAS THE PROBLEM IT SOLVED?

It taught me to be realistic at a young age—and detoured me away from a potential life of rejection.

5. CAN YOU CONNECT THE DOTS THAT LED TO THIS INSIGHT?

Despite being a decent hitter with a pretty good arm (I was a catcher), when I looked around and compared myself to other players my age, I began to realize my shortcomings. This may have been my first foray into research, analysis, and insight. To reach the top of any field, you have to be a cut above the next guy, not a cut below. And that goes for the next guy and the next guy as you climb up the chain. You always have to be at least a cut above. I like to think I rechan-neled that insight later on in the advertising I rejected or approved. The work always had to be a cut above what everyone else was expecting.

6. WHAT IS YOUR SECOND-BEST INSIGHT?

Recognizing that there was something else I wasn't cut out for. After baseball, I wanted to be a singer. I had done a lot of singing in high school, had a decent voice, and appeared in lots of small clubs in New York. But again, somewhere along the way, reality set in: I knew I would never be *great* at it.

7. AGAIN, WHY? WHAT DID IT SOLVE? HOW DID IT COME TO YOU?

The cliché of "one door closing and another door opening" is true. The door it opened for me was a job as a disc jockey in a small radio station in Virginia. It was there I discovered I could write a little and realized that a whole new career possibility was opening up to me: advertising.

8. WHAT IS YOUR DUMBEST INSIGHT?

That's an oxymoron. There's no such thing as a dumb insight. Only a right or wrong one.

9. HOW WOULD YOU CHARACTERIZE YOUR IDEAS?

I've always been passionate about ideas that were simple and easy to understand because they were true. People could see the ideas and then see themselves.

10. WHAT IS YOUR CREATIVE SIGNATURE?

Advertising that speaks to the heart as well as the head. In a world of parity products and services, advertising that packs an emotional wallop definitely gives you a big edge.

11. WHO ARE INSIGHTFUL PEOPLE YOU ADMIRE?

David Ogilvy for making advertising a bona fide respectable business. Bill Bernbach for revolutionizing the creative process and setting a standard against which even current advertising is judged. President Ronald Reagan for having more common sense than a roomful of presidents. Joe Torre for his expert management of baseball's highest-priced superstars and the game's most irascible owner. And Steven Spielberg for never failing to know what his audiences want, and for having the talent and insights to deliver it.

12. WHO ARE YOUR CREATIVE MENTORS OR ROLE MODELS?

As a youngster growing up in the agency business, I had the perfect mentor: my first boss at BBDO, John Bergin. John was an excellent writer who happened to be a great teacher: encouraging, demanding, honest, and tough. (We referred to his office as "The Nutcracker Suite.") But it was a music teacher, Nathaniel George Levine, the director of The Mixed Chorus at Brooklyn's Midwood High School, who had the most influence, even on my career. "Boss," as he was affectionately known, could tame the rowdiest ruffians with the healing power of music and by making them blend their voices in our chorus. He was so good at this that we performed at Carnegie Hall with the New York Philharmonic. Boss taught me a lesson that stayed with me all during my advertising (and somewhat briefer) screenwriting career: how to reach audiences on an emotional level, and thus have them reach for your product with their heart as much as with their mind.

13. WHAT DO YOU HAVE IN COMMON WITH THESE ROLE MODELS?

The commonality here, both with Bergin and Boss, is a fierce desire to swing for the fences, and never settle for second best. As true in advertising as in any competitive field.

14. WHEN ALL ELSE FAILS, TO WHOM OR WHAT DO YOU TURN FOR INSPIRATION?

Inspiration comes in many forms. For me, in the struggle for an insight or an idea, a long walk helps, or a hot shower.

Something about being alone in a silent chamber with water running down my skin makes me think better. Reading a book or seeing a movie works, too. But the best inspiration is just talking to people. Sometimes one word dropped into a conversation can get ideas flowing. I always liked John Steinbeck's method. He'd put a blank piece of paper into the typewriter and just type . . . anything: his name, his address, silly lists of things to do. Then, slowly, ideas would come. And then, as he put it, "ideas beget ideas, ideas have pups . . . and soon I'm powerless to stop them."

15. WHAT CRITERIA DO YOU EMPLOY TO JUDGE THE MERITS OF AN INSIGHT OR IDEA?

I first look at it with my gut. How does it feel? Am I excited? Am I bored? Am I delighted? Once past that, I look at it on a business level. And determine whether it's on strategy, whether it meets the essential objectives. And most important, whether it has the potential to lead to a great piece of advertising.

16. WHO ARE YOUR HEROES?

NYPD. FDNY. Rudy Giuliani. Roy Hobbs. Ronald Reagan. My mother. Jesus Christ.

17. HAVE THEY EVER TURNED UP IN ONE OF YOUR CONCEPTS? IF SO, HOW, WHEN, AND WHY?

Two have: Roy Hobbs as the featured character played by Robert Redford in a movie I cowrote, *The Natural;* and President Reagan who starred in the commercials our Tuesday Team created for his successful 1984 reelection campaign.

18. WHAT IS YOUR IDEAL CREATIVE ACTIVITY?

Coming up with a great idea or spotting one in some young person's work. Also mixing it up with writers and art directors in the give and take where great ideas are born. I also love total immersion in the post-production process, and working through the small details—the edit, the mix, the music, the effects—always in search of that little bit extra.

19. WHAT IS YOUR GREATEST FEAR?

Honest, I don't have any. Well, maybe one: that advertising will never again be quite so much fun as it once was before the demand for efficiency displaced the charming, nonchalant innocence that marked my time in the business from the 1960s through the 1990s. I fear that those who come after my generation won't have so much fun as we did.

20. DESCRIBE YOUR IDEAL CLIENT.

Someone who's reasonable, sympathetic, intuitive, empowered to make big decisions—and not afraid to make them. Mostly, it's someone who creates the environment in which great work can flower and flourish. If you want names, let's start with Alan Pottasch at Pepsi. Ideal client—for thirty-five years and counting.

21. WHAT'S YOUR FAVORITE YEAR?

1984 (with apologies to George Orwell). Three memorable events occurred: the launch of the original Michael Jackson spots for Pepsi, which was a game-changer in celebrity advertising; the release of *The Natural*; and the ad campaign we created for President Reagan. The documentary I wrote and produced for Reagan that year, "A New Beginning," is now a permanent fixture in the Reagan Library in Simi Valley, California. It was like leading the league in batting, home runs, and runs batted in—the Triple Crown—and almost made up for my answer to question 2.

22. A YEAR TO FORGET?

I can't remember one.

23. HOW DO YOU STAY IN CREATIVE SHAPE?

I prefer writing. All kinds of writing: letters, speeches, ads, films, you name it. Writing is just another way of *thinking*. And the more you think, the more ideas you'll generate and, therefore, the more you'll *create*. Writing is like weight lifting. The more you do it, the better shape you'll be in. Let it go and your creative muscle slowly turns to flab.

24. DEFINE LUCK.

Branch Rickey, the longtime president of the old Brooklyn Dodgers, defined luck as the "residue of design." I've always believed that you make your luck.

CHAPTER 5

HEY, I'M OVER HERE!

I n my experience, the biggest problem any enterprise faces is finding a way to tell the world "Hey, I'm over here."

The marketplace is so cluttered, so noisy, so overpopulated with other people clamoring for attention that getting heard can be a challenge—even if you have the right message, a good product, and an appealing way of beaming it into people's eyes and ears.

In theory, saying "Hey, I'm over here" should be the easiest thing for a business to do. If you're that Long Island wineshop, you can do anything from floating big balloons above your store to using a skywriter to etch your name against the clouds. You can even hire a guy to walk the streets of downtown Sag Harbor wearing a sandwich billboard with your name and address on it. It's a two-hundred-year-old advertising technique that's guaranteed to increase store traffic; it can't decrease it.

If you're any kind of small business, saying "Hey, I'm over here" takes more showmanship and flair than insight. I don't know any private business that does this better than the "small" supermarket chain called Stew Leonard's outside New York City. It was founded by a milk route driver named Stew Leonard, who started it as a modest dairy selling fresh milk to the residents of Norwalk, Connecticut. It expanded into a supermarket over the years. By 1980 it was a phenomenon, attracting long lines of customers who would drive one hundred miles just to shop at the store. Stew and his store gained fame by appearing in Tom Peters and Robert Waterman's influential best-seller *In Search of Excellence*. They were models of staying in touch with customers.

But Stew Leonard's store was even better at saying "Hey, I'm over here." It was a classic parity store, selling parity produce and packaged edibles. Its bell peppers and cartons of milk and boxes of Kellogg's Corn Flakes were no better than those at the A&P down the road. But Stew Leonard's store had P. T. Barnum's flair for attracting a crowd. Cows in the parking lot, a petting zoo (replete with llamas) for the kids, and even an architectural signature featuring an enormous farm silo. If you want to shout "Hey, I'm over here," put a silo on Main Street. People will notice.

Stew Leonard's fame, sadly, turned into notoriety in 1993 when he was sent to jail for tax evasion. But that didn't stop his son, Stew Jr., from keeping the company growing and prospering. Dad's "Hey, I'm over here" flair must have been genetic. Stew Jr. expanded the operation to Danbury, Connecticut. Then he opened a third store in Yonkers, New York, along the New York State Thruway. That's a crucial fact. The Thruway is a toll road. You can't just hop onto it every 100 yards; the entrances are 5, 10, 15 miles apart. But to the amazement of friends, neighbors, and rivals, Stew Jr. convinced the state of New York to build him a special exit so people could get to his store. Hey, if you're good at telling people where you are, you need to be even better at helping them get there. He even got the state to name the exit after him—Exit 6A, Stew Leonard Drive. But the most amazing thing he did was to build another signature silo in the parking lot. This time he built it very big. So big that he considered putting a lighted arrow on top of the silo to guide pilots to New York's airports: "JFK This Way." He was joking, of course. What he did instead was put a lighted sign on the silo for all the drivers to gaze at as they cruised up and down the Thruway. It said, "Milk 99 cents." You couldn't miss it. It was so big and bright that it lit up the entire shopping mall.

I mention this silo because it is classic "Hey, I'm over here" marketing. Stew Leonard Jr.'s store had two other anchor stores in its hard-to-get-to location—a mammoth Costco wholesale club and an equally mammoth outlet of The Home Depot. Both Costco and The Home Depot are major national chains, with annual sales exceeding $30 billion. They are paragons of retail savvy. They know what their customers want and how to give it to them. And yet if you were driving north or south along that stretch of Thruway, you'd hardly know they were there. You'd think they were humble tenants in Stew Leonard's mall.

There's a reason that, in terms of "Hey, I'm over here," the little guy skunked the big boys. When you're a small business, your life depends on telling people where you are and how to get there.

When you're a big national brand, you take it for granted. You've got all the brand-equity perks going for you: the familiar logo slapped on hundreds of stores, the carefully researched real estate that yields the most desirable locations, the years of national TV advertising. To spike store traffic, you can print millions of inserts in the Sunday newspaper. People know who you are. You don't have to yell "Hey, I'm over here!" because once you've built it, they will come.

In my experience, the "Hey, I'm over here" problem appears in three variations. When you need to:

- Announce your arrival on the scene.

- Remind people that you're still here.

- Tell people that they don't really know you.

In effect, you're either saying *I'm here,* or *I'm still here,* or *I'm still here but I've changed.* Let's look at all three, because the problems are sometimes more subtle than they seem.

I'M HERE

"Hey, I'm over here" was clearly the issue when we were invited to pitch for the launch of a new wireless phone service from a new entity called Cingular, an amalgam of wireless companies formed by the mergers of Southwestern Bell and BellSouth.

The wireless business is brutally competitive—largely focused on giving away cell phones and giving you lots of free minutes. It's an industry that spends most of its media budget on full-page ads in newspapers touting its latest pricing plans, trying to lure rivals' customers as aggressively as it tries to find new customers—and always dealing with the "churn," the loss of old customers. The category has featured some strong advertising. There was Sprint's long-running "you can hear a pin drop" campaign. And Verizon has done well featuring the silky basso profundo of James Earl Jones as its spokesperson. AT&T . . . well, it's hard to remember their advertising (all those who know what "mLife" means, call now; the lines are open). Upstart Nextel had a nifty success with its walkie-talkie feature that appealed to young people, and then Nextel pulled off a coup by replacing Winston cigarettes as the title sponsor of NASCAR, America's hottest sport.

As we began to circle the problem, we immediately dismissed the emotional route of showing loved ones talking to each other, using a cell phone to connect and maintain bonds. For one thing, Cingular was a new entity. It had no image, no name recognition, and certainly no track record of service. You can't claim to be great at connecting people if you haven't done it yet. There was also the wallpaper effect to think about.[1] Long-distance companies such as AT&T and MCI had been showing mushy family scenes in their commercials for a long time—most memorably in the "Joey Called" spot from 1981 showing an aging mother moved to tears by her grown son calling "just because I love you." (This was so effective that MCI spoofed it the next year with an aging mother weeping inconsolably. When her husband asks what's wrong, she cries, "Have you seen our long-distance phone bill?") Trying to "reach out and touch" wireless callers was not going to break through the wallpaper created by years of emotion-based telecom advertising. Nor were we ready to fight on price or make idle boasts about sound quality. The last thing the world was looking for was a new phone company, another name to learn, another promise to absorb, the usual baggage that comes with a launch.

Our job was to create a calling card that let the world know there was a new kid on the block—and this kid had a

---

[1] Wallpaper effect: You know the wallpaper is there, but no one notices, much less cares.

distinctive personality. Deciding that we couldn't resemble anything that had been done before in the category was a huge blessing.

Since we couldn't talk about the company's service or sound quality or pricing or technology or reach—in fact, nothing about the product itself—we turned to the remaining half of the equation, the end user of the product. This was the cornerstone of the BBDO philosophy, ever since 1960 when BBDO chairman Tom Dillon wrote a "white paper" for Pepsi explaining that some competing products, for example, soft drinks, were so equal in quality that it would be more effective to distinguish and celebrate the customer who used the product, rather than the product itself. This is how BBDO created a campaign for Pepsi themed "Now it's Pepsi for those who think young," and gave birth to "The Pepsi Generation." That perception was startling for its time (but it's not unusual anymore; when Volkswagen advertises "Drivers Wanted," it's celebrating the people who buy its cars, not the cars). But at BBDO, we never forget it.

Focusing on the consumer made us go through a quick Socratic Q&A with ourselves.

Q: What do you do on a phone?
A: You listen and talk.
Q: Why do you talk?
A: To express yourself.
Q: What's that called?
A: Self-expression.

That was our insight and strategy rolled into one. We would position Cingular as the company that emulated the consumer.

We would tell the consumer, "Hey, here's a company that, like you, believes in self-expression. We know you live in a world where it's important for you to get your piece said, whatever it may be. And we at Cingular will help you do that."

We added a clever lagniappe to the pitch. Cingular had already designed a logo, a stylish four-pointed jumping jack symbol. We decided to humanize the symbol, called "Jack," by animating it and making it an active part of every commercial. Cingular loved that, and it may have been the extra ingredient that landed the account for us. Phone companies face the perennial image problem that they're more robotic than human. Humanizing "Jack" humanized Cingular at the critical moment when it was about to shake hands with the world.

In a big, brutal, competitive industry, you can't say "Hey, I'm over here!" in a whisper. You have to shout. That's why our first spot aired on the 2001 Super Bowl. When you spend $1.6 million for a 60-second spot, you're shouting. After that, your only job is to make sure people don't cover their ears.

The commercial starred the renowned painter Dan Keplinger, who has cerebral palsy. It begins with an unsparing shot of crippled hands and legs and an unintelligible voice. A subtitle translates: "Yes, there is intelligent life in there." Then you see Dan Keplinger, bent over a splashy canvas, painting with a brush attached to his forehead. Images of him and his work alternate with subtitles translating his garbled speech. They read like Zen poetry:

I speak to the world in color and light.

Art gives me a way to express myself.

Most people think "gimp" means a lame walk.

Gimp also means a fighting spirit.

I am an artist.

I'm unbelievably lucky.

A graphic sums up: "There is no force more powerful or more beautiful than self-expression." Then the Cingular theme line: "What do you have to say?"

We thought long and hard about the political correctness of "gimp" in a Super Bowl spot. But we had discovered Dan from his appearance in *King Gimp,* which won the 1999 Academy Award for best documentary short. If it's okay in an Oscar winner, it's okay in a commercial. Besides, the spot's objective was to get people . . . *talking.* And it did. Subsequent commercials lightened things up, such as one featuring beefy football players "expressing" themselves in ballet class. "You're a peacock, you're a camel, you're a tree," says the dance instructor to the strains of Prokofiev's *Peter and the Wolf.*

Self-expression worked. But once the handshake phase was over and Cingular was properly introduced to the world, the push to say "Hey, I'm over here!" was as intense as ever. Cingular's new CEO, Stan Sigman, directed BBDO into a retail mode, putting the advertising on the prowl for immediate results. In a charming series of spots themed around the tag line "Cingular fits you best," the advertising took on a new and more aggressive stance. Like "self-expression," this worked, too.

But the most unexpected phase of "Hey, I'm over here!" was about to happen.

On October 28, 2004, Cingular swallowed up AT&T Wireless for $41 billion to become the largest wireless company in the world. Now "Hey, I'm over here" took on a new complexion: announcing the formation of a brand new company, Cingular's second such announcement within three years.

The news came in a torrent of new TV spots, print ads, outdoor sheets, and Internet ads. All wrapped around a simple compelling tag line, "Raising the Bar," a clever play on wireless phone graphics. Unless you lived on another planet, you got the message. Ten days after the campaign broke, the proverbial phone was ringing off the hook. Not only were consumers "getting it" and responding, Cingular was now pulling away from the pack and being perceived as the category leader: Numero Uno.

Of course, once that happy day arrives, new challenges begin to surface, such as making the business more profitable and moving the needle for Wall Street. And, naturally, the high-class headache that all market leaders face: staying number one.

I'M STILL HERE

Six weeks after the attacks of September 11, New York City's downtown was still smoldering and caked in soot. Nearly a thousand firefighters and police officers were dead. Two thousand more people who worked in the World Trade Center were gone. Hundreds of businesses were shut down south of Canal Street. Broadway theaters were half empty. Tourism wasn't merely off; it had vanished. No one was visiting New York. The entire city was in the dumps.

Which is why I found myself sitting with Mayor Rudy Giuliani in a makeshift command center inside the 55th Street pier, jutting out over the Hudson River on Manhattan's West

Side. The meeting had been arranged by a close friend of Rudy's, John Wren, CEO of BBDO's parent company, Omnicom. We were there to talk to the Mayor about the kind of advertising that would make people feel better about New York and bring them back.

It doesn't take much insight to see that this is a variation on "Hey, I'm over here," only it's a reacquaintance message. We needed to say, "I'm *still* here."

As we spoke, I started eliminating options in my mind. Images of the long-running "I Love New York" campaign with its rah-rah music and Broadway chorus girls and sweeping vistas of New York's Adirondack mountains would not work here. Nor would a heartwarming, emotional appeal. Our BBDO creatives had already done that the month before with a spot called "This Bell" for our client, the New York Stock Exchange. It was a moving testament to the fact that nothing, not even the 9/11 attacks, could silence the exchange's opening bell of freedom. It could give goose bumps to a mummy.

When drama and tears are out of the picture, the best option is always humor.

"You may think this is weird and inappropriate," I said to Mayor Giuliani, "but maybe we should do something humorous."

Rudy got it immediately. "That would be terrific," he said. "It would make people feel upbeat about all this. That's the idea."

So we went back to kick it around. Keep in mind that whatever New York was going through, we were living it every day. We all knew someone who had perished in the attacks; we had all been to memorial services. We realized that

New York was demonstrating how people can come out of the woodwork to fight and help and contribute and rise to the occasion. We decided to call this process the New York Miracle.

Now all we had to do was make that "miracle" concept stick. As we thought about ourselves, why some of us had gravitated to the big city, we realized that people come to New York because they have a dream. Everybody dreams of doing something big in New York. If we can get that message across to people, maybe we can bring them back here.

But how to show it?

That's when Gerry Graf, one of our senior creative directors, said, "Imagine Woody Allen ice skating in Rockefeller Center."

That opened the floodgates and the suggestions of famous people doing incongruous New York activities began to pile up. Ted Sann chimed in: How about Henry Kissinger finding his way into an empty Yankee Stadium to round the bases, slide headfirst into home plate, dust himself off, and ask, "Derek who?" Yankee Stadium suggested Yogi Berra. "But wait a second," I said, "how about Yogi conducting the New York Philharmonic?" Michael Patti suggested Billy Crystal and Robert DeNiro dressed up as a turkey and a pilgrim, arguing over who should play the turkey. They get up, walk out of the park, continuing the debate, and then you see them on a float in the Thanksgiving Day parade. Graf again: Barbara Walters auditioning for a Broadway show, butchering the song "42nd Street"! It was a creative free-for-all and we knew we were on to something exciting.

My favorite actually was a dowdy woman sitting down at the Stage Deli, where sandwiches are named after actors. Looking over the menu, she orders a "Ben Stiller" sandwich. "With bacon." The waiter shouts to the back of the deli,

"Hey, Stiller. Table three. With bacon." We see Ben Stiller and Kevin Bacon rise from a bench and sit next to the woman at her table. Mayor Giuliani pays off the spot, delivering the theme line "The New York Miracle. Be a part of it." Back to the deli, where the woman admires her handsome dining companions and says, "Waiter, can I have a doggie bag?"

The objective was to make people feel good about New York as a city loaded with possibilities, where dreams come true, and you should "be a part of it." (We borrowed that line from the city's unofficial anthem, Fred Kander and John Ebb's "New York, New York.") But plain and simple, it is a tourism campaign, announcing "We're still here."

I promised myself that I wouldn't talk shop in this book. I wouldn't describe the technical niceties of making commercials. But the New York Miracle was different. Yankee Stadium, Avery Fisher Hall, and Rockefeller Center opened their doors to us. We got six fantastic (if I do say so myself) spots written, cast, shot, produced, and on the air in three weeks. We had big names like Robert DeNiro and Billy Crystal and Woody Allen and Barbara Walters and Henry Kissinger starring in them. We had the great and impossible-to-book Joe Pytka directing. He flew in his entire production team from California. And everyone worked for free. Pound for pound, given the quality level involved, it has to be the lowest-cost campaign of all time. I guess that's the paradox when you're working with great professionals; they come through big time even for nothing.

The six spots took on a life of their own. Rudy Giuliani asked us to show them to the media at a City Hall press conference. The scene was like a Senate hearing, with rows of cameras and hardened City Hall reporters in every chair. Rudy introduced me. I ad-libbed my way through how it all happened. Then I said, "Let me just show you the first commercial if I may." They loved it. They started applauding (the press never applauds). So I ran through the other five spots and they continued applauding. I had been at the podium all of five minutes. I didn't know what to do, so I said, "Do you want to see them again?" And the entire City Hall press corps shouted, "Yes."

NBC *Nightly News* anchor Brian Williams, then at MSNBC, called to invite me onto his evening news program, promising to air all six commercials uninterrupted. "That's a twist," I thought. "Showing commercials without broadcast interruption." But when an adman hears the words "free media" for his agency's spots, the only thing to do is grab the DVD, jump into a car, and rush to MSNBC studios. All told, we got millions of dollars of free exposure before we ever paid for any air time. It proves the adage that people like to be entertained, no matter what the message.

I'M STILL HERE, BUT I'VE CHANGED

With Cingular and New York City we faced problems that were so familiar to us we could slot them into "Hey, I'm over here" and then deal with them. It was a little different with longtime client Dupont, because it wasn't immediately apparent that the problem fit into "Hey, I'm over here."

The year was 1987. Dupont had been a BBDO client for longer than anyone could remember. The agency had written the company's durable slogan "Better things for better living . . . through chemistry" in 1937. And over the decades we had done effective, serviceable (occasionally memorable) advertising every time Dupont's lab wizards created a miraculous polymer or material, such as Teflon, that would change the world. The account was so stable that when we needed a new slogan we simply crossed out the words "through chemistry." If it ain't broke, don't fix it; tweak it.

But things were changing. The year before we had done some breakthrough commercials for Dupont Stainmaster carpeting by showing humorous situations of people spilling things on a carpet and stressing how easy it cleans up if you have Stainmaster.

Stainmaster was not the easiest product to highlight in an entertaining message. What made it doubly difficult was that we weren't selling the carpet. We were selling the Stainmaster fiber coating. Getting people to walk in off the street and ask for a fiber product contained in a carpet was a tall order. It's like going into a Chrysler showroom and saying that you'll buy a car only if the transmission is made with a specific brand of aluminum alloy. We didn't want to go the boring route of demonstrating the product, as if it were any old carpet shampoo that cleaned rugs. Our solution—our insight— was to show scenes that people felt were familiar (in the best sense). Anyone could relate to a child in a high chair whizzing food onto the floor as he pretended to fly his airplane-shaped dinner dish. Young marrieds shopping for a rug could also see the relevance in a glamorous couple flirting their way into a food fight during a romantic candlelit dinner at home. Stainmaster sales took off. The approach moved the needle.

That's when the problems began. Dupont's head of external affairs, Jack Malloy, was so pleased with the work that he asked us to fashion a new corporate image campaign for Dupont. Not for any specific products, but for the company.

He gave us the one thing every ad agency prays for: *total freedom.*

"Guys," said Malloy, "you know a lot more about advertising than we do. Go to it."

Whom the gods wish to destroy, they answer their prayers.

Freedom is a double-edged sword. On one side, it lets you cut through anything. On the other is a sharp, cruel edge that can cut you down to size. Let me describe the worst-case scenario when the client gives you total freedom.

At first you are elated. The opportunity to alter the landscape. No ropes around the ring. Advertising heaven! You set to work with the usual rummaging around. You're determined to dig down deep and reach back for something extra. Visions of Gold Lions dance in your head. But five days pass and you've come up empty. Surrounded by wadded balls of paper, doodle pads, and perfectly aligned rows of paper clips, you stare into space, your forehead cold and moist. You feel the first gastric rumblings of panic. Your imagination has gone into vise-lock.

For the first time in your career, you wish the client interfered a little more—made you toe their marketing guidelines, suggested using the hot new celebrity, handed you a memo in bold capital letters listing the required product attributes: crispier, less filling, more refreshing.

You realize that the client has given you nothing to hang your hat on but your own head. You have no props to juggle, no client noise to worry into a snappy tune. You are a total blank.

That's what happened to us. When the manager lets you swing away at the plate, you tend to strike out. We were trying to come up with a breakthrough idea, but we hadn't yet articulated the problem.

We stepped back, took some deep breaths to quell the

panic, and looked at what we were being asked to do. A corporate campaign is a strange hybrid. It's hard to measure the results, and you're talking to a small carefully defined audience. Dupont is a giant industrial company, a lot like General Electric. And we knew that, like GE (which spends 80 percent of its corporate-image TV budget on the Sunday morning talk shows, where it can reach lawmakers, government officials, and CEOs), the Dupont campaign would be talking to a very select audience. So, we didn't have to swing for the fences with a universal concept that *everyone* could relate to.

As we looked at our client, and recalled that its slogan had not changed in decades—it was still "better things for better living"—we realized that Dupont was one of America's durable corporate icons. Who didn't know Dupont? It was big. It was science. It was miraculous materials where eggs didn't stick to frying pans, and garments didn't wrinkle, and hosiery didn't tear, and you could wipe spilled grape juice off your sofa without leaving a stain. It could legitimately claim "I'm still here." But it had changed as well. We needed to define that change, even as we extolled all that the company has achieved.

But how do you humanize a company that does all that? How do you remind people of what they already know, and yet don't know at all?

We couldn't talk about the myriad products that Dupont invents and manufactures. We weren't "selling" them to a Sunday talk-show crowd. Our insight eventually was the recognition that behind Dupont's significant successes is a continuing spirit of scientific inquiry that results in the creation of products that benefit individuals and society. That's a mouthful, perhaps, but we wanted our audience to infer that Dupont is a national treasure. It has always been around but now you see it anew.

The challenge we set ourselves was not to market products that we can see or feel or touch, but to dramatize the humanity of a company where everything starts in its labs. A suggestion by a Dupont department head, who had read about an artificial limb called the Seattle Foot that faithfully mimicked the springing action of muscles and bone, helped us settle on the Dupont plastic resin used in that prosthetic device. Vietnam vets, disabled in combat, were among the first to use the Seattle Foot. So we set about looking for a vet who was athletic enough to demonstrate the capabilities of the prosthetic.

We didn't expect Bill Denby, a Vietnam vet missing both legs. But our production people found him playing basketball in a competition for disabled athletes, where he was clearly benefiting from the double prostheses with the Dupont resin. The more our production people talked to him, the more we knew he was our man because he was telegenic and such a nice human being.

The 60-second spot, shot on a Manhattan basketball court, shows a young man limping past a schoolyard pickup game. An announcer tells Bill's story: "When Bill Denby was in Vietnam, he used to dream of coming home and playing a little basketball with the guys. That dream all but died when he lost two legs to a Vietcong rocket."

Friends greet Denby as he sits on a bench to remove his sweatpants and reveals his prosthetic limbs. It's a stunning moment. But the most gripping part comes, as the announcer describes Dupont's contribution, when Bill starts playing—and falls down. He lets out a soft groan; you wonder if he's okay. But he refuses help and pulls himself up as if his legs are no different from anyone else's on the court.

"Thanks to these efforts," says the voice-over, "Bill Denby is back. And some say he hasn't lost a step. At Dupont, we make the things that make a difference."

It was a powerful spot that instantly became Dupont's corporate signature for the next two years. It frequently appears in lists of the Top 100 commercials. But more than anything else, it changed people's impression of Dupont, particularly among the key constituencies we were aiming for: Wall Street as well as Washington, other businesses as well as consumers. It told them Dupont's message: I'm still here, but I've changed.

Remember this the next time you think your problem is not getting the notice you desire or the attention you deserve. Problems do not have to be complicated. Insights can be simple. As simple as a variation on "Hey, I'm over here!"

CHAPTER 6

SAUCE ON YOUR SLEEVE

The most salient feature of any insight is that it expresses an incontrovertible truth.

To *identify* a truth takes hard work, research, and a little luck perhaps.

To *express* it truthfully requires empathy—with the product, with the consumer, and with the client.

A lot of people in our field dismiss this or take it for granted. In a field guided by hard and fast results, empathy is warm and fuzzy. In a universe reliant on research, empathy is hard to test, even harder to measure. In a hardscrabble environment where consumers are fickle and clients scrutinize you on every expense, empathy is for sissies.

That may be arguable. But why take the chance? There's no better way to connect with the product you're trying to sell and the people you're trying to reach than by diving into their world and mixing it up with them. That's how you achieve empathy. Not by sitting at your desk and *imagining* it.

David Ogilvy, the magisterial founder of Ogilvy & Mather and one of the greatest copywriters in advertising history, preached that he would never take on a client whose products or services he wouldn't use himself. I am not sure whether he exclusively drank Guinness beer (one of his first clients) or wore only Hathaway shirts (another early client), but he certainly reached an empathic state with his client Rolls-Royce by using *that* product exclusively. His first Rolls, he boasted, lasted twenty-two years.

Ogilvy was also a stickler for doing his homework. When he first took on Rolls-Royce, he spent three weeks reading company literature, magazine articles, and customer mail about the car. This is where he came upon the extraordinary statement that "at sixty miles an hour, the loudest noise in this new Rolls-Royce comes from the electric clock." Those eighteen words became the headline for what Ogilvy, with typical bravura, called "the most famous of all automobile ads." The headline was supported by 607 words of heavily factual copy nestled in thirteen numbered paragraphs. By the way, I'm inclined to agree with Ogilvy's high opinion of this self-written ad. Its last line reigns as my favorite sentence in all of print advertising: "People who feel diffident about buying a Rolls-Royce can buy a Bentley." Such noblesse oblige. Now *there* is an ad guy with an empathic connection with his client and his customers!

I do the same. If you visited my office and asked for water, it would be Aquafina (a Pepsi product). If I gave you a lift home, it would be in a Dodge Neon or a Mercedes station wagon (both from DaimlerChrysler). If you came into our kitchen, you'd see nothing but GE Monogram appliances. My medicine cabinet holds only Gillette grooming products. I pay my restaurant tabs with a Visa card. My cell phone service is Cingular. When I reach for something sweet, it's never a Hershey bar or a Nestle's Crunch; it's a Snickers bar or M&Ms (both from Mars). I'll have to check with my wife, Susan, but I think all our rugs at home are made with Dupont Stainmaster. My agency only sends packages via FedEx.

You get the picture. We don't just bleed BBDO red. We bleed the colors of all our clients. (That's why I'm grateful that we work for Pepsi rather than Pepcid, GE rather than Geritol, Cingular rather than Singulair!)

I have to admit, though, that there was one client to whom I didn't pledge my undying fealty, to whom I didn't automatically turn when I had the urge to consume something in his category.

And it showed.

That client was Pizza Hut.

In 1987 it was fair to say that our agency, after a string of high-profile home runs for Pepsi, Dupont, Gillette, Apple, and FedEx, was on a hot streak. That probably explains why we were invited to pitch the $50 million–plus Pizza Hut account, because it certainly wasn't our understanding of the fast-food business in general and the pizza business in particular. Pizza Hut CEO Steve Reinemund (now PepsiCo CEO) and his marketing gun David Novak put our deficiencies aside and called us in. Novak had grown up in an ad agency environment at Tracey-Locke, so he understood that the disciplines of hard retail marketing and intuitive creativity didn't have to be strange bedfellows. I suppose it didn't hurt that Pizza Hut was then part of the PepsiCo empire, where we were regarded as "soul mates." But that was added pressure; we had to impress not only Pizza Hut but our pals at PepsiCo. They'd be watching us, and so was the rest of the industry because this was shaping up as one of the big account battles of the year.

For the previous four years, Pizza Hut's advertising had been handled out of Chiat/Day in Los Angeles—a super-hot creative boutique agency that had been the model for the ad agency in the hit TV show *Thirtysomething*. Chiat/Day had created a series of celebrity spots for Pizza Hut, and one of them was a real standout. Just days after his brutal fourth-round knockout of Tommy "Hit Man" Hearns, middleweight champion Marvelous Marvin Hagler is seen biting hard into a crusty Pizza Hut pizza. A voice-over announcer asks Hagler if he wonders what Hearns is eating. Marvelous replies, "Probably soup."

But despite the occasional gem, Pizza Hut believed that Chiat/Day's approach did not cultivate growth in the fastest growing food item in the fastest growing segment of the food industry: pizza. And a series of ads featuring *Saturday Night Live* comedian Rich Hall as a wandering Johnny Appleseed, spreading the gospel of pizza, was generally regarded as a flop.

That's why our then-chairman Norm Campbell got the call in February 1987 from his longtime friend David Novak, inviting us into the pitch (against incumbent Chiat/Day and Cliff Freeman and Partners).

We had a week to get our act together and dazzle Reinemund and Novak with strategic insights about fast food and our creative wizardry. I would like to say we blew them away. But such was not the case. Our presentation, resting solely on our credentials—no actual advertising—fell like limp pizza dough on Reinemund and Novak. Novak, who had put so much faith in us, was especially appalled by our clear lack of retail advertising savvy.

The next day Reinemund and Novak sat down to lunch with our chairman and told him in stinging terms that we had flunked miserably. We didn't know zilch about pizza. We had taken too much for granted, counted on the client/agency friendship and our creative reputation to save us. Not nearly enough.

Despite the bust, Norm Campbell somehow got us ten more days to reload and hit the target, except this time it wouldn't just be a friendly credentials march. Now it would be a winner-take-all strategic and creative shootout.

Some people like running from the front. Others prefer coming from behind. The world is divided into front-runners and underdogs. I guess we needed to feel like underdogs. We had ten days to get smart about the industry and Pizza Hut. To say we felt combative would be an understatement. This was war.

The next day we dispatched every person we could spare into the field to visit Pizza Hut locations all across the country, to speak with store managers, drivers, restaurant workers, and R&D people. Our aim was to blitzkrieg ourselves into a clear understanding of Pizza Hut's business and make our findings the analytical template for our campaign. Though there was still much to learn about the pizza business, we were confident that we had a solid grounding for our pitch. This time we'd walk into the presentation with some sauce on our sleeves.

The bedrock of our strategy was the assertion that no one gives you the pizza experience like Pizza Hut. We characterized that experience, first and foremost, as the superiority of the product itself. Then we spread that superiority around to include everything else that we had learned from the field about Pizza Hut: its in-house dining, its price value, its takeout and fledgling delivery service, and the fun and community of the pizza-eating experience. Excellence by association.

And we crystallized all those attributes into three words that became one simple concept: "Makin' It Great."

We were putting all our eggs into one basket: sell the "pizza experience," not just the pizza. That was our big insight.

When you stake a bold position, you better have vivid reasons for it. We thought we did. We dramatized the "pizza experience" with two contrasting scenarios. It's night. A guy returns from buying food to a semi-deserted office building where some people are laboring late into the evening. He walks back to his office, down a long corridor, past open doors with faint light drifting out of each, and people barely taking notice of his bag of burgers.

Now take the same situation, but the guy returns with pizza. He walks back to his office, past the same open doors, only this time people are popping their heads out and asking him, "Whatya got? Hey, that smells good." Soon everyone's in the conference room helping themselves.

That insight illustrated a simple truth—that unlike burgers and tacos, pizza is a communal fast food. It can draw a crowd. It's a celebration of sorts.

Maybe we would have come up with the same strategy if we'd never left our desks. But I doubt it. We'd already failed the week before with that sluggish approach. There's a lot to be said for going into the client's kitchen, tying on an apron, and working with the employees. As you sink your hands into the pizza dough and look out past the ovens into the dining area, catching glimpses of the patrons—who they are, how they dress, old or young, whether they're smiling or laughing or simply stuffing their faces, how they walk into a Pizza Hut and the difference when they walk out—you are stocking your previously closed mind with useful information. There's no guarantee that an insight will emerge by the time a finished pizza comes out of the oven. Insight and creativity don't work that way. But later on, as your brain starts sifting through the material, executing a pirouette of information triage, tossing out what's silly and keeping what's true, the faint shadows of insight may emerge. It may happen when you wake up in the morning, or after a hot shower, or during a walk around the block, or in the middle of a daydream. As Ogilvy liked to say, "If the telephone line from your unconscious is open, a big idea wells up within you." But, added Ogilvy, "Your unconscious has to be *well informed*." (Italics his.)

We did our research. We analyzed it. We came up with an insight and a strategy summed up in "Makin' It Great." As I've said before, once you have that, the execution takes care of itself.

Out of all this two campaign finalists emerged, one to warm up Reinemund and Novak, the other to close the sale.

We worked in two groups: Charlie Miesmer and a great young writer, Jimmy Siegel (soon to be crime novelist James Siegel, author of *Derailed* and *Detour*), came up with a nifty campaign wrapped around the theme line "Pizza Hut—Pizza with Everything." I split off with Ted Sann to work on "Makin' It Great."

Ten days seem about right for a relaxing vacation, but they're a fly speck when you're trying to pull together a great campaign, much less two or three. But we worked nonstop around the clock (where do you think that late-night, office-guy-with-pizza imagery comes from?) and by the morning of the presentation, we were feeling downright bullish about our chances.

We were told that we'd be the last of the three agencies to present. Not good news. I prefer going first—to set the bar at our level and see if the next guys can jump over it. But not to worry. Every move and moment of the presentation was choreographed, right down to the exact place at the table where Reinemund and Novak would be seated.

We flanked the room with two large Mitsubishi monitors and several Yamaha speakers. In addition to storyboards, we used rip-o-matics, industry lingo for existing bits and snippets of film from movies and commercials edited together to portray our desired image. Our setup narrative dispelled any doubts about our expertise in the fast-food category. We had all the facts and stats at our fingertips and wove them seamlessly through our strategy.

Now the first moments of "Makin' It Great" unfolded.

Our leadoff spots put on a happy face: bright and pumped-up moments exuding the scope and leadership that were missing from Pizza Hut's previous campaigns. Hey, these guys were the market leader, the flagship for the category, the biggest reason pizza was leaving other fast-food categories gasping for air. We'd be crazy not to exploit that, even crazier not to remind Reinemund and Novak that they were kings, not princes.

We were creating the impression that there was Pizza Hut and nothing else came close.

In the final hour of the meeting, we covered the waterfront: we showed eight thematic spots, a dozen retail price/value commercials, and a banquet of promotional ideas.

Rarely are you surprised when you win a new piece of business. You can sense it in a prospect's response to your work, see it in their eyes. And as we finished, I could feel the mood in the room becoming as warm and toasty as a pizza oven.

Two hours later Steve Reinemund called to say, "You guys came back from the dead. You're Pizza Hut's new agency."

Delirium. Bedlam in the office. High fives and champagne and nonstop grins all around. We even thought of ordering pizza, but Reinemund and Novak beat us to the punch. They sent over enough pies for the entire agency. Our hallways were smelling *gooooood*.

(Ordering pizzas on the spur of the moment was a Steve Reinemund signature. Once on a flight from Wichita, stranded with his fellow passengers on the tarmac for a couple of hours, Reinemund got on his cell phone and ordered pizza for everyone on the plane. A nice gesture—and not a bad PR move either.)

Over time, we would evolve "Makin' It Great" into more engaging and humorous executions. At the same time, sticking to the "experience" insight, we linked Pizza Hut with other experiences that attracted our target audience. Like NCAA basketball for which we created special spots to run during the Final Four in March.

We also came up with a special commercial that cemented Pizza Hut's association with Little League baseball. (Our experience on Pepsi had taught us that it's crucial to start winning over customers when they're young.)

The spot, a musical mini-drama called "Right Field," captures the irresistible charm of Little Leaguers urged on by their dreams of the big leagues but endearingly caught in the wonder of childhood.

From the viewpoint of the smallest kid on the team, stuck out in the distant meadows of right field (the traditional position of every team's weakest link), finding it hard not to let his attention wander, we watch a fly ball land totally by accident in the fielder's glove. And he is transformed into a hero. His innocence becomes glory and the viewer cannot help but feel good about baseball, children, America, and the company beneath the red roof where the whole team ends up in celebration. The spot, which came out of Charlie Miesmer's group, is one of my all-time personal favorites (and not just because it's about baseball). The lyric from a song composed by Willy Welch, and sung by Peter, Paul, and Mary, said it all:

Off in the distance
The game's draggin' on.
Two strikes on the batter
The runners are on.
Then suddenly everyone's looking at me,
My mind has been wandering,
What could it be?
They point to the sky,
And I look up above,
And a baseball falls into my glove.
I play right field,
It's important you know.
You gotta know how to catch,
You gotta know how to throw.
That's why I play in right field,
Way out where the dandelions grow.

Maybe it's me, but just retyping these words two decades later makes me swell with emotion. It also reminds me of the costly contrivance we needed to show the fly ball falling into the mitt of the amazed right fielder. Hurricane Hugo had blasted New Jersey after our first day of shooting, wrecking thousands of homes, our baseball field, and (let's get our priorities straight) our shooting schedule. Our producers had to pack up all the kids in the spot and put them on a plane to sunny Pasadena, California. So the pitched ball, which was hurled in Lodi, New Jersey, was actually swung at in Pasadena—and caught by our hero back in New Jersey. Without a doubt, the longest fly ball on record!

"Right Field" was a classy affirmation of Pizza Hut's dedication to youthful achievement and helped them take the high ground with its customers and franchisees, while solidifying its leadership position in the pizza industry. That's asking a lot of one spot—to say something different but appealing to several constituencies at the same time, to kids, parents, franchisees, and industry rivals—but when you have the right insight, it's almost easy to do. "Right Field" won two Clios.

Getting our act together for Pizza Hut taught us some valuable lessons about the burdens of leadership. At the agency we had marquee clients such as Pepsi and Apple that made a virtue of not being the clear leader in their field. They were willing to exploit their persona as the pesky David to the respective Goliaths of Coke and IBM—and it showed in their advertising, which reflected a greater freedom to take chances. But we were also working with Goliaths such as Gillette and Campbell's Soup and FedEx, all runaway leaders in their fields. We brought some of that experience to the pizza table.

Pizza Hut was a Goliath. But it had a complicated matrix of competitors. It was clearly number one in selling pizzas. Domino's was number two, followed by national upstarts such as Papa John's and Little Caesars. But Pizza Hut also competed with thousands of mom-and-pop pizza parlors named Gino's and Ray's—and many of these establishments made truly outstanding pizzas. Think about it: How many times has a friend proudly told you the local pizzeria in his or her town makes "the best thin-crust pizza in the world"? That's serious competition. It would be like Ford or Toyota having to compete with thousands of local garages, each one run by a talented auto mechanic who produced wonderful handmade cars that the townsfolk loyally scooped up. People would be cruising the local streets in a Gino 4.3-liter convertible or a Ray V8. That would be a strange and tough universe in which to compete.

Pizza Hut had to deal with that day in and day out. And it found out every Monday morning how it was faring. No business keeps its eye on the needle as fervently as the fast-food business. Pizza Hut, like McDonald's or Burger King or Taco Bell, tracks everything via computers at their 12,000 U.S. stores, and every Monday morning they receive their weekly report card: complete data on everything from national, regional, and per-store sales to volume gains or losses on each menu item. They can test anything in a week.

When we looked at the numbers, we were dazzled by Pizza Hut's number one status. But we weren't blinded by it. We knew that if Pizza Hut's sales sagged consistently, they could easily lose that number one footing, especially to a fierce competitor such as Domino's.

So we made Pizza Hut's leadership position an integral part of our advertising strategy. It wasn't obvious. It didn't require boasting or chest-thumping or self-loving testimonials. It was simmering below the surface—in the constant reminder to ourselves that the burden of leadership was a threefold task: act like a leader, look like a leader, and always defend your leadership position.

The first burden was more Pizza Hut's problem than ours. In the pizza business, *acting like a leader* is a delicate balancing act. It's a family-driven market, so you're always communicating that your price is right even as you're delivering a quality product, attractive ambience, and great service. The owner of a printing company I know has a sign on his desk that says "Quality, Speed, Price. Pick any two." Pizza is one of those rare businesses where customers expect quality, speed, and price all at once. At the same time, you have to keep the number one imagery going. In the pizza category, which is hungry for new product ideas, you act like a leader with innovation. You can't just advertise the same old extra-cheese pizza every day. You have to come up with new items relentlessly—from crusty calzones to bagel pizzas to a hundred variations on the deep-dish concept. If in-store feedback tells you that "everybody wants their own slice," you come up with a hit product called the Four for All—one slice per person with individual toppings. You're not scared off by the operational complexity of producing the Four for All in under 8 minutes 500,000 times a day; making it happen comes with the territory of being the leader. Your R&D people are madmen at coming up with evermore-amazing pizza products because part of being the leader is having twelve to fifteen marketing "windows" on the calendar where you are going to promote a new product to your customers. It lets you say, "Hey, we're the innovators. We're the guys coming at you with something fresh and new all the time. There's no reason for you to go anywhere else because we're constantly bringing you a delicious surprise."

(This is one reason why I always smile when people at creativity seminars limit their talk about innovation to the high-tech sector. If you want to understand innovation that truly feeds the demands of a hungry populace, study product development in the pizza world. What they have done with dough, tomato sauce, and cheese is mind-boggling.)

The second burden, *looking like a leader,* was up to us at BBDO. When people think of Pizza Hut, they think of bright red and green colors and beautifully photographed food. There's a reason for that. One of the smartest things we did was sign up Santiago Suarez, the foremost cinematographer of food, to shoot the food in every Pizza Hut commercial. Two decades later, he's still the only guy behind the camera for Pizza Hut. Our only brief to him was that the footage had to make people want to eat the screen. Any food company that doesn't do that is making a major mistake.

Of course, we didn't realize the intensity of labor involved in keeping Pizza Hut on top. For most of our marquee accounts, we'd create four or five major image spots a year. These are the commercials that get people talking, that win awards, that shape and establish brand imagery and get the agency more clients. But with Pizza Hut's R&D group innovating like crazy, and with all those marketing windows to fill, we were making sixty-five to seventy commercials a year for Pizza Hut. They weren't all $2 million production numbers with big concepts; they worked closer to the bone, touting a new product, its price, and the fact that you could get it only at Pizza Hut between June 6 and June 24. But still, those spots had to have the look of a leader; they all had to have that eat-the-screen "network sheen" or they weren't worth putting on national television.

Apparently it worked. By January 1991 Pizza Hut finally broke into the Top 25 rankings of America's best-liked/best-remembered commercials. But as any advertising pundit will tell you, life in the fast lane is never smooth. Just around the bend lie the potholes of uncertainty and surprise. This is where an agency really shows its stuff. This is where we learned the third burden of leadership: *protecting your leadership position*.

The dark unwanted surprise appeared in the form of a press announcement that sent shivers up our backs. McDonald's had decided to get into the pizza business. Though McDonald's had tried and failed before with an inferior frozen pizza, which we had spoofed by having a hockey team use it instead of a puck, this time they were back for blood with an improved product, much better than a hockey puck. They were trumpeting their huge investment in pizza as much to intimidate Pizza Hut as to signal to Wall Street that they were committed to being a hot growth company again.

We had no choice but to confront them head on and try to blunt the success of their trial entry into the category. Our strategy: to make the idea of pizza at McDonald's seem incongruous, even inappropriate. And while we recognized that bashing McDonald's could be risky business—you always want to think twice about attacking a beloved slice of American culture—we let the consumers do the job for us.

We staged our counterattack in Evansville, Indiana, a key city in McDonald's test market. In a home-movie style of filming, our BBDO crew captured locals ruminating about the "strange new menu item" at McDonald's in terms ranging from amusement to confusion to apathy. Three spots strung together the candid observations without editorial comment from the sponsor. *Advertising Age* created a new subgenre for it, calling it "anti-testimonial advertising."

"Does it come on a bun?" asks an eleven-year-old girl, laughing.

One child deadpans, "It definitely wasn't a Happy Meal," referring to McDonald's boxed children's meals.

"It wasn't that bad," opines a bicycle shop clerk.

"I'd just rather not talk about it now," says a dejected middle-aged man.

Not only had we safely skirted any rancor for criticizing McDonald's, but our target audience actually enjoyed the advertising. They laughed. More important, the advertising convinced consumers that Pizza Hut was still far superior as a product, and let us sleep at night again, secure in the fact that the McDonald's threat was fleeting and would never hit our homes. Our Patriot missiles had knocked down Mickey D's Scuds. We also proved that competitive advertising, even in the "going negative" form so common in political advertising, does work—as long as you do it with a wink instead of a sledgehammer.

Working for Pizza Hut not only reminded us of the value of getting sauce on our sleeves, it also convinced us to take a compensation gamble with our new account. In tough times, which come with the predictability of five-year locusts in the ad industry, the hot topic is agency compensation. While most of an agency's income back then was based on a fixed percentage of the billings—the more money you spent on media buys, the more you earned—it has since undergone radical alteration as consultants and consolidation have led to fixed fees and belt-tight cost controls. It's a complicated subject. Some of it started positively with our Pizza Hut relationship. We were so confident that our strategy would move the needle in so many ways for Pizza Hut that we struck a deal with them to tie some of our pay to performance incentives. While it would be foolhardy to bet everything on performance (inasmuch as we don't control a client's product, pricing, sales and distribution, R&D, and so on), incentive clauses in agency-client agreements can pay off for both parties. If we do our job and the client exceeds their performance goals, we earn a bonus. Not a bad incentive.

But perhaps the greatest incentive of all is when a client tells you they "love" you. And does it publicly. Nothing fuels an agency's creative juices like a client's outpouring of genuine support and praise.

Going into our third year with Pizza Hut, Steve Reinemund authorized a full-page ad in *Advertising Age,* which read in part:

In hundreds of ways, both big and small.

Every hour.

Every day.

Late at night.

Through the weekend.

Long past the point where others would have settled, you have dedicated your time, energy, and just plain smarts to grow our business.

Not just to make it, but to make it . . . well, you know the rest.

(Pizza Hut logo)

Makin' it great!

The glow from that lasts a long time. When I'm gone and for-gotten, my name will still be in the author credits on DVDs of *The Natural* and I might be a footnote in some history of Ronald Reagan's reelection campaign, but there is nothing else that makes me prouder than this ad. We're an ad agency; we make the ads for our clients. When grateful clients turn the tables and start making ads about us, that truly is makin' it great.

There's one beautiful grace note to our Pizza Hut experience. Ten years after we took on the account, David Novak moved on to bigger things—becoming CEO of Yum! Brands, the holding company that controlled not only Pizza Hut but Taco Bell and Kentucky Fried Chicken. He knew better than any-one else how we worked and how much we had learned about fast-food retailing. And he happened to be extremely unsatisfied with the performance of Young & Rubicam on the KFC account. So he picked up the phone and offered us the KFC account. No meetings, no review, no pitch contests. He turned over a $200 million budget to us on a phone call. He liked our performance when we got some sauce on our sleeves. Now it was time to get chicken crumbs on our shirts.

First thing we did was visit KFC headquarters in Louis-ville, Kentucky, and go through the same intense research drill. We were considerably smarter about fast-food retailing, but still we needed to get a feel for the restaurant experience. We needed to see how they prepare the food. We needed to stand behind a counter and take orders and then go around to the front of the counter and give orders. Most of all, we needed to taste the food.

On our last day in Louisville, our team of nine had spent all morning in meetings and we hadn't filled up on breakfast. By 1 P.M. we were starving. We were led down a corridor to the sparkling KFC test kitchens, where a feast featuring every known and in-development food item was set out for us. We all gorged on the food for over an hour, smacking our lips, licking our fingers, reaching across each other for more of everything. As we filled up and began to slow down our gourmandizing, we all looked around and had the same satisfied thought: "This is not fast food as we know it. This is home cooking. It's chicken and mashed potatoes and biscuits and beans. It's Sunday dinner at home."

A few days later we were back in New York, holding a brainstorming session in a BBDO conference room. We papered the walls with ideas, sketches, and one-liners, searching for an insight that would push us to the next step. As we did this, all of us in the room kept gravitating back toward the notion that KFC is not fast food. It is genuine good stuff. What if we position KFC in those terms? That it's not fast food. That it's something else.

Wouldn't that separate KFC from the pack? It's positive, it's differentiating, it's a parity killer. It could make a winning campaign.

That was the insight—a positioning statement asking, Why live in the fast-food ghetto if you don't belong there? It led to the theme line "There's fast food, and then there's KFC"— which David Novak ate up (so to speak).

Executing the commercials would have to live up to the theme line. If you say you're different from all other fast food, that you're not actually fast food, your commercials have to embody that. Even though we were selling the "comfort food" imagery of KFC, we couldn't resort to warm family scenes of people enjoying KFC by the home hearth. Family scenes would have created a "wallpaper" effect, blending our spots with everybody else's spots so that they faded into the woodwork. We needed to cut through the fast-food clutter and break out. To do that we hired Jason Alexander, famous to all for his jerky but almost sympathetic George Costanza on *Seinfeld,* to do a series of humorous spots. He would go up to people who were eating everything but KFC. A hamburger, for example, which he would pick apart for the tiny meat patty, the stale bun, the limp lettuce, and puny pickle. We had him poking fun at KFC's competition. Then he would tell people that they needed a little KFC in their lives— and bring out a bucket of chicken, which viewers could see was fresh and tasty and tempting. There's fast food, and then there's KFC.

Sales responded immediately, and the theme line stuck for more than five years, quite an achievement in a category known for fast and frequent change.

That's the beauty of getting some sauce on your sleeves. If you do it right, they let you scatter chicken crumbs all over your shirt.

CHAPTER 7

STANDING FOR
SOMETHING

Before you can tell the world who you are and why any-one should care, you have to understand what you stand for and how you will convey that information to strangers. In other words, you have to state your mission.

Everybody knows this—what company hasn't paid some form of lip service to writing a mission statement?—but many organizations have a tough time sticking to what they stand for. Their mission and vision changes with the seasons or the economy or with whatever strategy their fickle competition happens to be following.

This is dangerous, because consumers gravitate toward consistency. That is what they expect in exchange for their loyalty. Knowing what you stand for is the essence of building a brand. Without it, you are building the brand on sand.

Consider my experience with FedEx. It is a case study in insight and knowing who you are.

For some reason, I have always accepted the "legend" of FedEx's origins: how founder Fred Smith described the concept of overnight delivery on a college paper—and got a C for his efforts. People seem to enjoy the idea of a professor miss-

ing the boat on one of the more revolutionary business concepts of the last half century.

But Fred Smith set me straight on the facts.

In 1966, Fred was a senior at Yale in New Haven, Connecticut. In an economics class, he was asked to identify an
emerging business trend and analyze its implications. Fred
didn't write his legendary paper on Federal Express (that
insight would come a few years later). Actually, he wrote a
paper about automation—how America was increasingly becoming an automated society, more reliant on machine-made
than hand-made products, and how it would require a very
different kind of industry to keep it operating. The paper
must have been missing a powerful unifying insight, because
the professor indeed graded it a C.

Then again, it might have been C work because Fred didn't
have enough time to flesh it out. Even as a Yale undergrad,
Fred Smith was spending much of his time pursuing his passion for aviation, moonlighting as a charter pilot at Tweed
Airport in New Haven and the Westchester County Airport
in Purchase, New York. The Westchester airport was just a
few miles from IBM's world headquarters; it was here that
Fred got his first exposure to corporate jet pilots. He would
spend time in the waiting lounge talking to other pilots, casually asking about their passengers and where they were going.
What he heard surprised him. A lot of the pilots joked about
how often their so-called passengers weren't people at all but
rather packages, boxes, and small crates containing precious
technical equipment. Instead of flying a cadre of executives
to Washington, D.C., or Boston for the day, the pilots were
being asked to rush a two-pound box of replacement parts to
a factory in Ohio. Their beautifully appointed private jets

were becoming very costly cargo planes. The same thing was happening with Fred's "passengers." More often than not, he was strapping a box rather than a human being into the passenger seat.

Flash forward three years to 1969. The Vietnam War is raging. Fred Smith has graduated from Yale and completed his tour of duty as a U.S. Marine pilot in Vietnam. His war service has not only sharpened his flying skills and aviation knowledge, but it has also given him the time and real-world experience to get a handle on what he wants to do with his life. He knows he loves aviation, but he also wants a business career.

As he thought about his future, Fred Smith recalled his college paper focusing on the trend that the world would be automating the most basic functions, relying less on human labor and more on machines.

This is when the seeds of insight began to take root. Even though 1969 was more than a decade before personal computers would start appearing on people's desks and, therefore, long before computer-controlled robots would perform so much industrial work, you didn't have to be a genius to see that computers would play ever-increasing roles in all walks of life. Fred had seen this firsthand every time he flew into the airport serving IBM world headquarters. IBM was expanding so rapidly that even a greenhorn could see what it meant for the future of computers and automation.

Fred's wartime experience had taught him that as a soldier you lived and died with your equipment. From your weapons to your transport to your radio communications, you had to keep your equipment working. But the more you depend on that equipment, the more you give up the ability to control that equipment. He also remembered that in any war experience, only 20 percent of your forces are actual combatants. Eighty percent provide logistical support, from food to fuel to maintenance to medical attention.

Fred extended that personal wartime memory to his interest in business automation. As you automate, he thought, you give up the ability to control your equipment too. It means that you start to put a high premium on keeping that equipment working all the time. If you need a replacement part, you'll spend a lot of money to get that part—anything to keep the engines of automation humming and avoid even costlier downtime. This problem would only increase as the world was overrun by new computers and new amazing machines.

That, Fred thought, was the true significance of all those corporate pilots putting packages instead of people onto planes in Westchester County.

This is when Fred Smith had his insight moment. He knew how expensive it was to fly a small part from New York to Ohio. But it must be worth it, he thought, to deliver the part quickly. The cost of lost production through downtime was surely far greater than the cost of a chartered plane. He concluded that, until someone invented a way of magically beaming a mechanical part from one part of the globe to another, this need for speedy delivery would not end. In fact, it would increase, especially if the automation trend Fred had identified would continue growing.

Thus, a business is born: a company that would deliver as fast as possible—even overnight!—whatever American businesses needed to keep their factories and hospitals and offices running without interruption. That was the first part of Fred Smith's big insight.

The second part was how to do it. When you have an insight, you create a problem for yourself in that you still need to execute it. Again, Fred dipped into his war experience. In Vietnam—especially Vietnam with its dangerous, unmanageable terrain—people and equipment had to move in a carefully integrated system of air and ground transport. And much of this occurred through centralized bases, with planes and helicopters fanning out to distant areas. It was the only way to maintain a semblance of safety and control. You wanted your pilots to return to home base every night.

That gave him the germ of an idea for an air-and-ground enterprise that didn't fly willy-nilly all over the country but was anchored to one hub, one home. He refined it further based on his readings in an economics class about the Federal Reserve banking system, which consists of nine satellite banks all funneling into the central bank in Washington, D.C. I'm compressing here, but this is what gave Fred Smith the radical idea of using the centrally located airport in his hometown of Memphis, Tennessee, as the hub for his new enterprise of quick delivery. Everything would come to Memphis, get sorted, and fan out to its destination. The idea came from the structure of the Federal Reserve Bank. It's also the reason the company was originally called *Federal* Express.

If you ask Fred Smith about all this, he sees the insight part as obvious, a nifty piece of what author Rosabeth Moss Kauter calls "kaleidoscopic thinking"—getting ideas from everywhere, in pilot lounges, in the Marine Corps, in economics texts, and using common sense to synthesize them into a big idea. But he will also point to some of the lucky breaks, such as the 1980 deregulation of interstate surface transportation, which favorably changed FedEx's ground efficiencies and costs. And the emergence of the "fast-cycle" business model—the systematic shortening of each step from conceiving a new product to delivering it—which changed everything. Without that, companies from Dell Computer to Wal-Mart—the one a master at delivering equipment quickly to consumers, the other a master at shifting and distributing massive inventory in a blink—couldn't have done what they did.

He'll also point out that FedEx is one of the more misunderstood companies in the public eye. Most people still think of it as a company that competes with the post office in delivering mail, that it delivers valuable documents overnight. He quickly disabuses you of that by noting that only 6 percent of FedEx's $30 billion in revenue comes from delivering "mail." The majority is light to heavy equipment, which is precisely where his business insight started. With military-like discipline, the company has stuck to what it started.

More than anything else, though, the company knows what it stands for. There are plenty of competitors—and there were lots of parcel delivery companies when it started. But FedEx differentiated itself with two concepts: we'll do it faster and we'll not let you down. We know that if one component doesn't get there on time, you can't build the car. The line shuts down, and you start losing millions of dollars. Thus, FedEx stands for speed and reliability.

It was important to keep that, more than anything else, in mind when we had the chance to pitch the account.

I'd like to say that BBDO was there from FedEx's beginnings, but we were not. The company's first advertising was handled brilliantly for nearly two decades by the now-defunct New York agency Ally and Gargano. And if you study their work for FedEx, it's practically a primer on how to do sharp advertising for a successful start-up company through all the phases as it rises to category domination.

There's the start-up phase that required smart commercials to tell the world you're open for business. They did classic "Hey, I'm over here" stuff, not funny but serious and focused about their objectives. The first commercial FedEx ever ran performed like a calling card. "America, you've got a new airline," said a solemn voice-over. "No first class, no meals, no movies, in fact, no passengers. Just packages." And it worked. The average nightly package count increased from twenty-one their first year of operation in 1973 to 11,400 in 1975.

Once established, FedEx branched out. This began its competitive from-last-to-first phase, when it went after the established cargo leader, Emery Air Freight. The big idea began and ended with research. To prove that FedEx was better, the head researcher at Ally and Gargano filled forty-seven packages with sand and sent them on both FedEx and Emery to see which shipper was more reliable. The FedEx results were so good, they became the ad. A cruel tweak for which Emery had no response. Facts are facts. Within three years, FedEx was number one.

Your strategy and, in turn, your advertising usually change overnight when you become the industry leader. You no longer have to shout "Hey, I'm over here!" You don't have to pound on your chest and brag about your prowess. You do not deign to mock your competition. Your only job is to stay number one. And to do that, you have to (a) increase your market share, or (b) hold your share but grow the entire market, or (c) do both. That invariably means finding new customers in new places for your service.

That became the leadership phase for FedEx. Throughout their rise, they had aimed their message at middle and senior management, because these were the people authorizing the expense of using overnight delivery. That target audience had to expand once FedEx became the leader. They took their message not just to the corner office but to every department on every floor, including secretaries, mailroom personnel, and trainees. Shrewdly, they started talking to the enormous underbelly of corporate employees who, the research showed, actually made the decision on whether to use FedEx or someone else.

They did it with humor, most famously with the fast-talking John Moschitta playing an intense executive who talks at a 100-words-a-minute clip and operates as if everyone is slowing him down. It stresses the message that "in this fast-moving high-pressure get-it-done-yesterday world," you should be glad there's a company that can keep up with it all. It signed off with the timeless theme line "When it absolutely, positively has to be there overnight." The insight, as I see it, was to illustrate the urgent pace of daily business and at the same time appeal to the working masses by using the fast-talking character to mock management jargon. It was the 1980s, remember, when books like *In Search of Excellence* and *The One-Minute Manager* were in every executive's briefcase. It's one of the great commercials of all time (I wish I'd written it), and yet a few years later Ally and Gargano was no longer FedEx's agency. By the end of the 1980s, we were invited to pitch the business.

As we surveyed FedEx's twenty-year advertising history, it was pretty hard to knock our predecessors. They did some great work. FedEx was one company whose advertising and slogan lived up to its business reputation. What could we do to top all this and break through to an even higher level?

Our insight was: do nothing. Our strategy for the pitch was: give FedEx more of the same, but with a slick dash of humor.

The way we saw it, there have been two basic periods in FedEx's history: the speed period and the reliability period.

In the first half of its brief existence as a company, FedEx stood for speed. That was the company's revolutionary selling proposition: We understand speed. We can deliver your packages to anyplace in the United States faster. In fact, overnight. This was unheard of at the time. Many people consider FedEx to be one of those companies that "changed everything." Along with the semiconductor industry (where chip speed doubled every eighteen months), it ushered in our "accelerated age." At BBDO, we believed that. In its first decade if FedEx stood for anything, it was for the notion that speed pays—that accomplishing something 90 percent well but on time was infinitely more profitable than doing it to 100 percent perfection but six months late. That's why it could charge a premium price for speedy service. When FedEx appeared on the scene, other soon-to-be-extinct parcel-delivery services were stunned by its higher prices. Their pricing models were based on two variables: weight and size. They had no idea people would pay for speed. This period—let's call it Early FedEx—culminated in Ally and Gargano's "Fast-Paced World" commercial.

That is the moment when FedEx entered its Middle Period, the period of being reliable. By the mid-1980s FedEx had already closed the sale on the speed concept. Everyone bought into it. Even the U.S. Postal Service, hardly the paragon of speedy delivery, was offering overnight mail delivery. The difference between FedEx and all its Johnny-come-lately rivals was its reliability.

We weren't making this up. It was plain to see in everything the company said and did. Everything was geared to doing things faster and on time. Their whole existence, contained so pithily in their "absolutely positively" slogan, was reliability. As far as we were concerned, that was a damn fine virtue to own. Few companies could stake that claim. We saw no reason to change that. We couldn't think of anything better.

So, that was the insight for our pitch. We would stress FedEx as the paragon of reliability. In an imperfect world, where you couldn't count on much, you could always count on FedEx. In fact, you could stake your greatest hopes and your career on FedEx; anything less and you were jeopardizing those.

To illustrate this, BBDO's Jimmy Siegel wrote a heart-stopping spot showing a Latin American woman who ran a girls' orphanage reading a letter that accompanied the adoption papers, delivered by FedEx, from an American woman describing the kind of daughter she was hoping for, as images of a tiny girl wandering through the orphanage cross the screen. "I'm writing to you about a child. I don't really know what she looks like, but I can describe her to you perfectly. She is very dark or she is fair. She is very small or she is quite big. She is awfully shy or she is incredibly friendly. I don't know what to call her yet, but I think she will know to call me 'Mom.' Enclosed are all the documents you require. And one you didn't." The woman pulls a delicate silver locket out of the FedEx envelope. Voice-over: "Why does Federal Express treat every package as if it's the most important one? Because sometimes it is." The theme line, appropriate for the emotional tone, was "Our most important package is yours."

That was among the concepts we took with us to Memphis to pitch FedEx. I have to admit that at that point our creative reputation was so rosy, we were the odds-on favorite to prevail. FedEx's advertising chief, a blunt woman with a mouth like a sailor, was so happy to see us, I remember her saying that she was going to sit in the corner and listen to our presentation as if it were a sexual pleasure (I am paraphrasing). That's how excited she was to see us. When she called to say we got the business, her first words were "Let's get married."

As we got into it, we tightened our approach. We realized that FedEx not only meant "reliable" but that it had a humorous brand personality. People expected a light touch in its commercials. So we gave it to them, always careful to establish that FedEx's reliability was the difference between success and failure.

In one spot called "Mr. Calm" we had a late-night office scene, with long rows of desks and dimly lit computers. A young man is working late. An older executive, kind and avuncular, says on his way out, "You're working late, son."

"I'm kinda worried about a package I sent for Mr. Jones," he says.

The older man assures him that he's doing important work, that he's part of the team. And adds, "In over twenty years, FedEx has never let me down."

"What if I didn't use FedEx?" asks the young man.

"Well then, you're dead." And he walks out.

"Hit the lights on your way out" are his parting words.

FedEx's strong stand on who it was represented a great learning experience for me personally as a creative director—because it reinforced in me the notion that, even at an ad agency (hell, especially at an ad agency), where you are serving many different clients, each with strong assertive but radically different personalities, it was vital to your reputation and mental health to stand for something. Your commercials had to have a distinctive character so that they looked as if they couldn't have come from anyone else. You had to define that character to yourself, your employees, and your clients. And you had to have the discipline to always be true to it.

Ask me what that distinction is and I'll tell you that our advertising has to make you laugh or cry, or both, or something in between. Whatever it does, it has to make you feel *something,* because we want the viewer to associate that feeling with the client's product. That is how brand loyalty begins.

Now, I know that saying our *advertising makes you feel something* is a simple explanation. But when you stand for something, it doesn't have to be complicated. In fact, it's a good idea to express it simply.

Press me for specifics, though, and I'll direct you to one 60-second spot we made in 1998. It's not our most famous commercial; it didn't win a lot of prizes; it didn't run for twenty years and get lauded by the media. It didn't coin a phrase that became part of the lexicon. But in our agency's highlight reel of more than two hundred commercials, it's the first one you see. To me, it is the perfect signature spot. We made it for Campbell's Soup.

Chuck, a burly construction worker dressed in layers of sweatshirts and a down vest comes down to the kitchen for breakfast as his wife ushers three of their four kids off to school. She's packing his lunch box, pouring soup into a Thermos. A radio in the background predicts brutally cold, windy weather. Chuck holds up the Thermos, which is sheathed in bright orange plastic and emblazoned with Fred Flintstone.

"Fred Flintstone?" he asks his wife.

"The kids must have taken your soup," she says.

He holds up his hands in surrender. "I can't have lunch with Fred," he says. "The guys'll kill me."

Their fourth child, a toddler in a high chair, squeals.

"You stay out of this," says Chuck to his baby.

"It's gonna be cold," warns the wife.

"Fred's not seeing the light of day," says Chuck. "I'm not going around all day hearing, 'Yabba dabba doo. There goes Cave Boy.'"

Cut to the job site. Cold breath, snow flurries. The workers break for lunch in a large hall. Chuck stares at his gray metal lunch box, opens it up, reluctant to pull out his Flintstone Thermos.

He sees his coworkers pouring soup, saying, "Nothing like soup to warm you up."

Chuck yields to his hunger and quietly pulls out his Thermos, hoping no one will notice.

An enormous coworker with a deep menacing voice yells, "Hey, Chuck! What's that?"

Chuck removes his hands from his Fred Thermos.

The coworker mockingly shouts, "Yabba dabba dooooooo."

All the workers join in to shower Chuck with universal derision.

As Chuck begins to eat his soup, he hears the coworker shout again, "Hey, Chuck!"

He looks up, thinking, "Now what?"

The mess hall is silent as the coworker pulls out *his* Thermos and defiantly plants it on the table—revealing Pebbles Flintstone, Fred's daughter.

This time universal laughter.

Long shot of the two big men leaning across the table, clinking plastic Thermoses as if they held fine wine.

Theme line: "Campbell's Soup. Good for the body, good for the soul."

To me this spot has it all. An opening scene that all of us recognize, with just a hint of the ridiculous. A mild sense of dramatic tension with a man facing humiliation. And a funny surprise ending, while extolling the product's virtues unobtrusively because the product is integral to the story line. It represents a marriage of *logical persuasion* with *emotional drama*. It's true and it makes you feel something. It is our agency's most valuable creative strategy.

You could say we "branded" BBDO with that strategy. If you wanted a certain type of advertising—the kind embodied in this soup commercial—you came to us. If you didn't, you went with someone else. We would rise or fall with that brand identity.

The beauty of branding the agency with work that appealed to emotions is that it perfectly mirrored what we were doing for our clients. Emotion is how a branding relationship begins. The consumer sees the advertising, hears a memorable tag line, conjures up images of your previous advertising, and brings that association to the marketplace when he or she has to choose your brand over someone else's. (It's not the only factor, of course. Product quality, distribution, timing, the insight behind the marketing plan, and so on have influence too.) But to me, emotion is the nub of branding.

A lot of hot air has been released into the atmosphere by so-called experts on branding. At the risk of increasing the air temperature, here are my two cents on the subject.

Branding is not complicated. A brand is nothing but an expression of the consumer's loyalty and trust. It's a bond, a covenant with the consumer. When you see the brand's name attached to a product, do you trust that the product will deliver a predictable level of satisfaction? If so, you will be loyal to that brand—so loyal that you will stick with it even when a better product comes along. (That loyalty explains why it takes so much time and so much money to steal customers away from a leader. Leaders generate trust and loyalty—in that order. And loyalty makes them hard to unseat at the top.) So loyal that you will not only stick with that product, but when the brand name is attached to a new product, you will buy that product too.

The amazing thing to me is that loyalty—even when it is attached to the vagaries of emotion—is not a vague, amorphous concept. It's hard, it's real, it can be quantified.

One of the main goals of advertising—and by extension, any branding strategy—is to create lifetime customers, not just a short-term spike in sales. And that cohort of loyal lifetime customers lets you project your sales and revenues far into the future. The sales are ongoing and repeatable. They're the best thing in marketing—the guaranteed transaction. And you can attach a number to those transactions that defines the value of your company's name, what it stands for, what it means to the consumer. This is how branding consultancies such as Interbrand come up with their lists of the world's most valuable brands. This is how they establish that Coca-Cola is the world's number one brand, worth $67 billion, followed closely by Microsoft at $61 billion.

For example, if General Electric stopped doing business today, what would happen to its most ubiquitous branded product, those billions of GE lightbulbs? How many people would still be loyal to the GE brand of lightbulbs? How many would continue buying them while inventory lasts?

Those are purely hypothetical questions. Ludicrous what-ifs. But that's how security analysts think. When a security analyst looks at all those loyal GE lightbulb customers, he sees guaranteed transactions, or what analysts like to call "secured earnings." He can project those secured earnings for lightbulbs into the distant future. Then he will do the same for GE's other product lines, from medical equipment to turbine engines to hit comedies on NBC.

All those secured earnings have value to him. They help him figure out what GE shares are really worth. He taps his calculator a few times, matches all those secured earnings against GE's new revenue streams, and that is how $44 billion of GE's total $280 billion market value resides in the GE name—the brand.

That figure is, in essence, a measure of loyalty, of people's emotional attachment to your brand.

Kevin Roberts, head of Saatchi & Saatchi, argues that there are four levels of consumer attachment to a product or service, from commodities (the lowest), to fads, to brands, to what he calls "lovemarks" (these are super-brands that command both great respect and enormous love from the consumer). I'm not sure "lovemarks" will ever replace "brand" as an accepted marketing term (I suspect the word is Roberts's way of "branding" his agency's advertising philosophy), but I can't argue with the connection he makes between emotion and brand. A young marketer once came up to Roberts after a presentation and asked, "You say emotion is the key to building relationships. I'm in the brick industry. How do you make bricks emotional?"

"You don't," Roberts said. "But you talk about what the bricks stand for: homes, families sitting around the fireplace feeling safe and warm. Achievements. Buildings built by bricklayers whose inspirational dream was nothing less than to touch the sky."

That's a subtle—and yet simple—answer by a man who understands branding. Elevate the product by elevating the emotions attached to the product. You don't need to know much more than that.

This going-for-the-emotion approach doesn't work for everyone. But the freedom to choose either humor or drama, laughter or tears was right for me. It's certainly preferable to total freedom. With no lines on the road, you drive all over the place, including off the road.

I often wonder why I'm such a sucker for emotion. If I allow myself to spend any time on the self-analysis couch, I believe it goes back to high school and a teacher named Nathaniel George Levine. Mr. Levine was, among his 40,000 peers in the New York City public school system, the single most popular teacher in the five boroughs. He was called "Boss" by students and teachers, perhaps in ironic tribute to the fact that he was the kindest, gentlest soul I have ever known. Among other things he was the director of The Mixed Chorus at Midwood High School, where he turned hoods into artists, ruffians and rowdies into responsible citizens. Teen angels and devils were molded together into a 160-voice blend that one magazine called "the finest high school chorus in America." Standing in the middle of Boss's chorus, whether we were singing spirituals or Gershwin or Johann Sebastian Bach, I couldn't help but get caught up in the emotional surge that soft or swelling music inspired. I loved that feeling. Our biggest highlight was a November afternoon in 1953 when the Midwood chorus was invited to perform with the New York Philharmonic at Carnegie Hall. It was a day when wildness was tamed and reverence took its place. That incandescent moment has never left me, because I'm always trying to recapture it in every commercial.

After Boss retired, I visited him at his home, where he proudly showed me chests of drawers filled with thousands of letters from grateful students, each one elaborately filed by class and year. It was an astonishing catalog of one man's influence.

Boss Levine taught me the lesson that I brought into my little world of advertising: he not only had a passion to teach, but he knew how to reach people on the level of their emotions. I guess I must have subconsciously put one and one together—Boss's undeniable success as a teacher and his devotion to music, to kids, and to delivering a huge emotional wallop in his creative life—and decided that it would work for me too.

That's the best explanation I can come up with. Boss gave me a grounding. He forced me to stand for something.

This came in very handy when I started building my own

creative team at BBDO. It helped me choose people who would stand for the same things I wanted. And it really helped in establishing rules for the work that I liked.

My earliest mentor, John Bergin, taught me that your reputation rests more on the work you reject than the work you approve. If you don't have a kill rate of 10 to 1, he said, you're standards are too low. So I established criteria for work that wouldn't get out the door, such as:

- It's dull, boring, and unexciting. This should be self-explanatory. Commercials appear on TV. TV is an entertainment medium. Therefore, commercials have to be entertaining. (True since the birth of the remote control, truer still with the arrival of video-on-demand, and true to the point of pain with the invasion of TiVO.)

- It's not differentiating. It doesn't distinguish your brand from other brands in the category.

- It sounds, feels, or looks familiar. If it's been done before, you are, by definition, stripping yourself and your client of any originality. Even if you don't have a parity product, your copycat advertising will suggest that you do.

- It's off strategy, not saying what you want to say to your audience. It's the wrong message.

- It's reaching too hard. This is the creative equivalent of telling a joke that falls flat and then saying, "Well, you had to be there." The best humor or drama comes from real life. It's the shock of recognition, seeing in the advertising either yourself or someone you know, or someone you'd like to be.

- It's too expensive to produce. Self-explanatory. You can't afford it, and you can't do it justice for less. So why bother?

- It's offensive, tasteless. The only thing worse than not getting people's attention is getting it for the wrong reasons. Tasteless, offensive spots—for example, an old man passing gas and hearing Britney Spears's music coming from his rear end in an MTV spot—may have their place in advertising, but not in my shop.

- It can't be just a joke. That's a one-trick pony—a good idea for one spot but minus the legs to survive as a three-year campaign. And some jokes don't even work as one-shots. I can't imagine who approved a 2003 Verizon spot that shows a guy staring down a ferret sitting on his coffee table. (Did the ferret just drop in or is this the family pet?) The guy decides to have some fun and starts teasing the creature. So he sticks his tongue out in front of the ferret's face. Oops, bad idea. The ferret leaps up, latches onto the guy's tongue, and tries to yank it out of his head. Now the guy, panic-stricken, tries to shake the ferret loose with one hand as he dials 911 with the other. An end title mercifully appears: "Text with Mobile Messenger when you can't talk." This spot is painful to watch in more ways than one. (Even my cat left the room.) I can't understand how a scenario like this wins friends and influences customers for Verizon, much less enhances the company's public image. Anything that makes your viewers recoil in discomfort should get an automatic thumbs-down and never see the light of day. Plus, where does the campaign go after this? Answer: nowhere.

- It's poorly executed—in writing, art direction, casting. Or in the music, editing, and soundtrack. Even if it meets all the other criteria, a great idea done badly may as well be a bad idea.

These were some of the specific reasons why I saw danger signs whenever people showed me their work.

The most dangerous work of all, though, is the well-written, beautifully produced, on-message, tasteful, different from anything else out there, definitely not boring commercial—the one that meets all my criteria. It's dangerous because all those superior attributes might mask the fact that you are opting for cleverness at the expense of human connection. This is what almost happened to one of our top creatives, Michael Patti, with his award-winning Diet Pepsi spot, "Missing Link."

Patti traces the creative origins of the spot back to the afternoon he saw Matthew Broderick in the movie *Project X,* a heartbreaking film about chimps and euthanasia.

Years later Patti unearthed the memory of that film to use intelligent chimps for Diet Pepsi. The spot opens on a behavioral research scientist working on a study of chimpanzee intelligence. She hopes to prove that intelligent chimps are the long-sought-after missing link. But the elaborate tests she imposes on the chimps only prove that they aren't intelligent at all. A brief vignette shows her teaching one chimpanzee how to sign "Thank you" and "You're welcome," but the chimp fails at this too.

The viewer senses something better is coming. As the researcher types her disappointing report, the chimps perform remarkable feats of cleverness and ingenuity that directly contradict her words. She reaches for a Diet Pepsi by her desk; it's empty, so she tosses it in the wastebasket. As she types her last words about the chimpanzees' lack of organization and decision-making skills, we see the chimps making a "human" ladder to punch the buttons of the hallway vending machine. They set a new can of Diet Pepsi by her. She turns around and picks up the fresh can. Aglow with sudden understanding, she walks to the chimp's cage and signs "Thank you." The chimpanzee signs back "You're welcome," just like she taught him.

Patti was going to use a different ending.

Instead, the dejected researcher would turn off the laboratory lights and shut the door behind her. The camera would reveal the chimps alone in the darkness of the lab. We would then hear a sound emerge from the cage: the sound of Diet Pepsi cans being opened.

Now, that may be clever, in the sense that surprise endings tickle the funny bone. But removing the woman from the lab chops away at the warm emotional bonding between researcher and animals. In this ending, the missing link is still missing.

To this day Michael Patti shudders at the thought of how close he came to getting it wrong. Once he saw the link he was missing, he knew what to do.

Even the most clever, innovative, shocking, surprising gamesmanship cannot compete with messages that are truthfully centered on what we feel.

In this chapter, we've shown a few examples of "standing for something." You might ask: Why does standing for something help in the identification and harvesting of insights? Simple. It gives you a starting point. It reminds you of who you are, what you're really about, and what you expect to become.

As such you've moved closer to finding the insight that will help your company grow.

Remember: the clearer the starting point, the closer the finish line.

CHAPTER 8

FROM WORST TO FIRST

I t's the boldest stroke in business. The move from worst to first. But it's not easy.

Baseball teams can do it in a season. But no matter how many business-is-like-baseball analogies you may have heard—some of them in these pages—the two are not in the same league when it comes to letting you create dramatic turnarounds.

Baseball is a game, with strict rules that everyone must follow. Business is not so tightly controlled. Make a tactical move in a baseball game, and you have a good idea what the other team's options are. Not so in business, where your rivals can always be counted on to throw the unexpected at you.

Baseball standings are confined to one season. Business goes on and on, from one year to the next.

In baseball the margin between victory and defeat can be one pitch, one swing of the bat, one umpiring call. In business, your margin has to be decisive before you can claim victory.

Unlike baseball, there are no playoffs in business in case of a tie. (What's a tie in business anyway?) The fight goes on. It never ends.

Baseball has day-to-day matchups according to a strict schedule. You always know who you're playing next. Not so in business. You wake up in the morning and your competition that day may be someone you never heard of. Plus, in baseball you're playing only one opponent at a time. In business you're competing against dozens of opponents daily. They're all trying to eat your lunch.

The most important distinction, though, is that in baseball, you know how to define the leader. It's the team in first place in the standings. It's nowhere near that clear in business.

For one thing, how do you define the leader in your field?

Is it market share or market value?

Gross revenue or percentage growth?

Profitability or product quality?

Reputation or brand-name recognition?

Who's to say? What I do know is that you have to get creative and insightful about all of these factors, and pick one that is more legitimate to you than any other as your worthy goal. If market share is how you define leadership, then that's the criterion to use in going from worst to first. After all, before you can leapfrog the competition to the top spot, you have to know which frogs you're jumping over—and where you hope to land.

It's trickier than it seems. I was on a panel at an industry forum a few years ago when the question arose about whether Reebok, the perennial number two in athletic shoes and apparel, could ever overtake category leader Nike. (This is a truism of industry conferences. When branding professionals get together, at some point the subject always turns to Nike.)

Everyone gave Reebok their unsolicited advice about its advertising, its product line, its use of celebrity endorsers, and so on. One expert just held up his hands in surrender, advising Reebok to wait patiently for Nike to make a huge mistake. (Not the most reliable strategy. If you wait for the category leader to screw up, you might be out of business before it happens.)

I suggested that we were looking in the wrong direction. A great marketing strategy has to differentiate the brand. You can't be somebody else. You've got to be yourself. Nike is the perfect example. With its 40 percent share of the shoe and apparel market, there's no other brand image that's quite like it. They are global, they are unique, and everyone knows it. They also know when someone's copying Nike.

My idea was that since you're not going to beat Nike at its own game, why not cede that 40 percent market share to them—and start taking market share away from all the smaller brands behind you. The Converses and New Balances and Adidases of the industry. If number two can pick up 2 points from number three, 3 points from number four, and 1 point from the number five brand, that's 6 share points—which are a lot easier to lift from weaker rivals than from the top dog, who has more resources to protect himself.

In other words, I'd be telling Reebok, "Let's be realistic. You're never really going to close the gap on Nike, but we can make life miserable for your other competitors. After all, if they're doing their job, numbers three, four, five, and six in the field are already targeting you. You have no choice but to fight them."

What's interesting here is that no one else in the hall had considered this. That's one of the problems of trying to go from worst to first. The process sometimes clouds our vision about our real competition. We're so busy focusing on the top spot that we forget that there are other ways to make big gains.

But even when you have the right rival in your crosshairs, you have tough questions to ask yourself.

- Are you ready to make the leap?

- Do you have a superior product or service? If it is not, at a minimum, on a par with the leader's product or service—and hopefully superior in some way—there's no point in making the claim that you're better. Good advertising at the service of a bad product will eventually put you out of business.

- Do you have the budget to do what it takes—to ride out the downturns and wrong turns, and play defense when the leader fights back (and the leader *will* fight back)?

- Do you have the time? Unlike baseball, where you can leapfrog teams in a season, moving the needle in criteria such as reputation and brand value does not happen overnight.

But let's assume the best—that you have the product, the money, and the patience. At that point your big insight rests on knowing whom you have to fight to be the champion.

That's the issue we faced in the mid-1980s when we were invited to pitch for the Visa credit card account. In 1985 Visa was hurting, not only in terms of image, which was considered downscale, but also in marketplace volume. Master-Card, its chief competitor, was gaining market share because of solid steady marketing. As Visa's share eroded, so did its advertising funds, which were made available to it by the member banks. This was the beginning of a potential death spiral for Visa—shrinking share, shrinking ad budgets, shrunken card.

Of course, it wasn't that simple. The data about how people felt about credit cards, and Visa in particular, did not jump up and slap us in the face. More accurately, it stumbled on us, or we on it.

We were sitting around the room tossing out ideas for the Visa pitch. In the corner, Gary DePaolo, the designated executive in charge of the Visa account, was sifting through his research reports, patiently listening to our "creative" approaches. We could go to war with MasterCard. We could hire celebrities to endorse Visa. We could glamorize the Visa cardholder. This last notion was important since our research confirmed that Visa was perceived as the card people used to buy items like garden hoses, antifreeze, and athletic socks. The card had so little cache—it certainly couldn't compete with the American Express card for prestige—that Visa cardholders would sometimes try to conceal the identity of the card from fellow shoppers as they were using it to make purchases.

All these issues were roiling in the room as we desperately tried to top one another with clever advertising gambits that went nowhere.

Finally, Gary spoke up. "People," he said, "it's all about acceptance. The recurring complaint is that the card is not accepted at enough places. Which is kind of ironic when you realize that Visa is honored at five times as many establishments as American Express. Admittedly the establishments are downmarket. But the folks at Visa are really proud of their acceptance rate."

This analysis of the data piqued my interest. "Wait a

minute," I said, "are those numbers for real? Are you saying that we could walk into some restaurant and they don't take Amex but they would take Visa?"

"Yes," said Gary, "but the restaurant would probably not be the Four Seasons."

"That's sort of intriguing, isn't it?" I said. "We could do something with that."

"That's what I've been telling you all along," said Gary. "Acceptance is the entry point. We just have to make it attractive and believable. We have to invent an experience that people actually have in their lives, where they discover a great little restaurant or perfect out-of-the-way hotel that isn't well known nationally but that is a local legend. And we have to make it cool that these establishments take Visa. . . ."

"But not American Express," said the ubiquitous Charlie Miesmer, completing the thought.

The analysis was: *we're accepted in five times more places than American Express*. The insight was: *we can use that to our advantage against American Express*.

So that's what we decided to do. We positioned Visa right up against the gold standard of cards, American Express. We made it seem like a gilt-edge possession, only better because it was accepted at far more retail outlets. We were telling our customers to use Visa where they can't use American Express, implying that they used *both* cards and thus creating a parity between Visa and Amex where none had ever existed before. The implication was that Visa is everywhere or, as we put it in our theme line: "Visa . . . it's everywhere you want to be." This strategy had the additional (and huge) virtue of completely ignoring our true competitor, MasterCard—as if the two bank cards were no longer on the same playing field.

Executing the strategy turned out to be easy. One of our young creatives mentioned a restaurant named Rosalie's in Marblehead, Massachusetts, that was a local legend *and,* he was sure, did not take American Express. The exclusive just-waiting-to-be-discovered aura of such a restaurant was perfect; it would help us pump some upmarket panache into Visa's image. Thus, Rosalie's became the first of dozens of fine restaurants, exclusive shops, and luxurious vacation destinations (including the Olympic Games!) where Visa was accepted and American Express was not. The message: Visa was there for you wherever you happened to be in the world, and its entrée to the best places put you where you wanted to be in life.

The response was immediate and huge in all categories. Visa's numbers in total dollars spent, number of transactions, and number of venues accepting the card soared. American Express suffered an identity crisis, lowering its fees to retailers and cardholders in order to combat Visa's surge. As for MasterCard, they went into a marketing tailspin, hiring and firing five agencies over the next ten years (regrouping finally with their "priceless" campaign). The true test of our insight and strategy? Twenty years later, the Visa campaign still works—and is a prominent case study at Harvard Business School.

CHAPTER 9

BETTING THE FARM

Now that we've seen how insights can help solve the most fractious problems in business, from the challenge of distinguishing yourself from the pack to the issue of moving the right needle to telling the world where it can find you, it's time to address a much less common situation—when everything you've got is riding on the success of one product, one strategy, or one idea. What's the insight when you're betting the farm on a single notion?

If you're just starting out on your own or you run a small business, you're probably familiar with this. Any operation that's not diversified, that centers on one thing only, faces this problem every day. Whether you're running a plumbing supply store or that wineshop in Sag Harbor, every day is, in effect, a wager on your one service (good plumbing) or your one product line (wine). You don't have a choice but to place your bets on yourself.

It doesn't happen that often on a corporate level. Most big companies know how to spread the risk around. They're diversified, either in product line or industry or territory. When the Asian market is weak, they're bucked up by results in Europe or North America. They might never have all three territories firing at once, but each territory is a hedge against the others.

Every once in a while a bold company is forced to bet it all on one huge initiative. This is what happened when Apple introduced the Macintosh computer, when Microsoft launched the Windows operating system, when Intel put all its chips on the Pentium processor. None of these three seemed to have a choice. Failing to place that bet meant that each would stop growing and face inevitable extinction. Given the option of big risk–no reward or big risk–big reward, each chose the latter.

These big-bet initiatives should not be confused with huge product launches at other companies. They're not the same as Coca-Cola introducing the first diet cola in 1966. Bold as it was, it wasn't much of a gamble for Coca-Cola. If it failed, the company still had the steady cash flow from Coke. In fact, the company was so cautious, it didn't even dare to put the famous brand name on the diet cola. It was called Tab; Diet Coke came fifteen years later after the diet market was well established.

It was the same when Toyota introduced a luxury car line called Lexus. If Lexus didn't pan out, Toyota still had their full line of Camrys and Corollas and trucks.

These companies were extending the line, not putting it all on the line.

Betting the farm is a rare seismic event in business, but that's what we got involved in with Gillette in the late 1980s. The company was putting all its chips on a top-secret proprietary shaving system called Sensor, and they were looking to us, as their longtime ad agency, for a huge marketing insight.

I have to admit we were a little slow to understand how much was riding on this. We had achieved a nice comfortable equilibrium with Gillette. Too comfortable perhaps. A series of Gillette marketing chiefs had never really challenged our view of the way Gillette should be advertised. Any challenge came only from ourselves and somehow we were lulled into believing that the relationship was just fine.

In 1988, even in our smug comfort zone, vague unexpected rumblings of Gillette's disaffection began to echo in the halls of BBDO. The man who had set off the rumblings was John Symons, a dapper Brit who had recently been promoted from Gillette's top U.K. marketing slot to chief of all of Gillette's North Atlantic marketing. Symons's strategy was to revitalize the Gillette company as a whole and to spread the historic excellence of the Gillette shaving tradition through the entire range of Gillette grooming products.

That we had not taken the initiative on this, that we were a little passive, was a big mistake on our part.

We had heard of Symons from our overseas brethren who had worked with him in the U.K. From day one, I felt we were never quite on the same page. He was a pleasant enough chap but what drove us a little batty was his difficulty in making the mental leap from our storyboards and scripts to how the commercials would look on television. It wasn't until we presented our spots in "ripomatic" form—bits and snippets of film from movies and existing commercials, cut to a voice and music soundtrack—that he would "get it."

Symons had gotten along very well with Phil Slott, our creative director in the U.K., who had done some exceptional work for Gillette in that region. Gillette enjoyed a huge market share dominance in shaving in the U.K.—close to 90 percent of the wet shaving market—under Symons and Slott.

But things on our side of the Atlantic weren't as rosy. Symons's dissatisfaction with our performance on Gillette may have been justifiable. Successive consumer surveys had indicated a fall in Gillette's favorability rating. Top-of-mind awareness had been in decline. Certainly, a new generation had grown up unaware of the hallowed "Look sharp, feel sharp, be sharp" advertising promise of the 1960s. Some of that erosion could easily be laid at our feet.

It didn't help that Gillette's image was also being eroded by the growth of disposable plastic razors. Bic made them, and so did Gillette under the Good News name. Good News razors accounted for more than 50 percent of Gillette's sales volume, but a far lower percentage of the profits. The plastic throwaway razors were a necessary evil to maintain "share of beard," but as Symons remarked, "If the whole marketplace all of a sudden converted to disposable razors, you'd see a serious, serious problem in the shaving business."

Gillette divides humanity into two species: Plastic Man (people who use disposable razors) and Steel Man (those who use steel razor shaving systems). In response to a survey, one young stock analyst described Gillette as "hollow, plastic, and blue." This was Gillette's worst nightmare. Gillette's top brass did not want their company known principally for making a lowest-common-denominator product like Good News. They saw Gillette as an innovative high-tech company, a pioneer in the application of proprietary manufacturing processes that could produce billions—yes, billions—of low-cost, high-tolerance razor blades in every part of the world.

Their product, the steel shaving system, may not cost much, but as a piece of technology it was unique, elegant, and state of the art. And it delivered its big promise: a perfect shave every time.

This was how Gillette saw itself—as the avatar of Steel Man.

The image of Gillette as Plastic Man was extremely worrisome, so it was no wonder that Symons had asked us upon his arrival at Gillette headquarters in Boston, "Who will be my creative director?"

Oops.

Phil Slott, who had worked so well with Symons in London, had asked for and received a transfer to BBDO's sister agency, Tracey-Locke in Los Angeles, where he was to become chairman and creative head of the Taco Bell business. Somehow, we had neglected to inform Symons about this.

Not only was Symons angry, he was angry precisely at the time Gillette was preparing to launch the Sensor brand with a $175 million worldwide marketing budget. Instead of being ready to double our Gillette business, we were suddenly looking down the barrel of an agency review.

To be historically accurate, the advertising strategy that was being demanded here was applied to the Atra shaving system. But we knew that it was really a warm-up for the introduction eighteen months later of the top-secret Sensor system and an integrated line of new Gillette-branded grooming products including everything from aftershave to hair products to shaving gel to deodorants. There was so much money, staff time, branding, and prestige riding on this launch, that it was without doubt a bet-the-company decision.

That's what Symons told us at one meeting. But he was so

ticked off at us as he outlined his goals that he announced, "I don't think you guys can pull this off. You've had this account so long, you're sleepwalking on it. I don't think you know how to take Gillette to the next level."

As he spoke, I had a flashback.

Tough talk and tight demands from Gillette weren't new to me.

It was one of Gillette's extreme advertising strictures that forced me to write a commercial that propelled my career at a time when I was just another young face in the creative crowd at BBDO.

On my way to lunch by myself one day, I ran into Wally Butterworth, the account executive on Right Guard. Wally had just come back from a meeting with Gillette, and he had a worried look on his face.

"You won't believe this," he said as he collared me in the corridor. "They want to sell *two*—yes, two!—different Right Guards in the same thirty-second commercial. Regular Right Guard deodorant in the brown can, and this new antiperspirant in a silver can. They don't have much of a budget, so we've got to show both cans side by side in one thirty-second spot." Unheard of for its time.

Maybe it was the words "side by side" that flashed an image in my head. I told Wally, "Listen to this. We have two guys in adjoining apartments who are living on each side of the same medicine cabinet. But they don't know the other exists. One uses Right Guard deodorant, the other uses the antiperspirant. One day they happen to open their side of the cabinet at the same moment, which is the first time they meet."

It was one of the few times in my career that a complete concept popped into my mind the instant I heard the problem. It wasn't the result of deep linear thought; it was a reflex action—like a third baseman instinctively stabbing at a hot line drive and catching it. I have no idea where it came from. But I passed up lunch, returned to my desk, and wrote the script before the heat of the moment left me.

Two men open up two sides of the same medicine cabinet.

The one, a gregarious fun-loving bundle of comic energy (eventually played by Chuck McCann), is unfazed by the surreal sight of his neighbor in what he thinks is *his* bathroom. "Hi, guy," he says.

The other, a bookwormy worrywart (played by Bill Fiore), is not so nonchalant about it. "Who are you?" he says.

"I'm your neighbor," he answers as he reaches for his brown can of Right Guard deodorant. "Oh, I see you're using the new Right Guard antiperspirant," he says pointing to the silver can also in the cabinet.

Five seconds into a nutty setup and I'm already talking about the product.

The rest of the spot wrote itself.

We showed it to Gillette, and they loved it. Even better, the commercials were easy and inexpensive to produce. One medicine cabinet, which was probably the simplest set of all time. The cast of two actors, working at union scale, was one more than the minimum. You only needed two cameras. And you could shoot a whole season's worth of spots in one day.

If I were to permit myself some self-indulgent retrograde analysis (aka 20/20 hindsight), I could probably find the insight that drove this deodorant campaign. But the truth is, there is no big insight here. It was just an executional idea that worked. The insight was already built into the product—the brown and silver cans have the same name, but they're different, they solve different problems, they're targeting different consumers. All we did was come up with a concept—the two-sided cabinet—that metaphorically illustrated Gillette's insightful demand to show the two cans together.

The concept had legs. The campaign ran for seven years, moving the sales needle to the point where Right Guard unseated Ban and Mennen as the dominant deodorant brand. Subsequent creative teams picked up where I'd left off, even using celebrities in later years, such as Muhammad Ali and Don Rickles.

(The campaign also points out a paradox that crops up in a lot of our output over the years. The more constraints the client gives you on what you can do, the more your imagination fights to loosen those constraints. And in that struggle, the imagination often goes to wild and unexpected places. When you're locked in a bare prison cell, with few distractions, your brain goes a little haywire. This is how you solve the choking challenge of showing two products in one commercial by coming up with two-way medicine cabinets.)

Fond memories of the Right Guard campaign were going through my mind as Symons spoke, and I shuddered at the prospect of getting fired by Gillette. Through mergers and renamings and changings of the guard, our agency in its various guises had held on to the account since 1929. That's not longevity. That's eternity in the ad business. And yet here I was on the brink of becoming the creative chief who lost Gillette.

There are three great motivators in the ad business. Passion, pride, and fear. Fear was what motivated us to assemble an A team of creative, account, and research people and get to work on Gillette before Symons uttered the dreaded words "agency review."

We visited Gillette factories and saw the dazzling manufacturing facilities that could spit out thousands of razor systems an hour, to tolerances that would elicit awe from the best semiconductor plant manager. We talked to the scientists in Gillette's labs who explained the physiology of hair growth and the Sensor's twin-blade solution to the mystery of *historesis* (a facial hair's instant retraction after it is "set up" and cut by a razor blade).

The famous "look sharp" theme line had endured for three decades because of the word choice that cleverly linked Gillette *blades* with the desirable goal of being *sharp*. But Gillette was moving beyond sharp blades. In Symons's words, the goal was to make Gillette "the premier toiletries company in the world." Gillette was branching out. We had to come up with language that cut a wider swath than "sharp."

The answer and the insight, we found, was looking at us in every Gillette employee we met. These were very serious people. They did not see themselves as producing a low-interest product that people used in front of the bathroom mirror every morning—and then forgot about for the rest of the day. They saw themselves as committed scientists who were using technology to relieve men's suffering. Think about it. When guys don't shave on the weekends, it's not because they're trying to affect a manly image through excess stubble. It's because *they hate to shave*. Putting sharp steel to sensitive skin is tiresome and risky, demanding mental alertness at a time in the morning when many men would rather be sleeping. Shaving is a dreaded daily chore. Gillette's tech wizards were serious about producing the absolute best solution to the problem—from pioneering laser welding on a mass scale for shaving systems, a process previously reserved for making pacemakers, to earning twenty-nine patents for the Sensor system alone.

We also saw it in Gillette's management, from CEO Colman Mockler on down. When I say they were "steel men," it's not only because of their contempt for the disposable plastic razors that provided so much of their sales. They really were enthralled by metal technology and constantly making things better. If you hung around them for any length of time, you got the sense that anything they touched had to be the best it could possibly be. They couldn't imagine working any other way.

This notion of advanced technology applied to a worthy cause and of everyone at Gillette pushing to be not *good,* not *better,* but the *best,* eventually sunk into our cerebral cortex. And that's when the theme line appeared: *The best a man can get.* We saw it everywhere at Gillette. Why not trumpet it everywhere around the world to describe Gillette?

That campaign saved the account.

You don't ordinarily find advertising insight in the hearts of the employees who work for the client. You find it in research and marketing data. You find it in the CEO's statements. You find it in throwaway comments in meetings. You find it in customer complaints. But the more we looked at "The best a man can get," the more we appreciated how it fulfilled an absolute must for Gillette.

For one thing, it had the wonderful virtue of being true. Gillette, on the surface, looked like your classic maker of parity products. And claiming "the best a man can get," again on the surface, sounded like the same old cliché claim of superiority: our product is better. To which consumers reply, "That's what they all say." But when we looked at the heart of Gillette's big push, their shaving system, and when we talked to Gillette employees and when we actually shaved with the system, we knew this was the rare phenomenon—an ostensible parity product that was vastly superior to anything else out there. This legitimized our "best a man can get" claim. No small thing in a parity economy.

The theme also maintained the pipeline of goodwill that had made young men over the years as loyal to Gillette shaving products as their fathers had been. It acted as an umbrella for future male toiletry products and new shaving systems. Specifically, we were thinking of the soon-to-be introduced Sensor, which was to become the most important and expensive innovation in the history of the shaving industry.

The stakes in the Sensor launch were enormous, both in the size of the expenditure and what it meant for Gillette's entire corporate strategy. At the time of our meeting with Symons, Gillette had already secretly spent more than $200 million over a ten-year period devoted to conquering disposable razors (including their own market-leading Good News) with the Sensor system. Gillette was counting on the growth of Sensor to be achieved at the expense of all other razors, one third of which would be cut out of rivals Bic's and Schick's share of the disposable market. They were very determined to stay number one in the shaving category.

But all that diligent planning was being put in jeopardy. In the years leading up to the Sensor launch, while it was quietly spending on R&D, the then $3.2-billion-a-year Gillette was also prudently hoarding money for future spending, diverting its financial and human resources away from product marketing in a flat economy and saving it for future acquisitions. While Gillette was biding its time for the right acquisition, it became cash-rich, which made it a mouthwatering target for the aggressive takeover artists of the era. These were the go-go 1980s, the era of leveraged buyouts and Mike Milken's junk bonds and corporate raiders masquerading as sheriffs for shareholders.

The first raider to pounce was Ronald Perlman's Revlon group, which made two separate "greenmail" attacks on Gillette in the late 1980s. The other group was Coniston Partners, which had acquired 5.9 percent of Gillette stock in the hopes of winning control of the board and selling the company to the highest bidder for a tidy but handsome profit. Mockler fought off both suitors by buying back their shares at a 40 percent premium for $720 million. That premium purchase price was not available to other selling shareholders, which created a lot of ill will among the "owners" of Gillette. This was the poisonous, distracting atmosphere surrounding the Sensor launch.

Those of us privy to Gillette's Sensor project could only admire Mockler's steely fortitude. He was staking the company's future on a huge investment in radically new technology. He knew that if Sensor succeeded, the corporate raiders were actually selling cheap—that Gillette was ridiculously undervalued because none of the future earnings from Sensor were factored into Gillette's share price or future market value. For his bet-the-farm ballsiness with Sensor, Mockler earns my eternal admiration. (He died of a heart attack at work a few months after the Sensor launch.)

This was the crazy atmosphere around the Sensor launch. One product was being asked to rejuvenate, refocus, and restore the morale of an entire corporation. If we felt pressure when it looked like we would lose the Gillette account, that was nothing compared to the pressure on client and agency alike in launching Sensor. The numbers were daunting by themselves: the Sensor system was protected by twenty-nine patents, four alone for the new lubricating strip that softened your beard before the first cut; the manufacturing process was as closely guarded as the Coca-Cola formula; the development costs exceeded $200 million; the 1990 marketing budget was $175 million, to be spent in twenty countries, with $110 million earmarked for advertising.

I've said it here before that once you have a solid insight, the execution practically writes itself. It wasn't that easy with Gillette.

We were torn between two approaches, both valid. On the one hand, there was the sheer technical prowess of Sensor. It was without question the best razor ever created, and the more you learned about the technology, the more you wanted to brag about it. So we created animatics (an animated technical illustration) showing how the product achieved shaving perfection (not an outlandish claim) by softening the beard, cutting with one blade, and then swooping in with the second blade before the follicle retracted. Does that sound warm and uplifting to you? Well, it didn't to us either. While it highlighted pure product, the spots were also cold, taking no advantage of the emotional goodwill we had been building for more than a year with our pre-launch "Best a Man Can Get" commercials.

The other extreme wasn't much better. We wrote spots displaying pure emotion, showing very little of the Sensor and emphasizing soaring music and luscious photography instead. Does that make you want to buy, especially when we refuse to show you what you'll be buying?

One of my guiding theories about the creative process is a belief in *optimistic patience*. Insights and great ideas don't come to you with clockwork precision, perfectly timed to suit your needs when you snap your fingers. They come at their own pace, and you have to patiently wait for them. If you have had useful insights in the past, you will have them again in the near future. I can't say when exactly, but they will come. If you have written great copy before, you will do so again. Stay at your desk and be patient. There is no rational reason to think that you are blocked (whatever that means!), that you have dried up, that you have used up your full quota of good ideas (as if there is a quota). You simply have to keep scratching and clawing and groping for the answers—and trust that they will come. The only thing you *can't* do is rush the process, or grab on to the first idea that pops into your head because you're in a hurry. If you've benefited from these surges of serendipity, you know the feeling. Patience. Optimism. Optimistic patience. It's sort of what Kevin Costner develops in *Field of Dreams* when the voice from an Iowa cornfield intones, "Build it and they will come."

That's what we told ourselves as we tried to balance out the virtues of sheer product *vs.* raw emotionality. Our advertising message needed to be captivating, but it also had to be true. If you've discovered the cure for cancer, all you have to say is CURE FOR CANCER in big bright letters. And that would work. If you've just made a better razor blade—even the world's best razor blade—the majesty has to come from somewhere else. We found a big chunk of this mysterious majesty by hiring singer/songwriter Jake Holmes to write and perform the "best a man can get" music theme, which struck a perfect balance between a pop/country ballad and a national anthem. We then overlaid the music with stunning images of guys being guys—fathers and sons playing ball, a young man riding a Vespa, a young couple in love, a hard-body athlete lifting weights. And we left enough visual pockets in the spots so that we could fill them in with product shots of shaving systems, aftershave, or shaving gel. Unlike most other BBDO hits, they didn't have our customary signature of making you laugh or making you cry. Instead they made you swell with pride, simply for being a guy.

They also made the launch needle jump. In the first twelve months of its introduction, Gillette sold 24 million razors, 6 million more than projected. That meant that 24 million men had to abandon their current shaving method and accept Sensor as their new standard. This was a conversion rate never seen before in consumer goods. In less than a year Sensor became the number one selling shaving system in every country where it was sold. The biggest news coverage Sensor received dwelled on production struggles to keep up with the sold-out demand.

Proud of its success, Gillette asked my boss Allen Rosenshine and me to send special gold-plated Sensors to several VIPs. I sent one to Ronald Reagan at his California ranch. He wrote back that while he was not usually tempted by new-fangled technology, he'd made an exception for Sensor and loved it. Then Chrysler chairman Lee Iacocca said that he wished that we'd promote his cars as well as we did Gillette's razors. I told him that if he'd let us give away as many free cars as we did Sensors, I could guarantee equally impressive results.

CHAPTER 10

THE PHRASE THAT PAYS

In 1969, when I had been at BBDO for seven years, an investor offered to back me in the start-up of my own agency. It was a crazy, cocky thing to do because I didn't have a name in the industry or a handful of clients in my pocket who would follow me wherever I went. I hired a receptionist named Sally Hastings and rented a modest space on Fifth Avenue where she and I spent many weeks wondering when my first client would appear. It was 1969, the summer the New York Mets were in the middle of a hot National League pennant race, their first. The Mets played a lot of afternoon games back then at Shea Stadium in Flushing, Queens. And that's how I spent most afternoons—at Met games. I'd tell Sally, "If anyone calls, just say I'm out pitching the Flushing National Bank."

This went on for several months. Finally, I went to my backers and said, "Listen, guys. I don't think this is working out." But they had more confidence in me than I did.

"Don't worry, it's gonna happen," they said.

One day I got a call from a priest. I figured he was calling to give us the last rites. But he turned out to be a famous priest, Father Patrick Payton, who had created one of the great ad slogans: "The family that prays together stays together." He was looking for a new theme line and a new television campaign to promote prayer in American life.

I thought that was an interesting challenge. And since I had nothing else to do, I took it on—pro bono. We did some terrific commercials, totally on the cheap. To get the spots made, I used up every favor I had with New York casting agents, directors, editors, and production houses. We came up with a sharp theme line—you have to remember that this was at the height of the Vietnam War—that said, "The world hasn't got a prayer without yours."

I was proud of the work, but the agency was running low on money. With little left in the till, and even less to lose, I decided to throw a small cocktail party for the media to (a) announce the opening of the agency and (b) show our prayer commercials. One of the attendees was a great reporter named Phil Dougherty, who was the advertising columnist for *The New York Times*. He was, by miles, the most influential columnist in the trade. He liked the spots and came up to me at the party to ask about my agency. I said, "You know, Phil, I guess you could say we're the agency that opened on a prayer. Literally."

It must have been a slow news day because the next morning Dougherty used that line as the lead in his *Times* column—and he gave me credit for it! Within 48 hours we started getting calls from clients such as The Oppenheimer Fund and American Home Products, and the agency was on its way.

I can't say that's the moment I realized the disproportionate power of a few carefully chosen and arranged words. I'd been around clever slogans for years. But it was the first time I felt it in my wallet. A well-timed, well-crafted phrase can save a business, launch a career, even answer your prayers.

This shouldn't have been a surprise for me. One of my first bosses at BBDO in the 1960s and 1970s was a creative director named Jim Jordan who was probably the greatest sloganeer in American advertising history. He coined such memorable lines as "The one beer to have when you're having more than one" for Schaefer beer; "Delta is ready when you are"; "Us Tareytown smokers would rather fight than switch" (illustrated with happy smokers sporting black eyes); and perhaps most intrusively, "Ring around the collar" for Wisk detergent.

Jordan believed so fully in the power of a good slogan that he created a quasi-scientific subgenre of advertising to spotlight it. He made it his specialty and called it "nameonics." That was his label for a form of advertising in which every ad must make a consumer remember the product's name. Anything less and the ads were pointless. Thus, you got the ominous basso profundo chorus of "Tum ta tum tum" for Tums antacid, and "Aetna, I'm glad I met ya" for Aetna insurance. Corny as they sound, these tag lines imprint the client's name firmly in the consumer's mind (it's called brand registration), which for many clients remains Job One. (My admiration for Jim Jordan's theme line skill is practically boundless, but I drew the line at his nameonic solution for Chapstick Lip Balm, when he had the comely Olympic skier Suzy Chafee identify herself in a commercial as Suzy Chapstick!)

If and when you have the urge to dash off a phrase that pays, you may want to keep in mind what makes a slogan work.

- It has to be *memorable*—and force the reader to recall the brand name, either by rhyming ("The best part of waking up is Folger's in your cup") or spelling it out ("How do you spell relief? R-O-L-A-I-D-S") or employing a pun that works for the brand without eliciting a groan ("The Citi never sleeps" for Citibank).

- It has to *differentiate*: Miller Lite's "Everything you always wanted in a beer . . . and less."

- It has to be *strategic* about the product's use or benefits: Puppy Chow's "Don't treat your puppy like a dog."

- It has to reflect the brand's *personality*: Volkswagen's "Think small."

- It has to be *original*: "Nothing else is a Pepsi." You can't say "Simply the best," even if it happens to be true. A hundred slogans already say that.

- It has to be *simple*: Nike's "Just do it." Burger King's "Have it your way."

- It has to *make you buy*: Frito-Lay's "Bet you can't eat just one."

- It has to be *extendable* into a long campaign, such as the Absolut vodka series, or American Express's "Do you know me?" campaign showing celebrities whose names are more recognizable than their faces (author Stephen King, 1964 vice presidential candidate William Miller).

The rules can go on forever, and they will tell you what you can't do as well as what you should do. I don't believe in rules. I've yet to see the rule that says a good slogan should list the product's ingredients and turn it into a tongue twister. And yet that's what McDonald's did in 1974 to celebrate the Big Mac: "Two-all-beef-patties-special-sauce-lettuce-cheese-pickles-onions-on-a-sesame-seed-bun." For at least a year, everyone in the U.S was having fun trying to spit those words out.

At the least, a slogan or theme line must do something to focus your message or steer it in the right direction.

Sometimes the slogan is nothing more than the insight itself. It doesn't aim so high that it has to define the entire company. It's merely a utilitarian phrase that pushes a specific consumer hot button. If it's good, it inspires breakthrough advertising.

Something along those lines happened to me during those wilderness years away from BBDO—after the "on a prayer" episode but before I returned in 1977. The client was Castro Convertibles, a New York–based manufacturer of sofa beds. The Castro name was well known due to years of local TV advertising starring the owner's young daughter, Bernadette, showing how easy it was to open up a sofa bed. Basically, it was a product demonstration, introducing consumers to the then-radical idea of a couch that doubles up as a bed. The spots were so simple, they were almost goofy. But in truth, they were doing their job. They were attacking the problem of "Hey, I'm over here," educating consumers about a different sort of product and the company that makes it.

By the time the Castro account landed in my agency, people knew what a convertible sofa was. Castro needed to move to the next phase where they educated consumers about *why they needed a Castro,* not *what it is.*

Analyzing the situation, we concluded that Castro's target market was city dwellers—people who live in apartments and small houses. Apartments and houses are defined by the number of bedrooms. Apartment dwellers are always clamoring for more space and they *always* need an extra bedroom. That was it! Castro Convertibles, which lets you convert any room into a spare bedroom, solves the eternal city-dweller problem. "We make extra bedrooms" was the phrase that pays.

As we sifted through the everyday situations where you might need an extra bed, the usual scenes of visiting relatives and friends staying overnight came to mind. But we wanted to show that the need might be greater than anyone imagined. And we attacked the concept with humor.

The first commercial took place in a hallway late at night outside a bedroom with the door ajar. You can't see that much—just a glimmer of a husband and wife arguing back and forth. The husband is really steamed, saying, "Ceil, I can't take it any more. I can't sleep with a dog in our bed."

The wife says, "But, Jules, he's afraid of the dark."

"He's afraid of the dark? A two-hundred-fifty-pound St. Bernard is afraid of the dark?" says the husband. He continues ranting, finally laying down an ultimatum: "Ceil, here it is, either the dog goes or I go!" A pause, and the door opens and Jules comes out, carrying a pillow. He goes downstairs to the living room while a voice-over says, "Now and then, every family could use another bedroom. Well, we make extra bedrooms, and you can put one in any room you like." We see Jules pulling out the couch, still fuming. "Last week it was the piranhas," he mutters to himself, "and the week before that, the gorillas, and then the chimpanzees, and the dogs and . . ." He gets into bed, settling into a sound sleep. Then we see the dog's shadow as he leaves the bedroom and climbs silently into bed with Jules. In the darkness we hear Jules say, "Ceil, don't try to make up. . . . Ceil?"

The spot's humor kept people watching, but it was the "extra bedroom" that paid off by expanding people's idea of why you'd need an extra bed (like when you've had a fight and can't sleep in the same bed).

Slogans and theme lines grow in importance with vague intangible products. The more amorphous the product or service, the more you need a phrase that pays.

Insurance companies certainly appreciate this.

Some categories are very tough to advertise with a straight face. Insurance is one of them. There are thousands of insurance companies and it's impossible to tell them apart. They are prima facie evidence of the parity economy. Plus, the product is invisible. You can't see it or touch it or taste it or buy it in a store and take it home. On top of that rich sundae of invisibility, there's the whipped topping of gloom. Insurance companies provide a service that most people take no pleasure in paying for. The dominant emotions people feel for insurance are fear and skepticism: fear that disaster will strike, skepticism that they'll be covered when it does. Consumers need two aspirins to think about insurance.

How do we move the needle here? Better yet, which needle are we talking about?

Awareness is half the game in insurance—making people aware of your name and feeling positively about it. That's the needle. It explains why two of the most durable slogans of all time belong to insurance companies: "You're in good hands with Allstate" and "Like a good neighbor, State Farm is there." They know that claiming a superior product is an unconvincing argument. You can't persuade people or twist their arms. People hate insurance salespeople anyway. That's why the slogans are reassuring and say nothing about the companies' respective product lines. Instead, they bypass parity altogether and paint a friendly, reliable image of the people selling that product, so that when the dreaded insurance salesperson calls, consumers are more inclined to take the call rather than hang up. The slogan's only job is to put a friendly face on a faceless product—in effect, to humanize each company with images of Allstate's "good hands" and State Farm as your "neighbor." On that count, they have been succeeding for decades.

The same insight—let's put a friendly face on the company—was at work when MetLife introduced the "Peanuts" character Snoopy as the corporate spokescartoon in all its consumer advertising. A lot of people would look at that approach and say, "Gee, that doesn't seem to be an appropriate representation of a major insurance company." But MetLife's problem, like any other insurance company, was their need to get through the prospect's front door. In a field where insurance salespeople are seen as agents of gloom, Snoopy gave the sales force a new persona. Over time, the salespeople became warm and fuzzy and friendly because of their association with Snoopy.

That's the insight underlying the now-famous AFLAC campaign to sell supplemental disability insurance that you purchase through your employer. The significant difference that the ad agency, the Kaplan Thaler Group, injected into this insight was that instead of using a slogan or famous cartoon to humanize AFLAC, they used . . . a quacking duck.

I have to admit, if one of my creative people came to me with the idea of a quacking duck to drill the client's name into consumers' brains, I'd probably toss him out of my office. Too corny. But the spots, a series of humorous, technically ambitious vignettes showing everyone from synchronized swimmers to car mechanics to two guys on a park bench to Yogi Berra in a barbershop talking about insurance, while a kibitzing duck quacks out the AFLAC name, were executed with surprising élan. The campaign is a brilliant variation on nameonics (the duck quacking the client's name, AFLAC, so you remember it). And it does its job. It's not asking you to rush out and buy the product line. It only aims to pique your interest in the company. After all, the tag line of each AFLAC commercial is simply, "Ask about it at work."

The insight: we need to put a face on the company. The needle: awareness.

Some of my colleagues take the extreme position that no one watches commercials for the theme line. Theme lines are just the signal at the end of 30 or 60 seconds to let viewers know the commercial is over. They are window dressing. By themselves, they are meaningless. They only accumulate memorability because of the power of the commercial itself and because of constant repetition. A part of me can't argue with this.

For example, everyone agrees that the "Got milk?" campaign for the California Fluid Milk Processors, from a BBDO sister agency in San Francisco, Goodby Silverstein, is classic advertising. But it's the campaign, not the phrase, that is classic. By themselves, the two words "Got milk?" aren't *that* clever. They express a strong insight about how people feel when they're deprived of milk (based on focus groups asking people to not use milk for a week)—and what you can't eat without milk, such as cookies and cereal. But the words only acquire power when they're "illustrated" by a funny commercial. In the first spot, we are in a room with a collector obsessed with the legend of Alexander Hamilton and Aaron Burr. He's eating a peanut butter and jelly sandwich with his radio on. The radio announcer of a quiz show asks the big-money trivia question "Who shot Alexander Hamilton?" The phone rings and it is the radio announcer asking our mouth-stuffed history buff the question. He reaches for the milk carton to wash down the sandwich, but it is empty. Trying to say "Aaron Burr" repeatedly, the words come out muffled and unintelligible. He loses.

"Got milk?"

Only when you dramatize (with great wit) the idea that milk is great for washing down peanut butter and jelly sandwiches do the words "Got milk?" turn into the phrase that pays.

Another example: From 1961 to 1999 Hamlet cigars ran one of the most popular campaigns in U.K. history (though I doubt if one in ten thousand Americans knows about it). The slogan "Happiness is a Hamlet cigar" is innocuous. But when you couple it with more than one hundred hilarious commercials over 28 years, each showing people in exasperating or stressful situations finding happiness by lighting up a Hamlet cigar, the slogan works. Before the campaign went off the air because of a tobacco advertising ban, it moved Hamlet's needle to the point where the brand accounted for half the cigars sold in Britain. This is really an argument for *consistency* and *repetition*. This is the true secret of any phrase that pays: the phrases impinge upon the public consciousness if you repeat them with consistent execution.

I know from my experience with Pepsi that consistency can be more important than the actual slogan. Here are Pepsi's theme lines since 1960:

Pepsi. For those who think young. (1960)

Come alive, you're in the Pepsi generation. (1964)

Taste that beats the others cold. (1967)

You've got a lot to live, and Pepsi's got a lot to give. (1969)

Join the Pepsi people—Feelin' free. (1974)

Take the Pepsi Challenge. (1975)

Have a Pepsi day. (1978)

Catch that Pepsi spirit. (1980)

Pepsi's got your taste for life. (1982)

Pepsi now. (1983)

Pepsi. The choice of a new generation. (1984)

A generation ahead. (1989)

Pepsi. The choice of a new generation. (1990)

Gotta' have it. (1992)

Be young. Have fun. Drink Pepsi. (1993)

Nothing else is a Pepsi. (1995)

Generation Next. (1997)

Think young. Drink young. (2002)

The Joy of Pepsi. (2003)

It's the Cola. (2004)

None of these theme lines qualifies as poetry or, for that matter, graceful advancement of the English language. But at the same time, the lines never take their eye off the ball, which is extolling the youth and vitality of the Pepsi drinker. Hence, the recurring use of words like "generation" and "young." They also conjure appealing visions of American values such as freedom. Hence, the use of words like "free" and "choice." Team all that up with entertaining and often funny imagery in the commercials, populated by very attractive people and superstar celebrities, and you have a consistent message that—to agree with my colleagues—relegates some slogans to an afterthought.

More than anything else, a phrase that pays appears when you have the guts to stick with it and repeat it.

I learned this with Pepsi. Allen Rosenshine and I were driving from Manhattan to Purchase, New York, to show the Pepsi marketing team our new commercials. This was the best stuff Ted Sann and our creative team had ever done, a sharp break with the Pepsi Challenge and breakthrough advertising that was going to show the world that Pepsi was reconfiguring the playing field. We led off with a spot called "Shark," which showed an animated fin moving through a beach jammed with umbrellas to the theme from *Jaws*. Only at the end do you see that it isn't a shark but a cool kid with a surfboard. We followed that with "Soundtruck," again on a beach, where an entrepreneurial kid in a van broadcasts the thirst-inducing sound of a Pepsi being poured into a glass. Third came "Spaceship," showing an alien craft hovering over two soft drink machines—Coke and Pepsi, of course—taste-testing the two products, and beaming the Pepsi machine up.

All this creativity on cardboard, but we didn't have a theme line to sum it all up. During the ride uptown, Allen and I were weighing our options. We could wing it, tell Pepsi we'd fill in the blanks later—and trust them to trust us. But that's an imperfect sale. It could taint all the good work we'd already done. Somewhere on the outskirts of Manhattan, it dawned on us: "The choice of a new generation!" We both knew that was it. But we couldn't just say it. We had to show it.

As we arrived at PepsiCo headquarters with 20 minutes to spare before the big meeting, we snuck into the office of Pepsi's head graphic artist, Frank Rupp, and begged him to set up the slogan in type on a big card. He made up a beautiful design on the spot and that's the way we presented it: "Pepsi. The choice of a new generation."

Only problem: Pepsi president Roger Enrico didn't spark to it. He thought it was too long, not catchy enough, not . . . worthy of the work.

With nothing else on paper or in our heads, Allen, Ted, and I kept repeating the theme line through the rest of the meeting. Enrico still wasn't sold, even as the meeting broke up.

There's a story about the great German conductor Otto Klemperer, who was famous for his excruciatingly slow tempi. One day while he was rehearsing his orchestra, a cellist asked Klemperer, "Maestro, isn't this tempo a bit slow for this music?"

Klemperer replied, "You'll get used to it."

That's what happened with our theme line. Over the coming weeks as we kept meeting with Pepsi and began turning the storyboards into actual commercials, we kept repeating the phrase "The choice of a new generation." Until everyone at Pepsi got used to it. Most importantly, Roger Enrico.

The Pepsi folks liked it so much it became their slogan for the next five years. In fact, they liked it so much that after we abandoned it in 1989 for "A generation ahead," they reversed themselves and brought "The choice of a new generation" back in 1990 for a three-year encore.

You might say it became the phrase that pays . . . twice.

CHAPTER 11

GOING ORBITAL

Let's face it. Much of the work we do in advertising doesn't set the world on fire. At best, if we're armed with a solid insight, a sound strategy, and know who our target audience is, we're preaching to the choir.

We're reminding people who already like the product why they like the product. We're reinforcing our image so we hold on to our loyal customers. A worthy goal, often forgotten, in a world where rivals are trying to lure those customers to their side.

Maybe we're hoping to make some new friends, too, to keep the sales needle moving forward.

And if we put a dent in our competition's side, that's a plus.

That's about it. The commercials air, the print ads run, the coordinated promotions do their magic—even with all that diligent planning, we still run the risk that the majority of the population might not notice or care.

We've done our job. Made the impact we projected. Next.

On many days, advertising can remind you of the curiously comforting logic in the saying "No matter what happens, remember that one billion Chinese don't give a damn."

But every once in a while, if the advertising gods are smiling, something you do takes on a jet-propelled life of its own and lifts off into outer space. Your idea, your client, your message go orbital.

You might think I'm talking about Ronald Reagan's 1984 reelection campaign here, when we put together The Tuesday Team to create the President's ads. It doesn't get bigger than a presidential campaign, where you're targeting 100 million "consumers"—and we ended up getting more than 60 million of them to "buy" our product.

But even Hal Riney's "Morning in America" spot, which Republicans regard as the gold standard of political advertising (Democrats would pick the "Daisy" commercial that finished off Barry Goldwater in 1964), doesn't qualify as going orbital. That's because a presidential race isn't about the advertising. It's about the candidate, and Ronald Reagan was a helluva candidate. Even in my most vainglorious moments, I'd say his personal impact outweighed our commercials by a factor of 10 to 1.

Our insight to make Ronald Reagan the product was a good one. But this was one of those rare instances where the product was also talking. Reagan didn't need us to deliver his message. We just put a spotlight on him and added the soundtrack.

Unlike our experience with Pepsi-Cola.

BBDO had a long wonderful relationship with Pepsi, ever since 1960 when Charley Brower, a copywriter destined to become president of BBDO, created a new campaign for Pepsi with the theme line "Pepsi. For those who think young." It declared that there was something special about people who drank Pepsi. Pepsi's boss back then was a pragmatic, hard-driving man by the name of Al Steele. Though better known outside the company as the husband of movie actress Joan Crawford (which should tell you something about how tough he was), inside Pepsi his word was law. And the words he used after listening to our insight about Pepsi user differences were these: "I've had enough of this bullshit. We've got a very simple product here. We aren't selling steel-belted radial tires." To cap his outburst, he said, "You show me a guy with two lips, and I'll show you a customer."

So much for our groundbreaking theory about the customer as hero.

But we persisted and soon after initiated the concept that still prevails forty years later and still celebrates Pepsi as the soft drink for young-thinking contemporary people.

That concept—advertising that eliminated product attributes and competitive claims and focused largely on the end user—did not crystallize until BBDO copywriter Al Hoffman wrote three simple words: "The Pepsi Generation."

From that day on, Pepsi's advertising would exalt the user rather than sanctify the product. It was the start of lifestyle advertising. And it became one of our agency's signatures.

We developed other signatures over time, as we learned what you could and couldn't do in a commercial talking to a new generation. We learned the power of music—and we made people look at a commercial in a new way: with their feelings. This was a real "first." There were other "firsts." Pepsi was the first to use celebrities in a way that went beyond their celebrity; the first cola to publicly challenge the leader to a taste test; the first to use skywriting; the first to use entertainment as the primary appeal of a commercial, more primary than the selling proposition.

Okay, I'm bragging. But it isn't bragging if you've done it. That said, these firsts caught up with us as alert rivals caught on and emulated our style, stripping us of our parity-busting advantage.

By the 1980s Pepsi had lost some of its hold on its very own Pepsi generation, the 25 million baby boomers who were our target in 1964. But now those youngsters were adults and it was time to go after the next generation—their children.

That was one impetus.

The other came from Roger Enrico. He had just been named president of Pepsi-Cola USA. In a golden-boy career of steady successes at PepsiCo, Enrico was suddenly under more pressure than he'd ever seen before (and a company that has to face off with Coca-Cola every day knows about pressure).

Big multinational marketing operations such as Pepsi live and die by their projections, what they call the "plan." Company CEOs, division chiefs, and brand managers set their quotas for the year—the plan—and they are judged by whether they miss, match, or exceed the plan.

This is standard operating procedure at most companies.

But plans raise the deep philosophical conundrum, worthy of David Hume and Immanuel Kant, of how you write your plan. There are three philosophies. Do you set the quota low, and then come in like a conquering hero when you deliver numbers triple the size of the plan? (This is known as low-balling or "sandbagging the plan.") Or do you set a realistic target and then look like a consummate professional when you match it to the penny? Or do you set a super-aggressive quota, hoping it will inspire you to deliver heroic results?

All three approaches have their champions in the work-place. And as a rule, people don't cross over from one approach to the other. If you like to lowball your numbers, you will always lowball. It's not a bad thing if you deliver great numbers. It's certainly better than highballing the plan and missing by a mile. But it's not an attractive method; it implies deception or insecurity, which do not breed confidence.

Enrico's mentor and boss was known to sandbag the plan and deliver astounding numbers.

On his first day on the job, Enrico met with PepsiCo chairman Andrall Pearson, who told him that lowballing was not an option anymore. Pearson wanted a quota for Pepsi-Cola sales and market-share growth somewhere between high and aggressive—and he expected Enrico to "stretch" a little to exceed those numbers.

This is what was on Enrico's mind as we peered into Pepsi's future. He needed something big. He was ordering us to deliver big.

The Pepsi Challenge campaign had done its job and run its course. It was now showtime.

Critics say that when an ad agency resorts to celebrity advertising, it's a sign that the agency is out of ideas. That's true if you're still locked in the 1950s, plunking a familiar face like actor David Wayne in front of a camera to read the provocative lines "Hi, I'm David Wayne, and I'm here to talk about Preparation H." (I'm not making this up.)

But we had something else in mind. Use a celebrity, but not just any celebrity, the biggest one we could find, and put him or her in a carefully scripted scenario that functions like a mini-movie, with a beginning, middle, and end. We had done this with Michael J. Fox in "Apartment 10G," telling a story that aligned with his popular persona and yet moving it further along.

Now we were ratcheting up the stakes. Going after yet another Michael . . . Michael Jackson.

It started the day boxing promoter mogul Don King waltzed into Roger Enrico's Pepsi office to announce that he was now representing Michael Jackson exclusively for TV commercials. King was offering Pepsi the opportunity to sign the prince of pop for his first-time-ever TV commercial debut.

Recognizing a mega-idea when he saw one, Roger jumped on it. It doesn't get any bigger than having the number one star of his time pitch your product. This wasn't insightful, but when you're going orbital, insight often gets left on the launch pad.

Other forces were at work now—such as celebrity, glamour, global impact, sheer entertainment value. That's what Michael Jackson would bring to the table.

Mind you, this was the pre-weird Michael Jackson: still boyishly handsome, still face-lift-free, still years away from the tabloid frenzy that enveloped him in later years.

The irony for us was a role reversal. Usually it's the agency bringing an idea to the client. But here was the client bringing the idea to us.

Despite his enormous popularity in 1984, we knew we couldn't just put Michael on a stage and film him moonwalking. The commercials would have to make sense, integrate with our "Choice of a New Generation" message, and . . . uh, yes . . . show the product.

It was the week before the scheduled shooting of the spot

that Pepsi's Alan Pottasch and I met with Michael at his Encino, California, home (no, not Neverland). The estate had received a lot of attention over the years, mostly from hovering TV crews in helicopters, but the first time you visit the luxurious grounds with all the flora and fauna, you think you're in the first-class waiting lounge for Noah's Ark.

Michael was waiting for us with his father, Joe, and his attorney, John Branca (a nephew of the Brooklyn Dodger pitching legend Ralph Branca, the man who gave up Bobby Thomson's "shot heard round the world").

Our series of spots had already been approved and worked out in negotiations as intricate as the Israeli-Palestinian peace talks. Or so we thought. We were meeting to nail down the last-minute odds and ends that arise in any elaborate production. As we settled into a pleasant pro forma confirmation of what we had agreed on, Michael said in his familiar soprano tone, "I just have three things to say about the commercials.

"One, I don't like the storyboards.

"Two, I don't like the song.

"Three, you can't show my face."

It is a tribute to my cardiopulmonary vitality that I continued breathing. I shot a glance at Alan Pottasch, whose face was altering into the color of a ripe honeydew melon. Even Joe Jackson was stunned, running his hands through his hair and staring at his feet. He appeared to be loosening his tie, although he wasn't wearing one, and said to his son, "Let me understand this, Michael. You mean to say that you expect the Pepsi-Cola company to pay you five million dollars and they can't see your face?" With each word, Joe Jackson's voice traveled up the musical scale.

Joe knew what we knew—that the song and storyboard issues could be dealt with. But not showing Michael's face was a deal-breaker. No way we'd give in on that one.

An awkward silence followed. I hemmed and hawed and possibly sputtered. When you have nothing good to say, don't say it. Let the other guy feel awkward too.

Finally, Michael explained himself. "I just hate to see myself on television. I just hate it. How about showing just my glove? And my shoes and sunglasses. But not my face."

It occurred to me at that moment that, since the storyboards and song had already been approved, perhaps Michael, despite his soft breathy voice and gentle manner, was a shrewd negotiator using a string of objections to achieve his real goal—which was to mete out the precious seconds his audience would see the invaluable asset of his face. (In hindsight, given the radical cosmetic changes Michael's face has undergone over time, something else was going on here, something way beyond shyness.) From that moment—and I mean this literally—every raw scrap of screen time on Michael's countenance was a major negotiation. If you've got a stopwatch, you'll see we ended up with about a second and a half.

Not a bad thing, it turned out. Michael's instincts were right. The more you hold back, the more people will clamor. The brief, lightning-quick flashes of Michael's face actually made viewers eager for more of the sudden glimpses that had been so carefully portioned out.

Once Michael felt secure that we had understood his objectives, he became incredibly generous.

"As for the song in the commercial," he said, "why don't you take one of my songs?"

I thought: What song did he have in mind? Would this mean more tedious negotiating one week before the cameras rolled?

"Why don't you use 'Billie Jean'?" he suggested.

It was the last thing I expected out of him. For commercial use, most artists will pawn off one of their lesser hits, hoping to build more traction for them. Or sell you one of their mega-hits and charge you a fortune. But here he was offering the hottest song of the year, maybe the decade, at no extra charge.

Summoning up my best slick show business tones, I kept my cool and pushed for more. "That's great, Michael," I said, "but what about the lyrics? We need to include Pepsi in them."

"Well, change them," he said. "We'll make them Pepsi lyrics. Why don't we work on them together."

Suddenly I felt like $5 million.

Alan Pottasch and I took the red-eye back to New York, and by Saturday Ted Sann and I had worked out lyrics ready to try on Michael. I took the next 8 A.M. flight to Los Angeles and drove to his estate. At the door I was greeted not by Michael, but by his sister Janet, then a shy unvarnished teenager. (Her wardrobe-malfunction Super Bowl moment was twenty years into the future.) The resemblance to Michael was uncanny. So was the voice.

"Michael's not here, but he's expecting you. Make yourself at home," she said.

The house was empty, so I drifted into the kitchen. I couldn't help myself. Ever true to the client, I opened the refrigerator, delighted to find that it was jammed with cans of Pepsi. Not so surprising, since Alan had arranged to send Pepsi by the truckload to Michael.

As I surveyed the trophy room, which was a Michael Jackson museum of photos, Grammys, platinum records, and glittering costumes encased in glass—and he had just turned twenty-six—I heard a breathy voice behind me say, "Hi."

"This is going to be a first," I said. "I'm going to sing you the lyrics. Promise you won't laugh."

I then produced a Sony Walkman and, as we sat in a sunny nook of his den, sang over Michael's backing track of "Billie Jean" the Pepsi version of the lyrics.

You're a whole new generation
Dancin' through the day
Grabbin' for the magic on the run
You're a whole new generation.

You're loving what you do
Put a Pepsi into motion
The choice is up to you
You're the Pepsi Generation.

If future clients ever doubted my devotion to them, I thought, this is the scene that would back me up. An ad guy singing client-drenched lyrics to one of the most famous backbeats of all time . . . to the guy who wrote the song.

Michael listened, giggled over my singing, and said, "I like that." He unfolded a crinkled piece of paper to show me a two-liner he'd written for the chorus or the "hook." He sang,

Guzzle down and taste the thrill of today
And feel the Pepsi way.

I was concerned that the word "guzzle" was a beer term. But I didn't want to break our momentum. I could tell Michael was gung ho. He went straight to the phone, called his band, and arranged a recording session for the next night.

But he still hadn't signed off on the storyboard and I had carefully planned how to present it.

There is a peculiar danger in presenting storyboards. They tend to focus your audience on the literal details of the drawings, which makes it possible to miss out on the big picture and the spirit of the actual footage. So I had decided to act out the spots and let Michael fill in the blanks with his own considerable choreographic imagination. He listened and watched with remarkable patience as I dramatized and "danced" my way through a spot featuring a schoolyard pre-teen named Alfonso Ribiero, already a TV sitcom star at age eleven, jiving down a funky inner-city street, dressed like Michael Jackson, with the moves and gestures and élan of his hero. And then, as if by a miracle, lost in a moonwalk and a can of Pepsi, Alfonso bumps into Michael. Alfonso's face and body are suffused with surprise and joy. The viewer is swept up in the moment as Michael and Alfonso dance in unison with Pepsi fueling their magic.

Cue the tag line: Pepsi, the Choice of a New Generation.

"Oooh, this is great." Michael was squealing now. "It's gonna win every award in the book."

I remembered the trophy room. "Michael Jackson loves awards," I thought, "he's going to give us everything he's got."

With music and concepts now put to bed, all that remained was the shoot itself. Easy.

I don't want to give the impression that working with Michael Jackson was a seamless web of friendly cooperation, or that what you may have heard about his obsessive attention to minutiae is false, or that I see the world through a rose-colored Arriflex lens. That was dispelled the first day of our shoot.

Sparkling January Southern California weather was in sync with the good vibes coming off the set. Our director, Bob Giraldi (who had directed Michael's famous "Billie Jean" video), was filming from a "shot list" and a one-page synopsis that we had cobbled together. He had a crew of 200 people on the Universal Studios back lot in Burbank, and it was one of those days when all the gears were meshing. At least for the first 2 hours.

Bob came up to me. I wondered why he was the only face not smiling. Michael, he explained, was refusing to remove his sunglasses. You couldn't see his eyes or his expression. He looked as if he was doing the spot incognito. I hustled over to Michael's assistant, Sherry Dub, aka "The Dragon Lady" because of her fierce protective role.

I said, "Sherry, we're not shooting a Foster Grant spot here. We're doing a Pepsi shot. Please, let's lose the sunglasses."

Sherry gave me her practiced "drop dead" glance and said, "Michael likes his sunglasses. He doesn't take them off."

Inside me, anxiety and anger were having a footrace. I said, "Sherry, here it is. If Michael doesn't take off those sunglasses within five minutes, we're shutting this set down. And you can tell him he'll be in violation of his contract."

Poker time. I knew that during this ridiculous confrontation a crew of 200 people were standing idle, drawing paychecks. No way was I shutting the set down. But I hoped that Michael and his people believed I was crazy enough to do it. Sort of like Richard Nixon ordering the bombing of Haiphong on Christmas night.

Michael insisted. I persisted. Back and forth. And then a long silence. The minutes ticked by. I felt I was on the set of *High Noon*. Seconds before my 5-minute deadline, word filtered back through Michael's complex communication network that he would ungoggle.

The next three days went smoothly. We were getting great footage and Michael was on top of his game. Yes, he arrived late each day, but Michael had so much pride in his own abilities that he pushed to deliver his best.

He's also obsessively fastidious, with an almost religious devotion to the paraphernalia that makes him "Michael Jackson." Like his $10,000 bejeweled glove.

We were at the Shrine Auditorium in Hollywood on our last day of filming. Five thousand raucous, squirming, worked-up kids were in the audience as we prepared to film concert footage, complete with dancing and flashing lights and fireworks.

Michael and his brothers, the Jackson Five, were ready to storm onto the stage when Michael realized that he needed to make an urgent visit to the bathroom. The stomping audience continued to roar. Suddenly, from behind the closed doors of the bathroom, we heard Michael scream! Terrified, Alan Pottasch burst inside and discovered Michael, horrified and trembling, staring into the urinal where he had accidentally dropped his $10,000 glove. It was soaking.

By now several of us had gathered in the bathroom to fish

the glove from the bowl. (It is this moment, too, when I could remind clients about going the extra mile for them.) Outside, shouting, clapping, and whistling grew louder while inside we frantically patted the famous glove with paper towels to dry it off. Michael doesn't go on without it.

Finally, Michael was onstage, having regained his composure, prepared to do his magic, the soiled-glove episode behind him. The kids greeted him with tumultuous adulation. As the first take concluded, I watched with bemusement as Michael blew kisses to his fans with his still-damp glove.

Then we set his hair on fire.

It happened on an alternate take and would have been the last shot of the production no matter what happened. Michael's hair caught on fire from an exploding special-effects fireworks tower at the edge of the stage. It was a fluke, an errant leaping flame that somehow covered enough stage space to attach to Michael's hair. The rest is history. Within hours the accident was front-page news in every newspaper around the world—serious broadsheets such as *The New York Times* as well as lurid tabloids—and led the evening newscasts.

We had gone orbital—a little early and not for the right reasons.

That night Alan Pottasch and I visited Michael in the hospital, fearful that we had caused him terrible, irreparable harm. As we waited with Michael's family in a hospital anteroom, the atmosphere was thick with tension. Everyone was stunned into silence. And I couldn't help but feel that Alan and I were being viewed as the culprits. Then Joe Jackson, ever one to maintain good corporate relations, leaned over and whispered, "Don't worry, it's not that bad."

Joe was right. Michael's injuries were relatively minor,

bearing no resemblance to the life-threatening maiming the frenzied media were describing. He was released from the hospital within days and began reviewing rough cuts of our spots a week later. Less than a month after the accident, Michael appeared with his brothers onstage at Lincoln Center for the Pepsi bottlers' premiere of the spots. He received a tumultuous ovation.

I am a big believer in the law of unintended consequences, the notion that for every action there's a reaction, except that the reaction turns out to be the opposite of what you expected. Just as Michael's insistence on limiting his face time in the commercials ended up making his appearance more magnetic and alluring, so did the accident. It made the unseen backstage filming of a commercial a news event. It made the commercial itself, which aired a few months later on the Grammy Awards, an event too—perhaps the first time in history when a commercial was more anticipated than the television show surrounding it.

Back at BBDO, we took out our calculators and added up the "value" of all this. Crass as it seems, when you go orbital—when your commercials speed into the public consciousness in ways you never imagined—you have to check out the numbers to see if it's helping or hurting. We calculated that TV news coverage of Michael's accident added up to a minimum of $3 million in free airtime for Pepsi—and more than $10 million in newspaper and magazine exposures of Pepsi (sans Michael Jackson). It didn't hurt Michael's record sales either, which jumped immediately, going from their already orbital numbers to—what?—intergalactic.

Within a year, with no spending increase for media, awareness of Pepsi's advertising went up 24 percent, an astonishing number in a field where people slap high fives in agency corridors over gains of three-tenths of a point. Recall scores doubled the category norm. Nielsen shares increased a whopping two points in twelve months; that's $250 million a point.

Michael was also right about the awards. We walked away with more gold than Fort Knox—in all, seventy-four major creative awards.

Back at Pepsi headquarters, Roger Enrico was smiling too. He wanted big; he got BIG. He had always given us free rein. He also liked to say that he gave BBDO an unlimited budget and that we somehow managed to exceed it. But even he couldn't fault the results. Pepsi's market share continued its assault on Coca-Cola, and then the law of unintended consequences delivered its final ascending blow in our favor: New Coke.

I have already discussed in Chapter 2 how the Pepsi Challenge campaign induced Coca-Cola to change its formula, scrap its iconic flagship brand, and—in the greatest marketing bungle of all time—introduce New Coke. It wasn't just the Pepsi Challenge. It was the Pepsi Challenge followed up with the orbital impact of the Michael Jackson spots that sent spines quivering in Atlanta and made Coke blink.

We went orbital again the next year—this time with Madonna, the only female entertainer who young people would put on the same pedestal with Michael Jackson. Only this time the big news was our orbital crash landing.

We knew that Madonna would deliver instant consumer awareness and powerful attention to the product. Our aim was to give our young MTV-watching audience a reason to associate our brand with a personality they admired. We had chosen the first single off her new album, "Like a Prayer," as the music for our spot. We paid her handsomely, and if the spot ran continuously, it would work double-time to promote her album. A win-win.

The fact that Pepsi had hooked up with Madonna became a news event—more inside media circles than anywhere else, but still news. The fact that the commercial would air simultaneously with the release of her new album, her new song, and her new video was also attention-grabbing. Everyone was waiting for all four—album, song, video, and commercial.

At this point, a rabbi would say, "Oy." But it was the Catholic and Protestant communities that really howled. The "Like a Prayer" video was an incendiary, prurient mishmash of Christian church imagery that many people of faith regarded as obscene and sacrilegious. And because the video song was also the Pepsi song, all hell broke loose.

We weren't naïve. We knew that Madonna danced close to the edge of middle-American moral disapproval. But the video completely blindsided us; it went over the edge. That Pepsi and BBDO had nothing to do with the video, or even knew about it, didn't improve the situation. From the moment our spot aired on *The Bill Cosby Show,* Pepsi's fortunes were linked to Madonna's fall from grace. What was to be a triumphant marketing coup became a catastrophe. Viewers were confused. They did not differentiate between Madonna's video and our spot. The only way to end the confusion was to pull the spot and never air it again. Which is what we did. I had never understood what stockbrokers meant when they said, "Don't fight the tape." Something about a stock's momentum, I guess. But now I knew. When the tide is going against you, don't swim against it. We washed our hands of the whole affair, licked our wounds, and moved on.

Fortunately, we had other ways of going orbital, other ways of sticking with our strategy of high-risk, high-reward advertising—namely, the Super Bowl. At BBDO, we were slow to catch on to the showcase power of the Super Bowl. Keep in mind that this was the mid-1980s. The Super Bowl wasn't the catwalk venue where all the agencies got to strut their stuff. Not yet at least.

That all changed with Apple Computers' "1984" commercial, which ran on January 24, 1984, during Super Bowl XVIII. That was the commercial—a futuristic vision of a new world, symbolized by an athletic blonde sprinting toward the camera with a sledgehammer that she hurls at a screen showing Big Brother—that changed everything. Millions of people still recall that ad, which aired only *once*, but only football fanatics in California and Washington, D.C., remember that the Raiders beat the Redskins 38–9. That was the moment when the commercials began to overshadow the game itself.

At BBDO we watched the game and the "1984" commercial with awe and admiration. And envy. We wanted to do something mind-blowingly powerful like that too. The next few days, when we read how 200,000 consumers rushed to Apple dealers to check out the new Macintosh computer (which, incredibly, had not been directly shown in "1984"), we knew that the landscape had altered. The right spot on the

Super Bowl broadcast could, in fact, move the needle for a certain type of client.

If there's an insight here, it's the admission that times had changed and we were wrong. A mea culpa can be a very big insight. (What makes it an insight rather than just another idea, of course, is that it inspires action; it begets ideas.)

We had always known that the Super Bowl, perennially the TV event that draws the biggest viewership, was a magnet for consumers. But we always shied away from recommending it to our clients because reaching those 200 million American eyeballs was expensive—and anything you did would get mired in a cluttered commercial environment. Too many spots shouting for attention. On the other hand, it was a marketer's dream: the one day of the entire year when an advertiser can reach *every* demographic in the U.S.

As we dug deeper into the numbers behind the Super Bowl we also saw that people buy more soda, more pizza, more chips and snacks on Super Bowl Sunday than any other day of the year. An interesting fact that became *compelling* when we coupled it with some of our biggest clients—namely, Pepsi, Pizza Hut, and Frito-Lay. I remember the CEO of 1-800-FLOWERS describing Valentine's Day as his Super Bowl Sunday. He was using the Super Bowl as a metaphor for the biggest sales day of his year. Well, for many of our clients, Super Bowl Sunday was *their* Super Bowl Sunday, literally. And we were missing it.

The Michael Jackson experience—and response—emboldened us. The next year Ted Sann created a Pepsi spot specifically for the Super Bowl. Set in the future, it shows an archeology professor leading a class through a "dig" in a once-typical suburban home. The students drink Pepsi while they retrieve a baseball that the professor describes as "a spherical object they used to hurl at each other with great velocity as others looked on." An electric guitar is said to be a device that "produced excruciatingly loud noises to which they would gyrate in pain." When a student unearths an old Coke bottle, the professor examines it with zero recognition. "What is it?" asks the student. "I have no idea," says the sage. It was a cheeky spot, but not nasty, and totally in step with the hazing we liked to administer to our rivals from Atlanta. It turned out to be the most honored spot in BBDO history, winning the Grand Prix at Cannes, and was the first of a string of Super Bowl commercials from BBDO that were number one in viewer recall among all spots shown during the game.

That success opened the floodgates among our clients. Suddenly, they wanted to be on the Super Bowl, giving us the mandate (and the money) to make things super.

Visa, for example had us creating spots specifically for the game, and by 1989, Visa was the exclusive credit card sponsor of the Super Bowl, shutting out American Express again. Gillette launched the Sensor razor around the 1991 broadcast. Frito-Lay made it the linchpin of all its new product launches, from Jason Alexander for Rold Gold pretzels to Larry Bird and Kareem Abdul-Jabbar for Lay's chips to Elijah Wood daring folks to "eat just one" for Wavy Lays to former Miss USA Ali Landry introducing Doritos Puffs in a Laundromat (the Frito-Lay list is endless). Even FedEx, which had remained out of the Super Bowl fray since the early 1980s, came back to become a staple. In 1998 we produced the most inexpensive spot to ever run during the game. It was a commercial for FedEx. It showed a fictitious company scrolling an apology across a test pattern of color bars while the voice-over explained that the real commercial with dancing kangaroos and Garth Brooks couldn't be shown because "some boob" from the company's just-fired agency didn't use FedEx to send the tape to NBC. (I'm not sure which is more incredible about our "Apology" spot—that it cost so little to produce or that the FedEx brass had the courage to let us run with it.)

You could say that our insight about the Super Bowl also helped our agency go orbital, because it pulled in new clients like M&Ms and Snickers and Charles Schwab, who came to us, in part, for our Super Bowl work. At some point we were buying up so much time on the Super Bowl for our roster of clients that, as Bernice Kanner reported in her book *The Super Bowl of Advertising,* people inside the trade were calling it the BBDO Bowl.

But we didn't forget the power of using big-name celebrities to achieve liftoff for a client. From our "Madonna experience" we knew firsthand that celebrity endorsements were risky and could lead to public humiliation—something other agencies discovered too. They saw Cybill Shepherd claiming she doesn't eat red meat while she functioned as spokesperson for the National Beef Council. We saw her partner from the hit TV show *Moonlighting,* Bruce Willis, appearing in Seagram's wine cooler spots as headlines alleged he was in treatment for alcohol problems. Our eyes were open, but in the coming years our Pepsi spots would feature celebrated people ranging from Ray Charles to Billy Crystal to Cindy Crawford to Lionel Ritchie to Bob Dole to chess champion Garry Kasparov and NASCAR champion Jeff Gordon, all the way to Britney Spears and Beyoncé Knowles. And, oh yes, Don Johnson.

Remember Don Johnson? There was a brief moment in time when he capitalized on his 15 minutes of fame as the star of *Miami Vice*. In his suave Armani jackets as an undercover cop, he appealed to young people. Who knew he was playing a role?

I hate to be churlish about this so many years after the fact, but using Don Johnson in a Pepsi commercial is an object lesson in celebrity endorsement. We've given stage directions to billionaires. We've told Michael Jackson what to emphasize in a lyric (like he needed it). We've written lines for Ronald Reagan (like he needed them). We've given timing cues to Shirley MacLaine (like she needed them). In a career of working with hundreds of celebrities, I have only kind words for all of them—except Don Johnson.

It started out congenially enough: polite pre-production meetings, cordial phone calls on wardrobe and locations, even a relatively smooth contract negotiation. But as we drew closer to the first day of shooting, Don Johnson's amazing Amazonian ego appeared. He began an incessant patter of artistic differences with our accomplished director Ridley Scott, no slouch with *Alien, Black Rain,* and *Thelma and Louise* on *his* resumé. Every shot was followed by a mini-lecture by Don Johnson, throwing us into unnecessary hours of expensive overtime.

By not understanding Ridley's direction, nor wanting to, Johnson was diverting attention from the product to himself. He was breaking the unspoken rule of commercials: Nothing overshadows the product! No ego, no temperament, no fusillade of better ideas. Even Michael Jackson understood that when he changed the lyrics of his biggest hit for us. But Don Johnson thought the spot was about him and Pepsi was along for the ride.

Don had demanded contractually the right to refuse to touch or drink the product. It's a common practice, a celebrity's way of saying, "See? I really didn't sell out." That doesn't stop these same celebrities from "selling out" in Japan where their commercials won't be seen by friends and peers.

Once shooting began and we had grown weary of Don Johnson's charm, I went up to singer/composer Glenn Frey, whose hit song "You Belong to the City" was the musical backdrop for our spot. Glenn was a close friend of Don's and was costarring with him in the commercial. Feigning unfamiliarity with Glenn's contract, I asked him if he had a clause in his contract that let him refuse to touch or drink Pepsi. Glenn, as I was counting on, was surprised by my question. But he saw where I was going with this. When I told him that Don did have such a clause, he came up with a practical joke. Glenn knew that Don had been coveting the $200,000 Ferrari Testarossa that was a vital prop in the commercial. In fact, Don had been hinting all week that it would be a nice gesture if the Pepsi-Cola company would award him this car when the shoot wrapped—a nice thank-you for the privilege of Don's appearance.

No chance that would happen. Our $200,000 baby was going back to the dealership that leased it to us.

Our little joke was for me to call a "hold-it-a-minute" in the shooting at a point when Don was in the driver's seat next to Glenn. I would walk over to the car and gently ask Glenn if he would take a slug of Pepsi on camera. Glenn would adamantly refuse "what with the contract and all," leaving

Don to infer that they had similar product clauses. I then told Glenn that if he would put can to lips, I could convince the folks at Pepsi to give him the Ferrari.

I could see Don's jaw clench, then drop. But Glenn had not yet agreed.

Propping an icy, gleaming can of Pepsi on the dashboard, I said, "Please, Glenn, pleeeeeze. I really think I can let you drive these hot wheels home." (Hey, this was Hollywood. When in Rome, talk like the Romans.)

With perfect timing, Glenn waited a beat and said, "Give me the can."

The whole set cracked up.

Except for Don Johnson, who now realized that it was a joke, that he'd been set up.

From that moment on, with three days of filming remaining, Don would not utter a word to any of us. He cut off all communications and would only come out of his trailer to give us his professional but perfunctory performance.

Weeks later, Don's kettle was still simmering.

Just before we unveiled the commercial at the Pepsi bottlers convention in San Francisco, Don's agent, Steve Borno, called to say that Don would only appear at the convention, as he was contracted to do, if we came up with a cash "gift" to make up for the Ferrari joke.

When someone insults you, I've learned, it's best to make them repeat it. So I asked Roger Enrico to call Steve Borno and ask him to renew his "cash" request. Borno backed down. Don Johnson showed up at the convention, took a bow and left, and the commercial was a decent hit.

What Don Johnson doesn't know to this day is that before filming began, Ridley Scott had considered casting him as the leading man in his next feature film. Don's behavior on the set erased that idea and Ridley cast someone else instead.

I feel better now.

Lest you think I believe all actors have a great big soft spot in their hearts for themselves, finding it hard to settle for a Best Supporting Oscar while the product shines as hero, let me tell you about Billy Crystal and how well he fit himself into the complex, bewildering demands of a commercial production. It was a very happy experience.

It was a cold clear morning in February 1986. We were filming at New York's Silvercup Studios in Long Island City. Inside, on Stage 8, dozens of people were lounging on lipstick-red folding chairs, all gathered to shoot a spot introducing our new Diet Pepsi logo and packaging design. Billy Crystal was our star, playing his popular Fernando "You-look-mahvelous" Lamas. That phrase was sweeping the nation, and we aimed to capitalize on it.

The shoot began in earnest. Billy fired off his first line, gazing with mock affection at the new Diet Pepsi can. "You've changed your look, and, dahling, you look mahvelous!"

I stood at the back, silently watching a monitor. It wasn't happening. I wanted to pace but there was no room. I turned to Al Merrin, who wrote the spot, and said, "He's rushing the lines. It won't track when we intercut his words with our product shots. Would Billy be offended if we told him to slow down?"

This is what passes for lines of communication with a star on the set. The creative director turned to the producer who passed it on to the director, Patrick Russell, who hesitated for a moment, then cautiously approached Billy with soothing entreaties.

"For-get it!" Billy bellowed in his best Fernando accent. Everyone laughed.

I think Billy was putting us on, so I said, "Okay, bring in the better Billy Crystal."

He laughed again. Things loosened up considerably after that.

A crisis materialized, however, when we noticed that there was no room in the script or the camera setup to show the product—the can. It was a tight shot of Billy Crystal and it left out the product that was paying the bills! While we were solving this riddle, Billy started a private conversation with the Diet Pepsi can. He was entertaining himself as much as us.

"You not only look mahvelous, you taste mahvelous, too, my little twelve-ounce dahling."

And then he snuggled up to the can and gave it a little kiss. "Do you come here often?"

At that moment, I remembered what writer-director Nora Ephron had said about casting Billy Crystal in *When Harry Met Sally*: "You get Billy, of course, and you get free jokes." I prayed that the cameras were rolling and getting this stuff on film. One camera did. And we ran the spot pretty much the way Billy spoke it.

We showed it at the same convention where Don Johnson appeared. Billy's performance lit up the house, and as I watched the bottlers howling with delight, insisting that we show the spot again and again, I thought how pleasant the job can be when your star gets his ego gratification by energizing the game plan, not tearing it apart.

That's orbital, baby.

CHAPTER 12

PROTECTING YOUR INSIGHTS

There's no point in having an insight if you can't protect it. An insight that's been attacked—altered radically by compromise, or rejected by a client who doesn't "get it," or stripped by committee groupthink of its original insightfulness—is no longer an insight. It's just an idea or suggestion, no more valid than any other idea or suggestion casually tossed out in a meeting. If pursued it can turn into a boneheaded strategy.

To protect an insight you have to know the forces that are working against it.

- There are the forces of leveling, the people who try to reduce the insight to something familiar, something that they've heard or seen before. These are the people who judge an insight by its sameness rather than its difference with everything that has gone before.

- There are the forces of copying, the people who want your insight to be the same as what others are doing. "Give me one of those Nike campaigns," they tell you.

This is like leveling, only worse. You're not being asked for insights that bear a resemblance to other people's work; you're being asked to imitate other work directly. You might as well be tracing.

- There are the trembling midlevel forces at any organization who have the power to say "no" but not the conviction to say "yes." They can kill an insight simply by not being sufficiently confident in their own judgment to let it move up the chain of command.

- There are the people who don't share your standards. They lack either the experience or intelligence to take a chance with something new.

- Worst of all, there are the forces of mistrust, the people who do not cede insight, judgment, intelligence, or gut instinct to you, but prefer their own. This is the signal of a bad relationship that will end badly. When you do your best and the client doesn't agree, you both have a problem.

I don't mean to sound like an embittered advertising pro shuffling through his papers, remembering wistfully all the insights that coulda, woulda, shoulda happened if only the clients had been as smart as I was. But I've seen good insights choked to death, and I've learned a thing or two about how to protect them.

Protecting insights starts with a relationship. In the advertising business, possibly more than any other business in the world, relationships are critical. They're everything, in fact, because having a strong relationship with the client allows you to fail once in a while. You're not going to hit a home run every time out. But if you don't have that strong trusting relationship with the client, you won't be allowed to fail. You'll be looked at as a failure, rather than as a partner who has built up enough chips to be forgiven.

I recall the dark cold day in December 1982 when I went to Pepsi headquarters to present our new campaign for Pepsi. These are usually major events in our year, because Pepsi is a large showcase client. But they're also events at Pepsi, because we've been hitting homers for them for decades and the expectation level is high. We're a very important partner to Pepsi. Our proposed theme line for the next year, 1983, was "Oh, What a Time for Pepsi." And the spots we prepared were very slick in their use of music and film editing. Unfortunately, slick was all they were—and bloodless. They would not cause panic at Coca-Cola, nor inspire the Pepsi bottlers who actually sell the merchandise to the cola-drinking world. The silence at the end of that meeting with the Pepsi brass was chilling, like nothing I'd ever experienced before; the tepid response a week later from the bottlers was worse. But we had sufficient capital with Pepsi—in other words, trust—that we got a "do over." Our campaign deserved to be in jeopardy. Our relationship never was.

Relationships in the old days used to be the Good Old Boy network, East Coast division—guys who had gone to Princeton together, enjoyed three-martini lunches, and met for a round of golf in the middle of the week. Tales of a client admiring a pony for his daughter and the agency account executive delivering said pony to the client's home the next day were not apocryphal. This sounds like a cliché, but it wasn't back in the 1950s and early 1960s. The primary focus was on the *social* aspects of a relationship. This was the glue that held it all together. The creative work was secondary, and it showed.

That changed, mercifully, in the 1960s with the genius work of Bill Bernbach at Doyle Dane Bernbach and his acolytes. Suddenly daring work—landmark advertising for Volkswagen, Avis, Alka-Seltzer, among others—began to take center stage.

Nothing develops a great relationship with a client like great work. It's like opium. One taste of great work, particularly for clients who have never had it, and they want more. It gains their respect and trust.

I remember Allen Rosenshine bumping into Jack Welch on a Manhattan street corner once. Allen said, "Hi, Jack. You know Phil and the guys are coming up tomorrow to show you some new work. I hope you like it."

Jack said, "I'm sure I will. But if I don't, that's not a problem. I'm sure they'll get it right eventually."

That's trust.

But there's no point in developing trust with the wrong person. There's a clear pecking order in any client organization. It starts with what we call the "Junior G Men," the assistant brand managers who have the ability to kill your insight but not the authority to green light it. And it runs all the way to the chief marketing officer and the CEO. It's important to give lower-level people their due. But you should always be fighting for the eyes, ears, and minds of the people at the top.

There's a reason for this. The top people have access to more information. They know more about their company, their image, their strategy than anyone else. They're also very shrewd and insightful about their brand because they've grown up with it and they think about it every day. At companies where advertising is important, you're crazy not to see that the CEO is also the Chief Brand Officer.

The top echelon also know where they want to go because they are the final arbiter of where the company is going. And that has a positive effect on the work. When you have Fred Smith at FedEx or Jeff Immelt at GE approving your insights, it makes a big difference in the quality of the creative work—because it's people with their kind of vision and their sense of the future that can fuel the fires of great advertising. The top people also control your destiny. One time when I was feeling uneasy about our status on the FedEx account, founder and CEO Fred Smith reminded me, "Don't worry, Phil. Only Mike Glenn [chief marketing officer] and I can fire you."

Trust doesn't happen overnight. It starts with great work, of course. But you need a subtle (almost Machiavellian) strategy of increasing your face time with the top tier. It's happened so many times to me that I see it as part of a pattern now. You'll find yourself in a lot of meetings at the lower levels, and then one day the CEO decides to sit in on a meeting that his people are having with the agency. Or the lower-level people say, "We have to show this to the boss now." You'll present to the CEO and he'll respond to it. And he'll end up coming to other meetings, because he's discovering that the work we're producing—and the process itself—is exciting, entertaining, and fun. And it's teaching him, giving him other insights about the enterprise he runs. That's how relationships are built. At some point you discover that you can pick up the phone and call the CEO to suggest lunch or dinner, and he will accept the invitation because he knows you have his interests at heart and both of you might learn something.

It's a delicate game of diplomacy. The lower-level people you deal with on day-to-day matters are very sensitive about anyone going over their heads to the boss. If you play your hand with the top-tier people too aggressively, it can kill the relationship.

Some years ago a client CEO, who shall go nameless, called me on the road at my hotel room. It was an odd call at a late hour, but we had a strong relationship where I could be candid with him on many subjects. He said he was concerned about the people at one of his divisions (we handled their advertising and knew them well). He was talking about the advertising director, the marketing chief, even the division president.

"What is your concern?" I asked.

"I'm not sure they're any good. Can you—off the record—give me your opinion of them?"

"Off the record?" I asked.

He assured me it would go no further than the two of us.

So, I gave him the full-bore truth, that I thought his crew were some of the worst clients I'd ever dealt with. I itemized their errors in judgment, the opportunities they had missed, the weak links they had hired.

The CEO thanked me, assured me again that we were speaking off the record, and hung up.

The next day he called in his people and said, "Let me tell you what Phil Dusenberry thinks of you."

I know this is what happened because the division president, who kept his job despite my solicited diatribe, told me so when he fired us as his agency six months later. To this day I don't understand why the CEO did that.

That said, the best reason to cozy up to the top rung isn't just to get your work through unscathed. It's also to get direction from the proverbial horse's mouth. If no one at the client has a better idea of what makes the brand tick than the CEO, then it stands to reason that you need to get some direction from that person. There's nothing more dispiriting than creating what you think is a great campaign—based on an insight that has been applauded and approved all the way up the client ranks—and then hearing the CEO say, "That's not us." This happened to us when we had the Charles Schwab account in the mid-1990s. We developed the campaign working closely with senior Schwab executives. But when we presented it to the firm's chairman, Charles Schwab himself, he said, "That's not what we want to say about ourselves," dismissing weeks of work in a single sentence.

At that moment I felt my blood turn cold. I knew we were dead. Not just because Charles Schwab had his name on the building and knew his brand better than anyone else in the world, but because I didn't have a personal relationship with him that would give us another chance.

This is one reason why BBDO creative Charlie Miesmer won't lift a pencil on an account until he has sat down with the CEO, or as high up the ladder as he can get. Miesmer wants to sound the boss out on everything from what he thinks about the company to how he feels about humor or music in advertising. This is true whether it's a new account or a longtime client under new management. It's not that we want to spoon-feed the client what we think he wants, but there's no point in producing work that the client will never buy.

When it's firing on all cylinders, a great relationship will protect your insight even before it sees the light of day. I had a secret covenant for years with one CEO who insisted that I show him our creative work *before* his senior marketing people got to see it and approve it. And they had no idea. It was a surreal, delicious feeling to stand there and present our work to smart, demanding experienced marketing people, knowing that no matter what nits they could pick with it, it was already a "go." I don't believe this CEO's behavior was sneaky or evidence that he didn't trust his senior staff's judgment. As an ad guy, I welcome that level of intense involvement from the CEO. It showed me that he had a vision for his brand, and he knew it better than anyone else.

CEOs can get overinvolved though. In their enthusiasm for what you're doing, they can forget that an insight (and the campaign that follows) needs time to flourish. In their eagerness for something new and fresh, they might be too quick to pull the trigger and put a bullet into a concept still pulsing with life.

Many years back, we created a dozen magazine ads for our client, Shaeffer pen. Shaeffer's CEO was so pleased with the result that he had all twelve ads framed and hung in the hallway leading to his office, where he could proudly see them every time he walked by. Three months later, he called our then chairman Tom Dillon and said, "Tom, it's time to change the campaign. As much as I love it, I think it's worn out."

The normally unflappable Dillon hemmed and hawed, puzzled about how to handle the most premature withdrawal in agency history.

Finally he got the words out: "Bill, I don't know how to say this, but the campaign hasn't . . . run yet."

If you're in the insight-generation business (and this doesn't apply just to advertising), you have to think of yourself as someone imparting expertise, even wisdom. You have to think of yourself as an advisor, which means that people will be looking to you for advice. Age, title, and rank aren't the barriers here; you can be a rookie or a veteran. It's the quality of your thinking. That's how you build relationships with people at the top.

But if the old practice of martinis, golf, and gifts doesn't apply anymore, there's a new way to squeeze glue into a relationship. Be the client's advisor and friend, not necessarily in that order.

I learned this when I was a relative youngster, still in my thirties, and Alan Pottasch, head of creative services at Pepsi, asked me to help write an important speech he had to give at a Pepsi bottlers convention. A simple request; I was happy to do it. If you can help a client in this way, you are forging a relationship, and you are doing so *at his request* rather than on your own. It not only put me on Alan's good side, which would come in handy when I needed backing, but it forced me to see things from Alan's point of view, not just about a soft drink in a can but about one of his more important constituencies—the all-powerful bottlers. I was establishing my role as "advisor" rather than "ad guy." It was a new way of bringing a pony to the client's home, but it was an act of *friendship* rather than a *payoff*.

Bringing up Alan Pottasch leads me to my penultimate (and paradoxical) point about insight protection. The best way to protect your insight is to give it up; let the client own it. I've always found it interesting that in any successful campaign, the client thinks it's his success (and he's right) while the agency thinks its theirs (and they're right too). If you can create a seamless line of creativity where no one knows where the big idea came from, and no one cares, you are in the ideal position. As a wise man said, it's amazing how much can be accomplished when no one cares who gets the credit.

This has been my relationship, and BBDO's, with Pottasch and Pepsi. They say (and the history of the world bears this out) that no one is indispensable. But Alan may be the exception to the rule. How else do you explain that he has been influencing Pepsi's creative image for more than 40 years, through a dozen CEOs and a maze of campaigns and product launches, and that nearly 15 years after most people retire he's still on the job and on top? Alan Pottasch is the keeper of the creative flame at Pepsi, the one man who has seen it all, done it all, remembers it all.

Someone like Alan should exist at every successful company. I like to think of this person as the enterprise's Chief Consumer Officer, or CCO. Every company needs a CCO, somebody who is in charge of looking after the company's consumer, in terms of defining who they are, what they're doing, what their likes and dislikes are, what their latest urges and grudges may be.

At ad agencies in recent years this job has fallen on the broad shoulders of what we call the "planner," a senior person who doesn't have to worry about writing commercials or massaging clients. He's paid to watch the big picture, to worry about the clients' brands and the agency's relationship with them. Mostly the planner focuses on the clients' customers—the consumers. He makes it his business to understand their preferences, moods, and personal values.

It's different at other enterprises. In a restaurant the CCO might be the maitre d', who's keeping an eye on the tables, the front desk, the mood of the room, even what gets eaten and what is left on the plate. At newspapers it's the relatively new role of ombudsman, someone to review the paper's policies and performance as if he were the readers' advocate. At my wineshop in Sag Harbor, where a Chief Consumer Officer might be unaffordable, the owner might assume the role himself, manning the cash register, constantly surveying the shop and noting who's buying what and how much.

My point is, every business has someone like this in one form or another. It might be the head of marketing or the advertising director. Or it might be a sharp up-and-comer in the middle ranks. Find that person. Find clients who have the greatest personal interest and passion for protecting their brand. If you align your insights with their goals, they will give you all the protection you need. Because you and they are one and the same.

CHAPTER 13

BUILDING A FOOLPROOF INSIGHT CREATION MACHINE

A few times a year I run a three-day creativity seminar for BBDO's creative directors. It's a chance for the agency's top creative people from every corner of the globe to show their work and catch up on what's working and what's not in territories few of us ever visit or hear about. Not every great advertising idea or technique is born in the U.S. or the U.K. or Japan. Great insights materialize everywhere. That's why we get together, to applaud each other and to bat around notions on how we can do better. In 2004 in Barcelona I opened up the seminar with a formal "keynote" address. I spent two hours telling the elite 150 members of BBDO's worldwide creative team that "it's all about the creative work." If you do great creative work that hits the target and makes you strut with pride, everything else falls into place. You keep old clients, lure in new clients, move the needle, and win awards.

Extolling the virtues of being creative, especially to a group of creative directors, is kind of obvious, no? It's like going to a professional basketball players convention and reminding attendees to "be tall." But I know from experience that you can never remind the troops too often to stick to their creative guns. The anti-creative forces at any agency are powerful, pernicious, and numerous. They come in tricky shapes and sizes, but they all are after the same thing: they want you to compromise, to split the difference between your beliefs and someone else's, and settle for a little less than perfect.

You see it with agency executives and advertisers who only trust creative work that "tests well"; they're afraid to trust their gut. (And people who don't trust themselves tend to not trust others.)

Or work that keeps the client happy (even though it's our job to go light-years beyond what the client expects).

Or work that moves the needle, any needle (hey, lowering prices is a surefire way to move *a* needle, but it's not necessarily the right one for the long run).

Or work that copies the competition (though stunningly few "me too" campaigns have ever impressed the buying public).

Or work that wins awards (but doesn't move the needle on sales).

I could go on, but you get the point. Creative integrity is under perpetual attack in *any* organization, not just ad agencies. And people need to hear that it's all right to stick to your principles and your insights in the face of overwhelming opposition. People in any workplace need periodic pep talks.

It's no different from a football coach giving a rousing locker-room speech before each game. You'd think that players armed in helmets and pads and adhesive tape and gleaming uniforms emblazoned with their names and numbers, butting helmet to helmet, pad to pad, to prepare for on-the-field combat, would be sufficiently stoked before running onto the field, that they would *not* need anyone to tell them to "play hard" and "win." But they do. Every week, every game. And probably again at halftime.

It's in that Knute Rockne spirit of inspiring creative warriors that I offered that group in Barcelona my eighteen guidelines (not rules) for creative directors. They apply to any manager, big business or small, mundane or cutting edge, who needs to inspire ideas—and I share them with you here.

CAUSE INSIGHTS TO HAPPEN RATHER THAN CREATE THEM. You can't write every commercial yourself, or come up with every theme line, or deliver every great insight. It's not possible if you want your business to grow. You only have so many brain cells and only 24 hours in a day. In other words, you are limited.

Face it, accept it, and start relying on other people's creativity—and your business will take off.

Not long ago a group of my lifelong colleagues—guys I had hired and worked with for three decades—happened to be gathered around a conference room to go over some pro bono work we were doing for New York City. As admen are wont to do (especially elder admen), we started shooting the breeze about the good old days, with everyone recalling all the great ads they wrote for the agency, the songs they composed, the actors they discovered and cast, how they came up with the ideas. It was lively, entertaining chatter among seriously strong personalities, and I barely got in a word edgewise. After the impromptu session broke up, an objective observer in the room, noting how little I said, turned to me and asked, "Were there any ads that you wrote, Phil?" I knew it was a joke, but for a moment the remark made me bristle. Joke or not, was this guy challenging my creative chops?

But as I thought about it, perhaps I was overreacting. The time was long past when I had to prove I could write my own copy. If the agency had relied solely on my creative output, we'd have two clients instead of 200, one lonely office instead of 160 (and you wouldn't be reading this book). Somewhere along the way, I had made the subtle shift from *needing* to create insights myself to *wanting* to cause insights to happen in others. It's the difference between being a star and a manager—between being Derek Jeter and Joe Torre—and I had found a greater benefit in being the latter.

That's what I was trying to impart to the creative directors. If they could take as much pride of authorship in a colleague's good work as they do in their own, then their business would not only double over time but the growth could be exponential. After that, the remaining guidelines tell you how to make it happen.

HIRE PEOPLE SMARTER THAN YOU ARE. David Ogilvy said this a half century ago in *Confessions of an Advertising Man,* and I've heard it echoed in speeches by every great agency chief since then. But the fact that it needs to be repeated every year (and that I'm repeating it too) says something insightful about human nature and why some businesses will always prosper while others will always flounder. It starts with the people you hire.

As Jack Welch once said about playing sandlot baseball, "When you were small, you were always the last one picked for the team and put out in right field. The years passed, and then *you* were putting guys out in right field. You learned one thing as you got older: you picked the best players and you won."

Despite the slap-on-the-forehead obviousness about choosing great people, a lot of managers still don't do it. Who can say why? Perhaps they don't recognize talent when they see it (in which case they shouldn't be managing *anything*!). Perhaps they can't afford the best. (But that's why God created banks and credit lines. If you hire the best, there's little risk in borrowing against the future; the biggest risk is *not* doing it at all.) But when you dig deep, the root cause is the fragility of the human ego; people feel threatened by gifted, strong-minded people. It's such a powerful impulse that they will do it even though they know it's career suicide. Ogilvy said it best. "If you're a ten and you hire a nine and that nine hires an eight and that eight hires a seven, eventually you will become a company of midgets. If you hire people bigger than yourself, you will become a company of giants."

ALWAYS GAUGE A PERSON'S PASSION FOR AN IDEA. And give it a little more weight than it deserves. All things being equal, a passionate advocate for an insight will trump a dispassionate one. And you want that person on your side in the heat of battle.

When I was running my own agency in the 1970s, I found myself at a meeting with the marketing chief at a major home-products company. It was his job to eradicate cockroaches from the U.S. mainland, and such was the parlous state of affairs at my agency that I was trying to hold onto his account. It may be the most dispiriting meeting of my life.

I should have realized that the moment his assistant ushered me into his office. There he was, posed with his back to me, in his beautifully pressed seersucker suit, puffing on a pipe, gazing contemplatively out a window at a lovely lake below his corporate park office window in the wilds of Connecticut. I stood there for a few moments as he made a dramatic show of ignoring me. Then I heard a voice speaking. It was Seersucker. But he hadn't yet turned around to greet me, shake my hand, and invite me to sit down. He was saying something about his business, but the words were muffled by the window and the fact that he wasn't facing me. It sounded like he was the public address announcer at a very noisy stadium, and I couldn't quite make out what he was saying.

Finally he turned to me, faintly clicking his heels. I felt I was about to be briefed by General George Patton rather than by the marketing chief for the insecticide division of a home products company in suburban Connecticut.

He launched into a pep talk, psyching me up so that I would do my utmost to create the best conceivable campaign for his company's cockroach spray. This fellow literally foamed at the mouth with hatred for the vile cockroach. He painted a lurid picture of the many sadistic forms of torture we might visually incorporate into our television spots. I took him through several storyboards I had brought along with me. But the "kill aspects"—his favorite phrase—weren't sufficient. He demanded that we show the cockroach in evermore agonized death throes. This man, I thought, really hates cockroaches! That's very impressive.

At the same time, however, I was one step away from bursting out laughing because his ideas were so vulgar and stupid that I knew our relationship would end the moment I left his office. How could I work on this account? This was not a client I wanted occupying any share of my mind in the future, nor did I feel I could ever deliver the strange and cruel messages he was expecting from me. He was passionate about destroying insects. I didn't share that passion. Like a bad marriage where one partner loves the other more, much more, we got divorced. Amicably.

But what I took away from that meeting was an inviolate appreciation of people's passion for their job, their mission, their ideas. In this case, passion about something mundane, but passion nonetheless. In a perverse way, Seersucker remains the gold standard in my mind for passionate advocacy. (If I ever need someone to deal with a cockroach invasion, he'd be my first call.) Thirty years later he still flashes into my vision for a split second whenever I hear some young executive vigorously, even wildly, defending his or her position. The exec may be wrong, misguided, over the top, and out of control, but you can't discount the passion. Passion is good.

JUDGE AN INSIGHT ON ITS MERITS, NOT ON HOW YOU WOULD HAVE DONE IT. Easy to say, tough to do, particularly if you have a strong philosophy that's working. Your approach has been validated by success. Shouldn't everyone follow your lead? Not necessarily. If you force-feed every insight and execution through your prism, you are bringing otherwise smart people *down* to your level. If you insist that people only do it as you would have done, you are creating lesser versions of you. This is the creative equivalent of hiring weaker than you are.

If it isn't apparent yet, my advertising favors powerful emotions and humor. Not everyone works that way. At BBDO we had a fellow named Phil Slott whose work was consistently different from the precepts I had mandated. And yet it was undeniably good and effective. One of my favorites was Phil's campaign for Dry Idea deodorant that played on the phrase "Never let them see you sweat." In one spot he had the actor James Wood explaining the three rules for auditioning: "Know your lines cold, act as if you don't need the job, and never let them see you sweat." It was a great spot, not only because it cleverly dealt with the product's two big negatives: (a) deodorant is a low-interest category (few people think that their day won't be complete unless they get the right deodorant) and (b) you can't actually show the product being used (at least not if you want to keep people watching). But more than anything else, it had a powerful insight. With deodorants, people expect that it works immediately and that it will keep on working as the day wears on. Those are the essential desires for a deodorant. Phil's campaign leapfrogged those limitations by taking it to a psychological level and making an artful association between deodorant and success. Dry Idea not only did its basic job, but if you used it, you would get ahead faster. The campaign won awards, injected "Never let them see you sweat" into the lexicon, and moved the needle at a time when Dry Idea was being challenged by a dozen parity products. I would have been a fool to mess with it just because it wasn't emotional or funny. It was sly and effective, which more than filled the bill.

DON'T BE SURPRISED BY SURPRISES. In every creative endeavor it makes perfect sense to be open to accidents, messes, failures, and other disasters—and treat them as potential strokes of good luck. Because surprises, good or bad, whether caused by massive natural forces or the tiniest mishap, have a way of surpassing our earthbound imaginations and inspiring . . . magic.

The single most memorable Pepsi commercial our agency ever made—certainly in terms of generating favorable mail to Pepsi headquarters—was 100 percent accidental. We had a scripted vignette for a little girl visiting her grandmother in a bucolic farmhouse setting. The storyboard called for cute and heartwarming, so we "cast" a bunch of furry puppies for the shoot, hoping that something cute and heartwarming would materialize. Nothing worked out, and as the day wore on and the little girl and puppies became more restless (and less useful), we took a break from shooting. That's when a little boy on the set accidentally spilled some Pepsi down his shirt. You couldn't see the stain, but the puppies caught on very quickly. They were attracted to the sweet taste. Within a heartbeat, they were all over the little boy, licking him and jumping up and down. Everyone saw it. Fortunately, somebody got the camera going and caught the boy being tickled and laughing hysterically (while we prayed, "Please don't run out of film"). We punched in the boy's giggling later on in post-production. As I say, it may be the most beloved Pepsi spot of all time, and it's totally serendipitous. I doubt we would have had the imagination to create a tickling and giggling scene from scratch, not only because it's hard to get three-year-old boys and little puppies to perform on cue but because it simply would never have occurred to us. But that's the beauty of surprises. The only thing unsurprising about them is how far they exceed our imagination.

Somebody needs to be your group's Chief Serendipity Officer, alert to strokes of luck that others miss. Why not you?

DON'T COMPETE WITH YOUR PEOPLE. The biggest interpersonal flaw in any creative director's toolkit (and managers' too) is the constant overriding need to win. When it matters, we want to win. When it can go either way, we want to win. Even when it doesn't matter at all, we still want to win. When you're the boss, you can afford to ease up on this need to win. Cede a debating point, an execution of an idea, even ownership of a concept at least once a day—and you'll have people praising your open-mindedness and feeling much more free to think boldly (because they know you won't *always* be automatically stomping on their suggestions). It's a great habit to fall into. It doesn't mean you're weak and letting standards slip. It means you're strong enough to let others win their share. Most important, it shows that you're flexible, not doctrinaire, about what works and what doesn't. The payoff shows up in the more adventurous work people start bringing into your office for your approval.

RESPOND WITH YOUR GUT FIRST, YOUR HEAD SECOND. Not only because this is how consumers do it, but because it's the most trustworthy meter for an insight's power. If you laugh, it's funny. If you cry, it's moving. If you feel a jolt of any kind, it's breaking through the clutter. When you don't feel it in your gut, chances are the notion won't fly. Then your head can take over. Critique the work, send it back, and tell your team to do better.

ADD VALUE TO AN ALMOST-THERE IDEA. FORGET THE ALSO-RANS. Any sharp experienced creative director can add something to a bad idea. But why bother? You're only elevating the bad to mediocre. A bad idea, supported by nonexistent insight, should never see the light of day, certainly not for the less-than-persuasive reason that you spent a lot of time working on it. Save your brainpower for the undeniably good insights that are just a hair short of perfect. This is not only prudent time management, it's how great agencies are built. If you can add 10 or 20 percent of value to a concept or execution—whether it's by changing one word in the headline, tweaking copy, tightening up the edit, or brightening up the sound mix—then you're earning your keep and, in turn, raising rather than dropping the performance bar in your organization.

In November 1996, Visa assigned us the launch of the Visa Check Card. The card's benefit was simple: when you make a purchase with Visa's Check Card, there's no need to show even a single form of identification. We needed a breakthrough spot that would air in less than three months during the 1997 Super Bowl. Among several approaches we presented, one leapt to the top: a series of humorous scenarios showing well-known people prevented from paying with a personal check because they didn't have proper identification. The payoff: this doesn't happen when you have a Visa Check Card. But the concept didn't click for us until someone suggested casting Bob Dole in the first spot. Dole had just been defeated in his run for president against Bill Clinton. He had been on TV every day for a year and, at that precise moment, was probably the second best-known face in America. That suggestion added 20 percent to an already strong concept. And it made all the difference. Within minutes, Jimmy Siegel dreamed up a spot showing Dole returning to his hometown of Russell, Kansas, for a hero's welcome: a parade, banners shouting "Welcome home Bob," the locals greeting him by his first name. Dole ends up in a diner where even the waitress greets him with an affectionate "Bob"—until he offers to pay his tab with a check. She freezes him with an icy glare and asks, "Need to see a little ID, Bob." The spot won Visa immediate attention, not only for its wit but because casting the Republican nominee in a funny spot was newsworthy. But that's what happens when you push to make something a little better. It ends up making it a *lot* better.

BE REALLY TOUGH ON THE WORK. With the accent on "really." I learned this from my first mentor, John Bergin. He would get verbally, even physically abusive when people presented him with unacceptable work. He would throw people out of his office, tear up the work in front of them, threaten dismemberment and unemployment. It was childish, boorish, and completely persuasive. He once took a set of campaign storyboards that people had been working on for weeks, looked at them, then opened his window and tossed them out to the street 12 floors below. I'll never forget the cardboard sheets wafting down onto Madison Avenue and 46th Street— like a sad, pathetic ticker-tape parade for the rejected. He taught me that the power to stop bad work was the only true power a creative director possessed. You can't predict when the great work appears or if the client will appreciate its greatness or, for that matter, how the public will respond, but you damn well can stop bad advertising from getting out the door. Bergin taught me that your "no's" are far more decisive in setting your standards than your "yes's."

And I took that to heart. If something didn't feel right, if I felt the slightest hesitation or doubt, I'd press the reject button. Bergin also taught me to heed the siren call of compromise when a deadline was pressing me to approve something. Never let a due date or client meeting the next day convince you that something's ready when you know it isn't. Send it back. Make everybody stay at their desks all night if you have to. Cancel the meeting (as a last resort). And don't feel too bad about it. You'll feel a lot worse if you compromise and let something less than great get through.

BE DIRECT. DON'T LET PEOPLE LEAVE YOUR OFFICE WONDERING IF THEY'RE ON THE RIGHT PATH. I often made this mistake in my first years in a supervisory position. People would come into my office and, even though I knew I was looking at work that I would never let out the door, I'd mix my concerns with words of encouragement. But people, predictably, only heard my encouraging remarks; they tuned out my negative critiques. I would talk about the work and even be critical of the work, but by treating it seriously, I would dignify the work with more import than it may have deserved. People would leave my office not knowing that I really hated it. Perhaps I was a little more concerned about keeping spirits up than I should have been. But eventually I found a more effective method for delivering the brutal truth when I didn't like what I was seeing. This meant . . .

ALWAYS HAVE A REASON FOR YOUR OPINION. This lets you attack the work rather than the person who created it. I would never say, "You're an idiot for showing me this!" Not my style. And my reasons were fairly basic and predictable: The work wasn't memorable. It wasn't breakthrough. It's been done before. It's off strategy. It sounds familiar. Anything less than giving valid reasons for a rejection only solves half the problem. People knew I hated the work, but they didn't know why or how to do better. "I don't like it" is only the headline. *Why* you don't like it is the body copy. You don't have a complete message without both halves. And so I focused on giving people not only clear rejections but clear directions. You can't just be the creative rejecter. You have to be the creative director.

ONCE YOU SAY YES TO A CONCEPT, DON'T BACKPEDAL ON IT. Back your approval all the way. This should be self-evident. You will only confuse people if you hedge on your judgment, question your standards, and cave in at the first instance that a client doesn't share your enthusiasm for the work. This isn't a license to become adversarial with the client; you don't get far fighting the people who pay the bills. But your people are looking to you to display as much spine in supporting the team's concept as you exerted in bullying and browbeating the team to produce it. Anything less is phony.

BE THE BOSS EVERYONE WANTS TO WORK FOR. You will be that person if you do all of the above. That's the paradox. It's the really tough creative directors (and any other type of manager) for whom people most often want to work. It's not that creative people are masochists. On the contrary, they're fragile and sensitive. At every opportunity, they tend to go easy on themselves. That's why the best of them respond brilliantly to demanding bosses. They need the tough love because they rarely volunteer to administer it upon themselves. It's certainly true in sports. Given the choice, football players prefer to play for a really tough taskmaster than a coach who lets them slide by with less-than-total effort. They revel in the brutal workouts, the vicious sideline hectoring, and the outrageous demands the coach places on them. A more lenient, relaxed coach tends to earn their contempt rather than their respect. On that note . . .

MAKE YOUR OFFICE THE QUAKE ZONE. No matter how pleasant and easygoing your personality, your office—where everyone arrives to show their work—should not be an oasis of comfort and ease for visiting employees. They should feel a twinge of discomfort and fear, akin to stage fright, before they walk in. The more they quake, the less they'll waste your time with work that's less than their best. I never appreciated this until an observer noted how the demeanor of even my most senior people altered from confidence to nervousness when they came into my "lair" to display their layouts. He called my office the "quake zone." It was never my intention to scare people, but the effect has value. Develop a steely toughness (that look in your eye) and your people will respond accordingly.

NEVER LET THEM HEAR YOU BITCH AND MOAN. When people hear you complain, they take it as permission to complain too. Whatever misgivings you have about a client or a superior, keep them to yourself. They deflate morale, make you look weak, and create an environment that breeds negativity like a contagion.

KNOW YOUR PEOPLE AND PLAY TO THEIR STRENGTHS. David Ogilvy liked to say that in the advertising industry "we hire the kind of people our clients would never hire." He was explaining why clients, even with their deep bench of clever brand managers and marketing experts, could never do great advertising in-house. Too many constraints. Too many corporate voices. Too many by-the-book number crunchers. Too much groupthink. Not enough off-the-wall thinking.

It's true. The best creative departments are overrun by people who couldn't land a decent job (and keep it) in any other field. (My wife says I am one of those people.) Advertising attracts a healthy share of talented misfits, eccentrics, and people who (to quote Duke Ellington) are "beyond category." The best agencies indulge, pamper, and celebrate such people. They pay them well, envelop them in a serene corporate office environment, and don't ask them to conform to dress codes or regular office hours (whatever that means!). And they exploit any quirks as if they were a corporate asset.

For my entire career I always seemed to have at least one or two amateur guitar pickers on my creative team. They were smooth, serious guys who could comfortably have a dinner meeting with any chairperson of a Fortune 500 company and create business rather than lose it. But they also kept fancy acoustic guitars propped up near their worktables at the office. I'm sure that's why so many of the commercials that made our agency's reputation were driven in part by great music. Because these guys wrote the tunes and lyrics for General Electric, Pepsi, Gillette, you name it. I don't know too many fields where an employee's quirky hobby can exert such a heavy influence on the end product. But a creative director would be squandering corporate resources if he or she didn't exploit these quirks.

PLAY TO THEIR WEAKNESSES, TOO. If you know your people, you'll also figure out how to convert their weaknesses into strengths. I once had a fellow—we'll call him Nick— working for me, a terrific copywriter, who always needed a fire lit under him before he would work in earnest. Some of it was your basic-issue procrastination, not uncommon among writers, but I suspected that he had grown too comfortable working in a team. He always knew that if he didn't come up with the goods, one of his teammates would. The team was his cushion, and he took great comfort in it. Too much comfort, I concluded.

One day, as I was heading off for a two-week business trip to Europe, a very important project for Pepsi landed on my desk. It had to be delivered in two weeks and there was no one but Nick available to work on it. Everybody else was tied up with other projects, and I would be out of the office. With few options at my disposal, I thought I would try something different. I called Nick into my office and said, "I'm going away for two weeks. I need you to work on this, and guess what, Nick, you are the only one working on it. The entire campaign is on you." I removed his cushion.

He could have responded in two ways. He could have folded. Or he could have shouldered the responsibility for the first time in his career. I knew I was rolling the dice with Nick, but I also knew that I was doing him a big favor. If he failed, I was helping him see that he was at the wrong company. If he rose to the occasion, I was helping him convert a weakness into a strength.

When I came back two weeks later, Nick was jumping out of his skin to show me his concepts. He had literally papered every inch of his office walls with layouts and storyboards. It was the best work he'd ever done, and the client loved it. After that success, Nick never needed to be roused to action again. He could start up on his own.

GET A LIFE OUTSIDE THE OFFICE. Or you'll never be able to bring the real world into your work. So much of the insights and words and emotions that find their way onto the magazine page or TV screen have nothing to do with customer research or the client's brief or the account strategy. They're ideas that come from our personal shelf of experience. If you're a movie buff, that passion will somehow inform your work. If you regard baseball as a religion, you'll—consciously or not—find ways to use baseball as a vehicle for telling stories. If you're going through a tough romance, that heartbreak might end up in a commercial for something as unexpected as a soft drink—and yet it will ring true. Al Merrin, one of our senior creative directors, drew on his own experience of a troubled romance when he created the award-winning Pepsi spot "Something in Common." Two soon-to-be-former lovers angrily vow to have nothing to do with one another ever again and slam down their phones. Moments later, in their neighborhood grocery store, they are startled to nearly touch as they both reach for the same can of Pepsi. They remember how much they have in common. The viewer, in that brief moment, credits Pepsi as the catalyst of their reunion.

The richer your life beyond the business, the richer the work within. So, get a life. Before you can move the needle for others, you have to move your own.

CONCLUSION

In the introduction of this book, I mentioned how I wanted this book to be as useful to the guy who owned two Laundromats in Kansas City as it was to a brand manager at a major corporation or to a young person thinking about a career in advertising.

I didn't use the Laundromat example casually. Sometimes when I'm really bored or need to give my pulse rate a jolt, I think about what would be the absolute worst client an ad person could ever have. The answer I always come up with is a Laundromat. Think about it. A Laundromat has got to be the gold medal winner in the Olympics of commodified businesses. There is nothing special about a Laundromat. It's certainly not unique or special as a service establishment. It's so commodified, in fact, that there aren't any Laundromat employees on the premises to actually provide the customer service. You go in and do everything yourself. You bring your dirty laundry. You bring your coins (and if you only have bills, there's a machine rather than a person to make change). You even bring your own reading material and your own laundry detergent (which is like bringing your own beans to Starbucks and then brewing the coffee yourself). Basically, a Laundromat is little more than a noisy, uncomfortable reading room. I just shake my head when I think about trying to create great advertising for such a business.

If the mundane commodified attributes of the Laundromat industry weren't enough to give me the shakes, there are also the tough-to-pin-down features of the people who use Laundromats. They are either people who do not have access to their own washing machines and dryers, or cannot afford washers and dryers, or live in small apartments or homes that cannot accommodate washers and dryers, or have a transient lifestyle that requires them to do their laundry on the run. Whatever the reason that places them in a Laundromat on a Friday night or Sunday morning, these are hard people to identify, qualify, and reach.

Phew, what a tough business!

Then I played in a golf foursome with a prosperous looking gentleman named Ed. Ed was from Kansas City. He was a great guy, in his early forties, with a beautiful golf swing and a low handicap that suggested he spent a lot more time on the golf course than at work. He wore a multiple-warhead Rolex on his wrist, played in a golf shirt with an Augusta National logo on it, and had the latest Callaway ultra-super-titanium clubs in his bag. For a moment there, I wanted to *be* Ed. By the third hole in our round, when perfect strangers like us begin to schmooze about the lives we left behind that morning so we could play golf, I asked Ed what he did when he wasn't outdriving me by 60 yards.

"Laundromats," he said.

"Excuse me?" I said.

"I own some Laundromats back home in Kansas City," he explained.

"Omigod," I said, "you're the guy I've always talked about!"

Now it was his turn to say, "Excuse me?"

I explained how, whenever I gave a speech about applying the concepts I've learned in advertising to other businesses, I always talk about some mythical small entrepreneur who owns two Laundromats in Kansas City. "I didn't think I'd ever actually meet one," I mumbled.

Ed showered me with a wry, tolerant smile and then calmly approached his ball on the fairway (naturally) and hit a knockdown two-iron stiff to the flag 230 yards away. As Ed helped me look for my second shot near the out-of-bounds marker, I joked that the Laundromat business must be pretty good in Kansas City.

"It is when you own ninety of them," he said.

Ed was not only a good golfer, he had a keen understanding of market share and the economies of scale, not to mention the brilliance of repeating one success with another and another and another. . . .

But Ed's big insight, which I learned a few holes later as we made the turn to the back nine, was to go into a business that minimizes the cost of labor. That's the beauty of a Laundromat: it's a service industry that has essentially done away with service providers. His best-paid employees—thirty of them—maintain the washers and dryers around metropolitan Kansas City. His two younger brothers (whom he trusts implicitly) collect the money. As for Ed, he spends his days looking for new sites to either open or acquire another Laundromat.

"People say that the two big drives in life are food and sex. That may be true, but I gotta tell you, clean underwear runs a close third," he says. "Until every home in America has its own washer and dryer, I'll never run out of customers. And I'm sorry to say, Phil, but I don't need to advertise. When they need to do laundry, people will always find me."

Ed was proving to be a font of insights, but he left me with a parting thought at round's end. He was expanding—into coin-operated car washes. "People love a clean car as much as they love clean sheets and clothes—probably more. They'll be dropping coins in my pocket after every rain."

If Ed can have a parting thought, so can I. In this book I have stressed the difference between ideas and insights. Ideas are a dime a dozen; anyone can have them. They can be good or bad ideas, saving your hide in some cases, wasting your time in others. The best thing about a good idea is that it forces you to act. Insight is rarer, and infinitely more precious. A strong insight can fuel a thousand ideas, a thousand reasons to act and make something happen. That, more than anything, should be your reason to fight and persevere for your own insight moment. When you are armed with a powerful insight, the ideas never stop flowing.

INDEX